The Solution Tango

The Solution Tango

Seven simple steps to solutions
in management

Louis Cauffman

with Kirsten Dierolf

Copyright © 2006 Louis Cauffman

First published in 2006 by:

Marshall Cavendish Limited
119 Wardour Street
London W1F 0UW
United Kingdom
T: +44 (0)20 7565 6000
F: +44 (0)20 7734 6221
E: sales@marshallcavendish.co.uk
Online bookstore: www.marshallcavendish.co.uk

and

Cyan Communications Limited
119 Wardour Street
London W1F 0UW
United Kingdom
T: +44 (0)20 7565 6120
E: sales@cyanbooks.com
www.cyanbooks.com

A CIP record for this book is available from the British Library

ISBN-13 978-1-904879-91-6
ISBN-10 1-904879-91-8

Illustrations by cromheecke.com

Designed and typeset by Phoenix Photosetting, Chatham, Kent

Printed and bound in Great Britain by
TJ International Ltd, Padstow, Cornwall

Change is inevitable and the only permanent thing is change.
(Heraclitus)

Warning!
Reading this book may be hazardous to your problem-oriented
expertise.

For Ella

Table of Contents

Introduction

If I have seen further it is by standing on the shoulders of giants.
Isaac Newton

The scope of this book

According to one of the many classical definitions, management is the process of planning, organizing, leading, and controlling the efforts of the members of an organization and of using all other organizational resources to achieve stated organizational goals. This very broad definition includes all possible technical aspects of management. The managerial alphabet goes from auditing, budgeting, controlling, decision making, environmental analysis, finance, group behavior, human relations, IT, joint ventures, knowledge management, leadership, marketing, negotiation, operational control, planning and production, quality control, risk assessment, sales management and strategy, time management and team building, and the list goes on and on.

Since we feel safe to assume that our reader is an expert in the technical aspects of management, this book does *not* deal with these "hardware" issues.

This book is about "management as the art of getting things done through people." After all, that is what we managers do for a living, we get others to do what is necessary to achieve the goals of the organization. Bertrand Russell taught us "Change is one thing, progress is another." The solution-focused approach is a utilitarian approach — it's more about progress towards goals than about change in itself.

In order to get closer to the goals of our organization, we need to act both as a leader and as a coach. Leaders define the direction of the organization and develop action plans that guide their employees on the way. Coaches are enablers that help their employees to make the best of themselves. The days of the manager-boss, who orders around and imposes his or her decisions top-down, are over. On the other hand, coaching without leadership creates a managerial style that is like the ocean: vast and ever moving but going nowhere. Therefore, we see coaching and leading as two sides of the managerial coin.

This book offers a multitude of new insights and tools that will sharpen both your leadership skills and your coaching skills.

As you go, you will gradually discover the innovative elegance of the solution-focused model, you will start looking at the everyday challenges and problems of your (business) life from this new perspective. You will learn ways to let go of the problem fixation that we are all trained in at business school. This will open up the road towards more useful ways of dealing with the issues that you have to face daily in your job as a manager. Like Marcel Proust said: "The real voyage of discovering consists not in seeking new landscapes, but in having new eyes."

What to expect from this book

This book is intended as a hitchhiker's guide to the world of solution-focused management. It is designed to be a practical guide for people who want to add the innovative insights and practical tools of this new approach to what they are already doing well in their job of influencing others. So, the book is written in a conversational and informal style, illustrated with some cartoons and packed with business cases and examples from real life. Since it is a hitchhiker's guide, it is a book for the road and not necessarily for reading behind your desk.

A word of caution for the reader is appropriate here. If you like reading complicated and theoretical books about management, this book will disappoint you. However, if you like a fun read while simultaneously having a gentle brain massage that relieves the stress of your daily management challenges, you should go for this book.

Chapter 1 teaches the basics of the solution-focused model. Once you understand why *analyzing* the causes of human and managerial problems is not the quickest shortcut for helping your employees find solutions, Occam's Razor will trim all unnecessary complicated management theories down to the powerful "Simple works best." The power of common sense is demonstrated in the four basic tenets that underlie the solution-focused model: "Do not repair what is not broken," "Stop doing something that does not work," "Do more of what does work," and, "If something works teach it to or learn it from someone else." You will join in at a team meeting at both Problems Inc. and Solutions Focus Inc. where you will witness the differences between the problem-oriented style and the solution-focused style.

In chapter 2, you will learn how to improve your language skills and the increased power of words that results. What is still working for you and what will you do to avoid perpetuating your problem? You will learn how to use **solution talk** to maximize your efficiency as a manager, and how listening yields more results than speaking. You will find out that asking solution-building questions is more helpful than just giving suggestions. You will be introduced to the magic of words that will help you become a solution wizard.

The third chapter takes you to a dancing school where you will teach yourself the **seven steps** of the solution tango. The seven different steps of this dance show you what you can do in the interaction with your employees. Since it takes two to tango, the first thing you must do is to invite your employee to the corporate dance — establishing a sound working relationship as the motor for change is always the first step. Exploring the context sets the stage for finding out which are the most useful goals to work on. For example, asking questions about exceptions to their problems, and exploring the resources of your employees, gives you the ideal chance to compliment and encourage them to do more of what works. Offering your employees a colorful and differentiated view on their problems, instead of allowing them to remain stuck in the blackness of their problem fixation, miraculously propels them into a future where the problem is solved.

Chapter 4 offers you a **flowchart** that will help you navigate the jungle of business life safely. You define your position on the flowchart by answering a set of four fundamental questions: "Are we dealing with a problem or a limitation?", "Is there a request for help?", "Is this request workable?", "Are you able to use your resources?" For each position, we have designed specific interventions. The flowchart tells you which intervention works best at which moment in order to help you to achieve more with less effort.

At this stage, you are provided with the three most important toolkits of the solution-focused manager: solution talk, the seven-step dance, and the flowchart.

In chapter 5 you sit on the front row to witness the adventures of managers on the corporate battlefield. It tells the fascinating story of Solutions Focus Inc., a company that has just merged with another company, and is in the middle of a strategic reorientation. Written in the form of a play, it will teach you how the solution-focused model operates in real life. Witness how Ronald solves the power struggle between Peter and John. If you are curious and want to get a quick feel of what this solution-focused model is all about, you might start out with reading the dialogues in this chapter.

Finally, in chapter 6, we talk about special issues you might come across as a manager in a non-perfect company, working with non-perfect people. Here we provide some answers to frequently asked questions that nobody dares to ask in the open. Topics range from: "The three-minute elevator ride during which I get a once-in-a-lifetime opportunity to explain to my CEO what this solution-focused mumbo jumbo is all about" or, "Help, half of my team are morons" to "Teams at war and how to handle them," and many other useful topics for solution-focused hitchhikers.

Rubik's cube

This book can be likened to a Rubik's cube, with each of the six chapters representing one side of the cube. You can twist and turn it so that the cube looks different, but the overall shape remains the same. In a similar way each chapter is multi-layered and contains the messages in the other chapters, just viewed from a different perspective.

With each chapter you read, you will add new insights to what you are already doing that works in your (business) life, and you will also gradually deepen your understanding of the solution-focused approach. The solution-focused method offers additional tools to hone your interactive skills.

While reading this book, it is highly likely that you will have thoughts about how you can apply what you learn to your own work. We encourage you to constantly make comparisons with your own work situation.

How to read this book

What we call the beginning is often the end
And to make an end is to make a beginning.

T.S. Eliot

If you are eager to learn quickly, if you don't have much time to read books or if you are just an impatient person, you only need to read the chapter on basics, which is a synopsis of the complete book.

If you have a little more time, or if your curiosity is tickled after reading this chapter, you might skip to the fifth chapter, the story of "The man in the middle," where you will find how the solution-focused approach works in real life.

If you are curious about specific topics, you might jump to chapter 6 and find answers to frequently asked questions.

If you are more into fun than learning, you might flip through the book reading the many cases and looking at the cartoons. It will give you a flavor of the approach, and while you are having fun, learning will come automatically.

If you want to be thorough, if you like to discover the many layers of the book and grasp the richness of this new way of thinking and working, just sit back and go for the whole book. It is simple, although not easy, and the fun will come automatically.

Why this book?

In the beginning of the eighties, the solution-focused model was developed by Steve de Shazer and Insoo Kim Berg in the context of psychotherapy. Since then, the model has spread rapidly and it still continues to do so. Due to its remarkable applicability to all kinds of work contexts, the solution-focused model as a process driver found its way to the business field.

This book is written to help managers and corporations profit from the combination of both worlds. There is synergy and added value in combining the wisdom and techniques of the solution-focused model with the stringent rules of business life.

Crossovers from one field to another often are fruitful, yet, sometimes dangerous. This book wants to work as an antidote to oversimplistic notions or "allergies." Allergy number one results from psychologists who insist on pushing their — however well formulated — psychobabble ideas into the business world without any knowledge about what real life in business is all about. Allergy number two is the politically correct stance of many diehard business people pretending that the human factor is more a liability than an asset.

This book wants to bridge the worlds of human interaction and business in such a way that both sides profit from the simple yet powerful contributions of the solution-focused model.

Reality is the best teacher

The many examples and cases that you will find throughout the book all come from our daily practice. No case or example is made up. Every problem and every solution we use to illustrate the solution-focused model comes from our experience.

For the sake of clarity, most cases in the book are examples of one-on-one interventions. The same insights and techniques are equally valid when you work with a team or even with a corporation as a whole. This book is written from the perspective of the manager, but the solution-focused technology is applicable for internal or external consultants, HR managers, business owners, intra- and entrepreneurs, trainers, and for everybody who earns his or her living by influencing others.

All the characters that you will meet throughout the many cases are real persons in real companies, and they actually acted as described in the stories. For reasons of privacy and discretion, we have changed the names and circumstances of each case so that the real persons and companies become unrecognizable. If you think you recognize your own case, this is pure coincidence but it does show that the problems you encounter in daily life and business are universal.

Although in essence the solution-focused model is simple, this does not mean it is easy. Encourage yourself to take the concepts of the solution-focused approach seriously and learn the smart way of managing yourself and your company.

Create your own solution-focused book

The goal of this book is to help you become even better at what you are already doing well. Theoretical considerations are reduced to the minimum; instead the cases, techniques, tools, and tips enhance the fun of reading and will facilitate your learning.

Please feel free to translate the ideas, tips, techniques and examples given in this book into your own working life. Take notes while reading so that you create your own personal solution-focused organizer.

When problems arise — rest assured, they always do — this personalized "book" will be your assistant solution-builder.

Please feel free to write in this book. After all, it's yours.

Chapter 1

The Basics

May God us keep
From single vision and Newton's sleep!

William Blake

Introduction

Leadership out of the box

Nicole has recently been promoted to assistant director of the financial department in one of the plants of Solutions Focus Inc. Her boss asks her to supervise the department during his upcoming extended absence. He has only been gone a few hours when his employees and staff members start wandering around the department, engaging in long conversations in each other's offices, and disappearing behind closed doors for meetings with vague content and purpose. The atmosphere is jovial, but no one is getting the work done on time. The situation worries Nicole a bit, but, still green in her new position, she decides to be flexible.

However, after a few days Nicole notices that some colleagues keep breaking the newly implemented rule that all dividing doors in the department should remain open. She isn't sure what to do about this. Should she ignore the problem, or should she remind her colleagues of the rule? Perhaps she should open the doors herself when she notices that they are closed? Should she feel undermined as an acting director in charge and respond by circulating an angry memo or publicly reprimanding offenders? Should she try to find out the reasons why her employees are behaving as they do? Is it because they don't accept her authority? Is she a bad manager and is that what her employees are trying to tell her by behaving as they do?

Nicole could respond in many ways. After serious consideration, she decides to call the technical department and asks them to lift all the dividing doors off their hinges, literally and metaphorically solving the problem.

This is a beautiful, true-to-life example of solution-focused management. Nicole's intervention does not send shockwaves of political correctness through the company: people immediately grasp the meaning of the unhinged doors and accept it with a smile.

But is it really that simple?

Change is inevitable, both in life and in business. On top of this, the only thing that is guaranteed is change. Yet, change is what people often find most difficult. This book will teach you how to facilitate this difficult task of change, step by step, without alienating your staff but keeping them on your side.

Oh no! not another management model please!

Classical management models all start with the problem. Confronted with a problem, we are all trained to take the following steps. First, we investigate the history of the problem and analyze all possible aspects of it in depth. Second, we speculate about the root causes of the problem, trying to make sense of the hows, whos, and whys of the problem we are facing. Only then, so goes the classical reasoning, can we find a proper solution to the problem. The solution is found in the elimination of the root causes. The third and final step is to prescribe what should be done about the root causes.

This cause-effect model is particularly useful for dealing with relatively simple, mechanical problems that can be traced back to simple, unambiguous causes. Therefore, this model is ideally suited for solving medical and mechanical problems. If you are sick, the doctor takes a blood sample, sends this off to a lab. The lab finds the specific germs causing your illness, and the doctor prescribes a specific germ-killer. If your car doesn't start in the morning, you might open the hood to find out what is wrong. Similarly, if you hit the cue ball with a certain amount of kinetic energy and it then hits the eight ball, the cue ball will pass on its kinetic energy to the eight ball.

However, when dealing with human interactions in the classical problem-oriented style, we encounter many difficulties:

- People tend not to respond like germs, engines or billiard balls. Human beings are not as neatly organized as cue balls or car engines. When delving into the complexity of human and managerial problems, it is often hard, if not impossible, to find one single root cause. One can come up with numerous and complex reasons to explain why people behave as they behave. Looking for reasons for undesirable behavior in your employees often leads to blaming someone for being the "cause" of the problem. Getting caught in "blamestorming" does not move the organization ahead.

- Since cause precedes effect, most classic management models force us to look back into the past, and the future gets lost in process. Analyzing the problem in depth can be intellectually rewarding, but unfortunately a detailed report about the history and details of a problem doesn't solve it.

- Problem-oriented managers are supposed to be experts who know — if not best, then at least better. They are supposed to tell others what to do to solve their problems. However, we all know how others tend to react when someone tells them what to do. Giving strong advice invites the other person to find reasons why this is not going to work: "If you insist, I resist." Of course, then the expert can go on blaming them for not responding positively. But, again, not much will come out of this — instead lots of spent energy recycles itself into frustration.

Strategy meeting at Problems Inc.

Witness a strategy meeting at Problems Inc., and see if you recognize how they handle things.

Monday morning, strategy meeting at Problems Inc.: in order to find out what the company needs to do next, managers at Problems Inc. feel the urge to deeply analyze the "what, who and why" of what went wrong. What is not good enough? How come our competitors are so much better? What should have been done already? What is the reason why we did not meet the deadline, quota, or target? Whose fault it is that we are in this mess? How much time is already lost and how little time is left?

They then ask everybody about their ideas on how these problems have arisen. They deepen the analysis by asking what is behind every mentioned problem. What are the deeper causes and, furthermore, what is behind these causes? Who is responsible?

Slowly but surely, everybody becomes absorbed by the constant deepening of each problematic aspect. In the world of Problems Inc., professionalism and business cleverness is measured by the creativity to discover and bring forward the ever deeper hidden sides of the problem that is already at large.

No wonder people at Problems Inc. tend to become depressed, frustrated and hopeless. After all, the managers at Problems Inc. are trained to do just that: go into all the possible details of the "whys" and the "why-nots." As everyone attempts to reach the deepest causes of the already weighty problems, they forget to focus on what the solution might be. With every round of the discussion, another problem is unearthed, making the issues seem insurmountable. The chance that positive changes will arise from this is minimal.

Although this example is a little overdone, many elements of the problem-oriented approach are recognizable. But surely managers are always occupied with problems? Yes, of course. But if you are not happy dealing with frustration and headaches, there is a different way.

The power of common sense

Creating solutions is what management is all about. Managerial problems are similar for everybody. However, the way one approaches these problems can differ radically from one approach to another. The way you look at problems changes the way you solve them. Throughout this book you will find many examples and cases that will illustrate how creating solutions works.

It is important to clarify the basic and simple assumptions of the solution-focused model. A very long time ago, around the year 1300, William of Occam declared that: "no more things should be presumed to exist than are absolutely necessary." In plain English this means: "do not complicate things unnecessarily." Or even more to the point: "simple works best." Throughout the centuries this logic has guided and shaped most, if not all, philosophical and scientific developments.

Following this tradition, the solution-focused model uses this famous medieval rule of philosophy to remove all unnecessary complications. With Occam's adage in mind, the solution-focused model uses the power of common sense to tackle managerial problems, and create quick and robust solutions.

The following four tenets sum up the common sense inherent in the solution-focused model, in the most elegant way possible. These tenets are so self-evident that you need to make the effort to take them seriously or you might miss the point. If, however, you make the effort to think these tenets and their consequences through, then you are fully armed for the corporate battle. Simple works best:

1. If something is not broken, do not fix it.
2. If something works (better), do more of it.
3. If something you do doesn't work, stop doing it and do something else instead.
4. If something works, teach it to or learn it from someone else.

We would like you to think for a moment about the problematic situations that you have recently encountered in your (working) life. Reflect on the situations where you were able to find good solutions for the problems you or your company were facing. Chances are high that you have been using one or more of the above-mentioned tenets, without even being aware of it.

Now, for the sake of the exercise, think of some situations where you failed to solve your problem. Chances are high that you will find out that you have ignored one or more of the tenets.

The solution-focused worldview

In the solution-focused model, problems only interest us in as much as they provide us with clues to the possible solutions. Although problems can be overwhelming, there are always moments when the problem is not there or when the problem is less severe or slightly different than at other times. In other words, there are always *exceptions* to the problems. These exceptions interest the solution-focused manager because they indicate that there are partial solutions that can be enlarged into total solutions.

The solution-focused manager asks: "What does work in spite of the problems you are facing?" Even amidst the worst possible mess there are always things to be found that still work or can be made to work. All human systems — from individuals, to teams and larger organizations — have resources available in spite of their problems. The solution-focused approach constantly taps into these resources.

Questions help to shape the answers you get and vice versa. Solution-focused management is about asking useful questions in order to elicit useful answers. When asked the right solution-building questions, everyone will uncover resources that can be used to build solutions.

Solutions belong to the future while problems belong to the past. The solution-focused model offers a wide range of interventions that channel your attention towards constructing possible solutions. Instead of concentrating on the (why of the) problems in the past, the solution-focused model concentrates on the desired outcome: "What do you want to accomplish tomorrow and next week?"

The solution-focused model offers you insights, tools, and techniques to survive and even thrive instead of drowning in a sea of problems.

Strategy meeting at Solutions Focus Inc.

Now witness a strategy meeting at Solutions Focus Inc., and notice the difference.

After welcoming everybody, the chairman asks the following questions. "What is it that we need to talk about during this meeting to make it helpful for you and for the company? What are the things that still go well in spite of the problems we are facing? What are the strong points of our company? Thinking about past successes, how did we achieve them? What is it that this company certainly wants to keep going? How did we proceed that last time we encountered a similar problem?" He then invites the team members to openly discuss all of this.

After a while, he summarizes all the information and asks: "Now that we all agree on what we want to achieve and now that we know what our strong points are, it is a lot easier to tackle our problems. What would be the smallest difference that you, your team mates and our clients would notice if we make a little progress towards a solution?"

Rapidly everybody becomes more and more enthusiastic. They share their knowledge and hopes for a better future. Professionalism and business prowess is measured by the extent to which everybody adds new ideas towards possible solutions. Yet, there is no room for naivety — everybody realizes that dreams are nice but bring in no money. So they ask each other questions that help translate the dreams and wishes for the future into precise and concrete actions. Of course they know that they will encounter setbacks and difficulties, but they have learned that difficulties and even crises are opportunities to act out their expertise. They are not problem-phobic, they are solution-focused. Together they move towards positive action and plan the initial small steps.

Conclusion

This first chapter of your hitchhiker's guide has offered you a general description of the land of the solutions focus. You have been given a quick glimpse of all the basic insights that underpin the solution-focused approach. In the coming chapters, your hitchhiker's guide takes you on a more detailed tour that will turn you into a connoisseur of the solution-focused approach.

During this fascinating trip, keep in mind William Blake's words:

To see a world in a grain of sand
And a heaven in a wild flower
Hold infinity in the palm of your hand
And eternity in an hour.

Chapter 2

Words Are Magic

Words were originally magic and to this day words have retained much of their ancient magical power. By words one person can make another blissfully happy or drive him to despair, by words the teacher conveys his knowledge to his pupils, by words the orator carries his audience with him and determines their judgments and decisions. Words provoke affects and are in general the means of mutual influence among men.

Sigmund Freud

Introduction

Communication is action by interaction with your staff. Communication is bi-directional — you send and receive information. This chapter will suggest many techniques to hone the two most important skills of an effective communicator: listening and talking.

Learning how to become a better listener will enable you to help your staff to become more active and effective, which in turn will make your life as a manager much easier. Learning to use solution-focused language, and more importantly the art of asking solution-building questions, will enhance your effectiveness in dealing with your employees. The combination of asking solution-building questions with the art of listening is the most powerful tool a manager can have.

In short, you will discover how words can work magic for you and your organization. You will be able to test the benefit and pay-off immediately. Read this chapter with its many business examples; add these insights to what you already do well; put down the book; step out of your office to test your new skills, and be amazed.

Skill number one: LISTEN!

Listening is more than simply letting your eardrums be touched by someone else's sound waves. To listen means to be able to hear what others say without distorting that information by your own preconceptions. Being uninhibited and open-minded about what others say requires a fundamental attitude of unprejudiced intellectual openness. In simple words, listening is the art of genuinely hearing what the other says and avoiding hearing just what you want to hear. Of course we can never listen to anybody without some degree of interpretation; the ability to listen as if you know nothing about the subject, however, is proof of genuine wisdom. Listening with this type of "not-knowing" attitude sounds simple, but it is far from easy to do. It requires practice and effort to constantly put you in a "beginner" position. You must be brave, wise and agile enough to put your own ego aside, whilst avoiding a childlike naivety.

Experts know and speak, wise men ask and listen.

As a solution-focused manager, you will listen for different things than those that problem-oriented managers do. As you will learn in more detail in chapter 3, you should mainly listen for exceptions, tools, resources, and positive messages. In short, you look for the elements in your employee's train of thought that provide natural links to possible solutions. While you don't *ignore* the problem elements in the story, you make sure that you stay attuned to everything that hints towards a solution, even the smallest element of a possible solution.

A good listener can hear solutions growing in the thickets of problems.

If you listen, you will receive more information than when you speak. Giving your full attention and interest to what an employee is saying always leads to more useful information. Listening also improves your relationship with the employee. The reason for this is very simple — people react positively when others listen to them attentively, they feel appreciated and that they have been taken seriously. Actually, listening attentively is one of the main ways in which you can empower your staff. For managers, listening tops speaking.

If you are speaking, you won't hear anything.

The language of solutions

Reality is always "our" reality and never "the one and only" reality. The way we look at things and talk about them defines what we see. Alfred Korzybski taught us that: "the map is not the territory." We live in the territory, yet we only know the territory through our maps of it. Language is the main method by which human beings "map" their territory. Solution-focused language offers us a very different way of mapping out reality. As you will see, this map offers you far shorter roads to solutions. In the paragraphs that follow, you will learn how to use your standard English in a slightly different way. The rules of solution talk are very simple, yet not easy to master.

> **Essentials of solution talk**
>
> 1. Permissive language
> 2. What still works?
> 3. How does the problem end?
> 4. Solution-building questions
> 5. What else?
> 6. "How" works far better than "why."

1. Permissive language

Managers sometimes take pride in their skill of not beating around the bush and getting "to the point" very fast. Their language is often very macho. After all, taking a firm position and using firm language gives us the illusion that we have a strong personality and we therefore come across as very competent and firm. Some even think that talking with a bossy attitude makes them better managers. But look in the mirror and see how you react if someone talks to you like that. You will notice that there is a good chance that this style will incite you to listen less well and switch to a defensive attitude. The thought of "Who do they think they are ..." will soon come into your mind.

The solution-focused manager is less interested in their own image and more concerned with effective results. The language we endorse is more permissive than directive, more inviting than steering. This does not mean that you do not possess the skills to be directive or that you don't make corrections when your employees perform under par.

Using permissive language invites your team to think for themselves. This, in turn, empowers them to the point of optimal performance and makes room for their own learning cycle.

If you always seem one hundred percent sure and direct your team all the time, no learning will happen — if you use more tentative and permissive language and listen, your team will learn to be agile, flexible, and cutting-edge.

Permissive language increases the chance of cooperation and prevents opposition. Examples of permissive language are: "What would you think if we...". or, "What if you opted for...". Expressions such as "maybe, possibly, it could be, probably" turn out to be far more effective than "certainly, now, immediately, I know for sure that...".

2. What still works?

When you use solution talk, you concentrate on what still works *in spite of the problem*. It is far less useful to speak in terms of deficiency and matters that don't work — that is problem talk. Showing interest in the working parts invites people to talk about their resources — what are their strengths, and how can these be used to solve the problems they are facing. The question: "What still works in spite of the problem?" also directs the attention of your employees towards situations and instances when the problem is not so bad. These so-called exceptions to the problem are partial solutions and serve as perfect launching platforms for solution building. In the next chapter, you will learn more about the techniques involved in this essentially solution-focused approach.

For now, it suffices if you get a feel for this innovative approach by reading the next example:

The owner of a very successful plastic extrusion company, Mr. Kingsley, is caught between his son-in-law and the non-family CEO. His son-in-law is a board member and shareholder, and he is demanding an increasingly central role within the company. There is a long-standing tension between him and the non-family CEO. The straw that broke the camel's back was the son-in-law's purchase of an entirely new computer system without prior consultation with the CEO. The CEO threatens to quit. Mr. Kingsley is furious at his son-in-law, but his hands are tied: the son-in-law acted upon his own authority and the deal with the computer company is already closed.

Instead of venting all the negative feelings towards his son-in-law or conspiring with the CEO, Mr. Kingsley decides to take a long walk. After fuming for a while, he reflects on everything that goes well in his successful family business, on every smart move his son-in-law has made in the past, on the important role of the CEO for the further development of the company. Instead of analyzing the "whys" of his son-in-law's solo action or the history of the conflict between his son-in-law and the CEO, Mr. Kingsley visualizes all the occasions on which his son-in-law and the CEO collaborated for the best of the company.

Mr. Kingsley's anger soon passes and he decides to have an open conversation with his son-in-law.

Mr. Kingsley: "I do not appreciate nor approve of your solo action, let that be clear. Yet, what is done is done and we will not dwell on it. I would like to talk about other things with you. Let me ask you the following question instead: 'What, in your opinion, goes well in our company, and how did both you and our CEO contribute to that?'"

The son-in-law is startled. He was expecting a heavy rebuke from his father-in-law and had prepared his arguments extensively. He immediately realizes the wisdom of this question. Knowing the tenacity of his father-in-law, he drops his prepared arguments and answers in great detail. Their conversation steers towards the future of the company. The son-in-law is able to see the importance of a better cooperation with the CEO. At the end of the conversation, they both agree to initiate a project on corporate governance.

Mr. Kingsley then sets up a meeting with the CEO and starts off with the same question. Their conversation ends with the same conclusion.

Talking about what goes well in spite of the problems allows all parties to voice their opinions in a constructive manner instead of remaining stuck in the classical "who is right and who is wrong" discourse.

3. How does the problem end?

Analyzing how problems start and how they develop further and further is typical of a problem-oriented approach. However, the result of such an analysis is all too often a further intensification of the problems.

The solution-focused approach takes a radically different stance and concentrates on how the problems end, because this information directs you down the shortest road to possible solutions. The reason for this is simple — once you have determined how the arguments end, you can learn how to stop the argument cycle much faster.

Let's take an example from our daily life. Everyone who has a partner occasionally has an argument with him or her (which, by the way, is perfectly normal and healthy). Most people can predict with surprising accuracy how these arguments usually develop. If you think about it, you know all too well what your partner has to do or say to drive you up the wall. As a matter of fact, you do not need the actual presence of your partner to become angry towards him or her! However, it is so much more useful to concentrate on how your conflicts usually end — you only have to use those words and the conflict is likely to evaporate into thin air.

The same, of course, goes for discussions and problems in the office! Teams that work together for a longer time all develop certain routines in how they interact. This is very functional and useful, unless they develop routines that get them into trouble. When you work with a team that frequently quarrels, you might be tempted to analyze the routine that starts their quarrels. Chances are that the answer will be that someone is to blame. If however you ask the team and yourself how they stop their quarreling, and who does what differently, then you will get information that is far more useful for it will help them to stop their quarreling considerably faster.

A fast-growing distributor of electronic parts runs into liquidity problems. It is clear that they need a much higher turnover to cover their increasing costs. The credit lines are already stretched to the max.

The sales director, heavily supported by the marketing manager, sees a solution in extra advertising budgets, extra sales effort, and a "highly necessary" investment in setting up a big website. The financial manager has designed a cost-control program and insists that serious efforts in cost-control are imperative.

You can easily imagine the field of tension — without sales effort (which costs money), no extra turnover will occur; without cost-control (through which a higher margin is achieved), there will be no improvement in the cash position.

The ensuing conflict is predictable — the salesmen want to invest, but the financial manager wants to save money. The salesmen blame the financial manager for being shortsighted while the financial manager blames the salesmen for being careless with money. The salesmen then blame the financial manager for not believing in the vitality of the company while he blames them for living from one day to the next without facing the consequences of the financial position of the company, etc. If this discussion continues it simply will result in "more of the same."

Instead of asking unproductive questions like: "Who first started the blaming?", "Who is right?", "Who should admit they are wrong?", it is far more useful to ask "How did your discussion stop?", "What do you do differently when you aren't at odds?", "How did you tackle these dilemmas in the past?", "What did you do differently then?", "What will you do differently once you have reached an agreement?"

In other words, solution-focused managers are far more interested in what happens after the problem is solved, and use this approach as a way out of the situation, rather than concentrating on how problems arise.

Mind you, it does not follow that because we are solution-focused we then become problem-phobic! Of course we talk about the problems that pop up in front of us, but we make sure that we do this in a different manner. The goal of the solution-focused model has more to do with finding solutions than with eradicating all possible problems. We prefer to speak in terms of the presence of desired behavior rather than the absence of problems.

4. Solution-building questions

As we have already mentioned, listening is the number one skill for the effective manager. We do not mean that we listen to all the white noise coming out of deeper space, nor to the meaningless chatter that sometimes fills the air between people. On the contrary, we search for information: differences that can make a difference.

We can elicit this kind of useful information from our employees by asking questions of a special kind — solution-building questions.

Questions shape the answers you get (and vice versa). Therefore, asking solution-focused questions helps to set a collaborative tone and invites your employees to cooperate in building solutions. Questions that are focused on solutions will help in building solutions! This is in sharp contrast with questions that are focused on problems — those questions have a tendency to enlarge the problem.

Since solution-focused managers are not interested in intensifying the problems at hand nor in quick fixes that have no sustainability, it is useful to remember the words of Francis Bacon: "A prudent question is one-half wisdom."

Ask solution-building questions and solutions will echo.

ASKING QUESTIONS HAS MULTIPLE ADVANTAGES OVER TELLING PEOPLE WHAT
TO DO.

1. People usually ask questions to receive information. However, solution-focused managers go one step further. The solution-focused manager asks questions which help staff to evaluate their own perspective on the problems and to direct the conversation toward solutions. Asking good questions is the ideal way to lead from one step behind.
2. Asking questions is a more inviting and collaborative way of having a conversation than constantly taking the expert or boss's position.
3. Furthermore, everybody likes to express their own ideas, and asking your employees questions shows them that you care about their opinion. This is a sure way to enhance their motivation and morale.
4. Asking questions promotes listening: talking too much wears on those around you. By asking questions you invite others to speak, to contribute. After all, that is the essence of your goal as a manager — to empower and encourage people to use their own creativity, to be motivated to maximize their own contributions, and to help them to take on their own responsibilities.
5. Asking questions helps you to refrain from talking too much yourself. It has the added benefit of sharpening your concentration on your counterpart's story instead of on your own thoughts.
6. On top of all this, there is one crucial advantage to asking questions instead of telling your employees what to do: the ownership of the answer lies with the respondent and therefore the respondent is more likely to do what he or she just answered that he or she would do.

SOLUTION-BUILDING QUESTIONS COME IN MANY "SPECIES"

Every question points the nose of the respondent in a specific direction, namely the direction that is implied in the question itself. Thus each question contains a suggestion of the direction of the answer.

Throughout this book, you will find hundreds of solution-building questions. According to the purpose of the question, each question belongs to a specific category. Here is a list that you can use to help you to design your own questions.

1. **Clarification questions:** "Could you tell me something about the way your team functions?", "What else can you tell me so that I can see this situation even more correctly?", or later in the conversation, "Is there anything that I have forgotten to ask or that you have forgotten to tell me that is important for this issue?"

2. **Continuation questions:** "What are the practices that work well in your company, that you definitely want to keep going, in spite of the changes that your organization needs?", "What should remain the same?", "What part of your job is going so well that you want to make sure you keep it going?"

3. **Goal-setting questions:** "What do we have to talk about to make this meeting useful?", "How are you going to know at the end of this meeting that it was useful?", "What will be different after this meeting that will tell you that it was worthwhile?"

4. **Pre-session change questions:** "Since you scheduled this meeting, has anything changed regarding the conflicts in your team?", "On a scale of one to ten, where ten is that your issue is completely resolved and one stands for the moment in which you decided to call the meeting — where are you now?", "What tells you that you are at X?"

5. **Differentiation questions:** "Are there moments when the problem is less intense?", "What is different then? What do you do differently?"

6. **Resource-oriented questions:** "What still works well in spite of the problems in your team?", "Besides the difficult situation that your company is facing today, what are your company's strengths?", "What are your team's strongest assets?"

7. **Exception-generating questions:** "Have you ever solved similar problems?", "How did you do it?", "Who helped you?", "How did he or she help you?", "What did you find most useful during that previous crisis?"

8. **Future-oriented questions:** "Imagine that this problem was solved. How would things be different then?", "What would you do differently?", "How would the department function differently?", "What would be the smallest step you could take to solve this problem?", "Now that you have achieved that, what is the next small step you could take?" These questions become even stronger when you use the word 'will' instead of 'would'.

9. **Triangular questions:** "How would other departments notice that you are making progress?", "What would your boss say you would be doing differently if things improved?", "What would your boss need to see you doing so that he can trust you with the management of this new project?", "What will your colleagues notice that will tell them that this meeting was useful?"

10. **Suggestive questions:** "Would it be helpful if you were to try...?", "Have you ever thought of...?", "Do you think it might help if you...?", "What if your team mates were to...?" Experimenting with suggestive questions will show you that even straightforward suggestions work better when you put a question mark behind them: "Now, how about doing X? Would that be helpful?"

SPICE YOUR SOLUTION-BUILDING QUESTIONS WITH IMPLICATIONS

Now that you have learned about the power of asking solution-building questions, we will add some extra spice to that technique. You remember that questions shape the answers you get (and vice versa). If we add specific assumptions and/or implications to the questions, chances are high that the answer will be based upon this implication. In one move, the implication will be accepted without discussion.

This may seem complicated yet the following list will show you that it is actually rather simple (although not always easy to do). When you study this list, you will get a feel for this technique.

By practicing and designing your own questions, you can learn to transform this technique into a skill that comes naturally.

Here are a few examples:

- "How will you know that this meeting was useful?" (Implies that the meeting will be useful and the question is just a matter of how you will become aware of it.)
- "What needs to change so that we no longer need to discuss this problem?" (Implies that the problem can be solved.)
- "How did you handle being understaffed for so long?" (Implies that the team did their work well despite being understaffed and there is plenty of ability in the team.)
- "When is the cooperation between your team mates better?" (Implies that lack of cooperation isn't always a problem and focuses the attention on the positive moments. Notice the contrast to "Was there a time when your team cooperated better?")
- "How did you solve that situation so quickly?" (Implies that they can find solutions because they have done it before.)
- "How will the top management notice that you have finished this project successfully?" (Implies that they will be successful, helps to translate "success" into concrete terms, and sets a future goal. It also helps them to answer in such a manner that prompts them to think about how to show this success to top management.)
- "What concrete signs will let you know that the merger is successful?" (Again, implies that success is possible and invites the team to hypothesize the outcome of a process that in fact hasn't begun yet.)
- "What will be the first small sign of improvement?" (Implies success and focuses the team's attention on small steps that can gradually lead to bigger improvements.)
- "What was most helpful the last time you thought the project

would run over budget and miss the deadline?" (Implies that the present situation doesn't have to be seen as hopeless and focuses the team's attention on solutions that were effective for previous problems.)

All these different ways of phrasing questions imply that you have trust in your team's abilities to find solutions to current difficulties. This attitude generates staff confidence and induces hope for a positive outcome.

Questions are midwives for solutions.

5. What else?

An extremely important question that the solution-focused manager cannot do without is: "What else?" This question encourages staff to provide more detail and generate more realistic perspectives. The simple "What else?" question might be the most important follow-up question you can ask.

However, there is one single condition here, namely, that you use the question to elicit more detail about aspects of the solution. In talking about problems, the use of the "What else?" question is counterproductive. By delving more deeply in the possible aspects of a problem, you run the risk of aggravating the problem.

When it comes to details of a solution, more is better.

6. Avoid "why?" questions

If you take a close look at the previous list of questions you will notice that it includes many "W" questions: who, when, where, what. The only W question that solution-focused managers try to avoid is the question "why?"

Now why [sic] is it best to avoid this question? The main reason is that "why" questions turn very rapidly into "who did it," "who's fault is it?" Brainstorming about the why of a problem between team members rapidly becomes blamestorming about who is the culprit responsible for all the misery. That is not at all useful.

There are far better and more useful questions then asking why. Instead of asking "Why did you not meet the budget on time?", it's a lot more useful to ask: "How will you meet the next budget on time?" or, "What do you need to meet the budget on time?"

Forget "why?" and ask "how?"

Solution-focused questions at work: Miles & Son Inc.

Let's see how solution talk works in real life. Try reading the following case and see if you recognize which kind of questions are used. You may even want to think about which questions you would ask in such a case.

Miles & Son Inc. is a family business which specializes in developing and manufacturing packaging solutions for the pharmaceutical industry. This company is one of those "hidden champions," extremely successful yet unknown to the general public. Mr. Miles (fifty-nine) is the founder of the company and Chairman of the Board. Mr. Miles is half inventor and half businessman. His business acumen, combined with some inventions that he has patented, has been the basis for the corporate growth story. His only son, Stephan Miles (thirty-two), is working for the company. Stephan's job is not clearly defined. He is seen as his father's son and aide. Although Stephan's business card states that he is marketing director, he is all over the place like a butterfly. As happens frequently in closely held family businesses, there is a great-looking organizational chart, yet the roles and mandates of top management are not clearly defined. The emphasis lies on how the business actually runs, not on how it should be run. The working relationship between father and son has always been good to great, even if Mr. Miles senior keeps a tight rein on things.

Lately, Mr. Miles senior has experienced serious health problems and consequently has been in and out of the office over the past six months. During that time, his son Stephan stepped up as CEO. He has made a few small, significant changes in the way the business is run, especially on the organizational side.

Once recovered and working again full time, a friction develops between Mr. Miles and his son. It started out small, with Mr. Miles senior expressing his amazement about things that, during his absence, had been changed within the company. On certain topics, this grew into bewilderment. Stephan was not amused by the fact that his father shared his bewilderment openly with the board of directors. Mr. Miles was happy that the business was run well during his absence, but he was less happy with the changes that Stephan had introduced, especially since Stephan had not informed him about these changes. Stephan, on the other hand, felt that as an acting CEO (and CEO in waiting) it had been his responsibility.

A serious brawl erupted between them when, unannounced and in the middle of a board meeting, his father bluntly cancelled a fact-finding trip to China that Stephan organized. Stephan reacted furiously. The board members were flabbergasted by this extreme falling out between the two — a kind of open hostility that had never occurred before. Over the next few days, both parties completely avoided each other, and this avoidance then continued on for weeks. Mr. Miles and Stephan went on giving instructions without consulting with each other. Soon the personnel received contradictory orders and felt like they were being used as pawns in the struggle between Mr. Miles and Stephan.

How should this problem be approached? Studying the history of the conflict and analyzing the reasons behind their conflict would probably lead to more arguments and more conflicts.

Another approach might be to encourage Mr. Miles and Stephan to "express openly" what they feel and think about each other — but then you run the risk that they hurt each other even more.

Some might even think that discussing the psychology of the father–son relationship will do the job, but there again you risk making their problem even more personal.

Conversely, the solution-focused approach is very utilitarian — our aim is to help both parties cooperate again, like they always have been cooperating, and preferably to do this in the swiftest way possible. In other words, to help them help themselves. Throughout this book you will learn many different ways of doing this, but for now it suffices to look at the vehicle for change — solution talk.

Mr. Miles was convinced that Stephan had seized the opportunity to take charge of the company. The son believed that it was his duty to keep the business running, and that he had earned the right to continue managing the company in the same way as he had done during his father's absence. They had already tried to convince one another of the correctness of their own position by rational arguments. This only led to a harshening of their conflict. Soon they were simply blaming each other in front of the other members of their management team. They asked staff to give their opinion but nobody dared to take a clear stance for the simple reason that both the father and the son were very successful in running the business. The staff members were caught in their loyalty towards both men. Plus, staff members realized that whatever they said, they would run the risk of getting trapped in the conflict. (And it is very difficult to get people to bite the hand that feeds them!)

After some months of growing tensions, John, the technical director who had been working for the Miles family business for over two decades, could no longer stand it. During a meeting in which the same old disagreements paralyzed the discussion yet again, John is no longer able to refrain himself and blurts out: "Excuse my bold language, gentlemen, but you are messing up this company with your personal conflicts. You simply paralyze the company. If you don't stop this, this company is going to grind to a halt and we'll never get it going again. Please, shape up!"

Everybody in the meeting, and especially Mr. Miles senior and Stephan, are startled. Nobody expects this kind of language from the usually silent John. Mr. Miles senior feels the urge to take over as big boss yet he refrains from doing this. In a split second, he realizes that John is correct. The same goes for Stephan. John's outburst is a wake-up call for the both of them.

John tells everybody that it would be inappropriate to continue the meeting: "I do apologize for my outburst. But hey, I am one of the veterans of this company and I know that both of you are very concerned with what's best for the company. I share that concern, as do all of us around this table. If you agree, I would like to have a private talk with both of you. Let's see how we can solve this."

Before Mr. Miles senior and Stephan can answer, the other participants stand up and swiftly leave the room. Both Mr. Miles senior and Stephan agree with John that it is necessary to let things cool down a bit. They agree to meet again the next day.

That evening, John ponders on how to tackle the next meeting. Thoughts like: "Why did I have to stir up the hornets' nest" cross his mind. John is aware that, in order to avoid getting trapped in a pure rational discussion with the same old arguments, he needs a different approach. It dawns upon him that asking lots of questions might work best. John learned this method a few months ago when he and his team were working with a solution-focused consultant on team coaching.

At the same time in their respective homes, father and son are also thinking about the next meeting. They both are aware that doing more of the same, arguing and analyzing the other's behavior, will be of no help.

Next day, ten o'clock in the meeting room, Mr. Miles opens the meeting by thanking John for the wake-up call: "I am so glad that you spoke your mind, John. This disagreement between me and my son has been going on for too long now."

John: "OK, I have been thinking about how we could solve this problem. In the past twenty-two years that I have had the honor of working here, it has always been very clear to me that the Miles family is crucial for this company. The same goes for your cooperation at the top, Mr. Miles and Stephan. It has never before been a problem, on the contrary, your cooperation has propelled this company towards its success. Now, if my words in the meeting yesterday were a little harsh, I apologize for this. Yet I could no longer stand to see how both of you are suffering as a result of the tension and how this tension threatens to spread throughout the business. I am certain that this situation is something that the both of you never had in mind but that you just got caught up in it. I am sure that you both prepared for this meeting. But, if you agree, I would like to start out with something completely different."

Both: "Go ahead, John."

John: "Instead of remaining focused on the negative, I would like to invite you to look at more positive aspects. What are the things that — in spite of the tension that has arisen between the two of you — still function well in the company?"

Mr. Miles: "Well, that's an open book, John. You know perfectly well what works well in our company. But I understand the reason behind your question. Actually this would be a good question to ask every employee. It would turn their heads away from complaining about everything that goes wrong towards more positive insights. For now, I can list many things but maybe the most important issue here is the cooperative style of the business."

Stephan: "I agree with my father, although it sounds a little silly coming from the two people in the company that lately have not been cooperating." (All laugh)

John: "I'm glad that you have kept your sense of humor, Stephan. Now, what is it that we should talk about so that this meeting will be useful?"

Stephan: "I would like to get some clarity about what is going on between my father and me."

Mr. Miles: "I would like to find order and peace again between us so that we can pick up our cooperation where we left it a few months ago."

John: "What would be the smallest sign that your relationship has improved and that you are making little steps towards cooperating again?"

Mr. Miles's answer is quick: "My son has to stop shutting me out."

When John asks the same question to Stephan, he says: "Dad has to stop interfering with my work and leave me alone."

These answers are not very useful. They both answer with what the other should do differently and John realizes that this isn't going to help progress. Of course, John is not going to give up easily and so he continues his line of questioning.

*John: "Let me ask you again. What are **you** going to do differently to make things easier? And by 'you', I mean each of you. So would you please be so kind as to talk about yourself."*

Mr. Miles: "What I could do differently to make things easier? Well, we sure can't go on this way. I will try to be friendly to Stephan but I'm not going to butter him up."

John: "Fine, Mr. Miles. Now how about you, Stephan. What would you be prepared to do differently to make things better?"

Stephan answers: "I could invite my father to join the meetings of the steering committee that I've organized. But only if he promises not to snap at me during the meeting."

Nothing is solved here, but it's a start.

Feeling that these answers open up possibilities, John proceeds: "When you think about the last few months, have there been any instances — however small — when there was a little less tension between you? And what did you do differently then?"

Stephan: "Sure. I remember. The week before our falling out concerning the China trip, we were in a meeting together with some clients. The clients were complaining about our announced price raise. It was very nice to hear my father backing me up totally when I explained the reason for the raise. That support was very welcome and it made me feel good."

Mr. Miles: "Yes, I remember that meeting too. I was glad to be invited. It was the first time that I got to meet one of our main clients again after my sick leave. Stephan told the clients that he and the rest of the company were very glad that I was back. It was the first time that I felt welcome again in my own company."

John: "Great. Are there other moments that you can recall when things went OK between the two of you?"

Mr. Miles and Stephan continue to talk about other examples and the tension between them slowly abides. John compliments them on the many examples of exceptions to their problem.

John: "So if I understand you correctly, what you are saying is that whenever you cooperate, you notice that this eases your tension. What do you need in order to be able to act more and more cooperatively again?"

Stephan replies directly to his father: "I would need to feel more at ease and not be so on edge when you are around."

Mr. Miles answers: "For me, the smallest sign of betterment would be that you stop avoiding me."

As the conversation progresses, both men become more willing to change their attitude towards each other.

John: "What are the things that you can do in the next days and weeks so that you know you will make further progress?"

Mr. Miles agrees to try to act positively toward his son. He translates this into being more friendly, inviting him again for the family's traditional Sunday aperitif, and agreeing with him in the presence of their employees (or remaining silent if he doesn't agree).

Mr. Miles: "I know I am not good at this, never have been and probably never will be. But I will try to do my best to say something positive when you do something well, Stephan."

Stephan says he will inform his father weekly about all matters concerning production and sales figures.

John ends the meeting by complimenting the two of them and wishing them good luck.

In the weeks after this conversation, all parties concerned notice an improvement in the relationship between Mr. Miles and his son, much to the relief of everybody in the company.

Mrs. Miles discreetly sends John a case of champagne!

What did you learn in this chapter?

You learned the new language of solution talk that provides you with essential tools for becoming an even better leader and coach. Combined with the art of listening you enhanced your skill in the magical use of words.

You also learned that asking solution-building questions is the core tool to empower your employees to find quick and sustainable solutions themselves. Armed with these basics, you are now ready to learn the seven-step dance to solutions in the next chapter.

But before you take this next step, we would like you to take a few minutes for yourself to think about the following questions:

- Which insights of this chapter do you think you are already using?
- What do you need to do so that you further enhance what you already know?

- What are the three most important lessons you learned?
- What are the suggestions that you think you will try out first in your daily work?

Chapter 3

Seven-Step Dance

You manage people by interacting with them — just as dancing is an interaction. You lead, follow, move to different rhythms and try to work as a harmonious unit while trying not to bump into anyone! In this chapter you will learn how to dance elegantly towards solutions. You will learn solution-focused leadership and management techniques, which will help you and your staff to perform at their very best. As in dancing, you will also learn how to have lots of fun while doing it.

The solution tango

Since management is the art of getting things done through people, it is about interaction between people, and is a process of mutually influencing each other. Therefore, managing people is not a one-sided monologue but a dialogue between the parties concerned. Thus, solution-focused management is like a dance — and the solution-focused tango has seven basic steps. So far so good — this is the easy part.

As you know from learning to dance or learning to ride a bicycle, there is much more to learning than just content. Learning always consists of two components — the *content* of what you are learning and the *process* of how you will be using what you have learned. Or to put it simply, the "what" and "how" of learning.

The seven steps structure the pattern of the interactions between you and your employees. They shape the process of the interaction, and by process we mean the form of the interaction not its content. All interactions between people are made up of content (what you talk about) and process (how you interact). How you phrase a request, and the order of topics you choose to discuss, are part of the process of the interaction. What you talk about, the budget, an employee's performance, etc. is the content of the interaction.

The solution tango is a metaphor for the process side of this interaction. When you have read the following paragraphs, the different steps of this "process stuff" will become much clearer. For now, please trust the fact that these steps are present in every interaction, be it a meeting, a conversation, even an email. Actually, you will recognize most of these steps, or at least some of them, because you are most probably using them already to some extent. The solution tango provides you with steps that add elegance to your already proficient performance. Of course, you, the manager, are the leading person in the corporate dance — you set the pace and direction into which you and your employees are going to dance.

Presenting the different steps in an orderly structure has big advantages for remembering it. However, let us make a few cautionary remarks.

First, we present the different steps in a certain order. However, this order serves only as an *aide mémoire*. In reality, as you will see in the case studies, the only fixed step is the invitation to the dance (by which you establish the working relationship), which always comes first (or you would not have a dancing partner and therefore no dance). The order of the following steps depends on the situation (the issues, your partners, the circumstances...). However, just as an elegant dance is never purely random, your solution-focused ballroom movements will always look more like a fluent tango than like hopping around in an unorganized and chaotic manner.

Second, you will probably not use all of the seven steps in every conversation. You will select and use only those steps that you deem important and necessary for the situation you are dealing with. Your main criterion for selection is the usefulness of each step.

The solution tango is simple — yet the possible combinations of the steps are endless.

The process protocol embedded in the seven-step dance is an orderly, ever-changing way of cooperating with your employees. Isn't it our job as solution-focused managers to help our employees help themselves, or to help them regain their capacity to help themselves?

For your convenience, we have designed icons for every step. You will find them in the margins throughout the book to help you to stay on track. We hope these icons make it easier to learn the different layers that are hidden in the text and that they add to your enjoyment of the book.

Music, Maestro!

THE SOLUTION TANGO

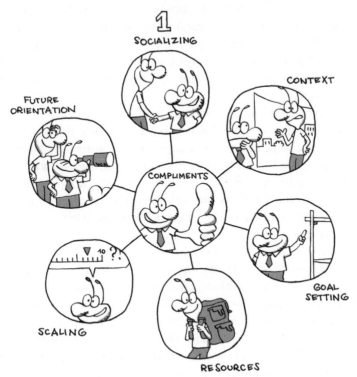

Step 1: socializing

Now think for a moment... what is the first thing you do when you come into the office in the morning? Do you storm head down towards your desk, coffee cup in left hand, briefcase in the right, without looking

around or speaking? Of course not. You walk in, look around, say "good morning," you might even shake hands with some people. You take a moment to say hello to your secretary, maybe ask how his/her weekend was or how his/her kids are doing. This is how you start the corporate tango. Unless you prefer to tango on your own, you need to invite someone to dance with you. This means making contact, reaching out, in short: socializing.

As much as this seems self-evident, if you look around at your own workplace, you might be astonished to see how often this is forgotten. Sometimes it is simply taken for granted that it is not necessary. People seem to think: "Oh, but we have been working together for years now, so there is no need to say hello..." Imagine what the atmosphere in your home would be like if everybody in the house suddenly decided that it's no longer necessary to say hello to each other because you have been a family for so long now...

Socializing is more than merely being friendly or acting like "Mister Nice Guy" all the time. Socializing is about establishing contact with others, and the goal of socializing is to create an optimal working relationship with your co-workers. Socializing implies reaching out to others — you make sure that your colleagues and staff feel that you are interested in them and that you value them both as a person and as an employee. Socializing is as easy to do as it is to forget to do. You can start socializing by shaking hands, saying hello, being interested in what is interesting to the other person, asking and remembering personal things about the other person, remembering and reminding people of specific details from the past that show that you make the effort to remember, etc. There are a myriad ways of socializing with other people, just pick the ones that suit you the best, and that you feel most comfortable with.

As a manager, you can use this process of socializing to create the most constructive and collaborative atmosphere possible. Actually, there are some very good reasons to do so. For one thing, most people prefer to have a good time at work, and it is simply more enjoyable to work in a positive atmosphere. Experiencing happiness at work does not mean that you party all day. Being happy at work, however, means profit in all possible meanings of the word and for everybody involved.

Second, if you have a good relationship with your co-workers, they will allow you room for mistakes. When you do or say something wrong, you will be forgiven far more easily when you are on friendly terms to begin with.

Third, and maybe most importantly, is the fact that management sometimes has to deal with difficult situations. Tough decisions with negative outcomes for people sometimes need to be taken, communicated, and acted upon. Sometimes people need to swallow hard decisions that require difficult changes. The more you have taken care to create a good relationship with your employees, the easier it will be to move into a constructive direction, even when the going gets tough.

Hints for boosting your working relationships

Basically, all these hints can be reduced to one bottom line — build a working relationship that is as positive and as strong as possible. It is imperative that your employees and co-workers are willing to work with you, and the more positive the working relationship, the faster you will jointly come to solutions.

TIP

A powerful working relationship is the motor for cooperation and change.

So what is the recipe for creating a powerful working relationship? The following ten hints will get you started.

1. Make sure that you develop a positive and respectful working relationship. Ideally, this will ensure that the people you are working with are in the right cooperative frame of mind.
2. Focus on their way of thinking and speaking, and adjust to their language. If you want to communicate with someone, it helps to speak the same language — both verbally and nonverbally.
3. Be quick, clear, and concise in your analysis of the situation. To be accepted as a manager and leader, you must demonstrate your ability to put your finger on the right issues. Non-committal statements, five-thousand-dollar buzz words, complicated terminology that primarily serves the purpose of obscuring things rather than clarifying them, theoretical *tours de force* that aren't linked to reality, and demonstrations of your intelligence might be standard in many companies, but they don't contribute to a solid working relationship. You may impress others and boost your own ego, but you won't accomplish much else.
4. Keep it simple — reality is already complex enough so there is no need for complicating things .
5. Build on whatever is already working for your staff. In spite of all the problems which your employees consult you about, there is always

something that they are doing well. All problem situations contain elements that can be built upon in positive ways.

6. Commitment is essential. Play the non-committal technical expert and you will be kicked out swiftly. Be honestly committed to your co-workers and employees.

7. Stay clear of the fantasy of being their savior. ("Without me you can't do anything. I am indispensable because I am the key to your solutions.") Refrain from playing the role of an apostle. ("I have seen the light, and if you do what I say you will be granted eternal life in this company.") Bear Carl Whitaker's famous words in mind: "Guard your missionary zeal or you will be eaten by the cannibals."

8. Cooperate. You can't work successfully in a vacuum. Working in a company means working together. As you will learn throughout this book, T.E.A.M. stands for *together everybody achieves more!*

9. Go slow and go with the flow! "Love at first sight" is rare in a business contact. So you'd better take the time to allow your working relationship to develop from initial contact into cooperation.

10. **Golden Tip:** Evolution tops r-evolution.

Turbo on the cooperation booster: yes-set

Language is a conveyor belt that transports and transforms meaning to and fro between you and your employees. The different aspects of solution talk that you have familiarized yourself with in the second chapter (see page 29) are lubricants that facilitate the working of the conveyor belt. The yes-set technique will double up the speed of the conveyor belt, and therefore it is a great way to open a conversation.

Using a yes-set is a technique that comes naturally to good salesmen. They use this technique without necessarily even realizing it. In the "yes-setting technique," employees are prompted to answer positively to a series of obvious questions or statements. After several positive reactions, chances are high that the mood in the interaction automatically becomes more positive. This "yes" frame of mind makes it more likely that your counterpart will react positively to questions or statements that may be less easy. When handled with subtlety, the yes-set creates a positive atmosphere and serves as a booster to your cooperation with your employees.

Most daily and non-business conversations begin with opening comments about trivial matters: "How are you?" or "Nice weather!" These seemingly trivial remarks can be used for yes-setting. It doesn't matter that these issues aren't really relevant to the actual conversation — the goal of yes-setting is to create a positive context.

Handling the yes-set well means adapting your opening comments to the actual context. Opening a board meeting with "Nice weather today" is probably neither particularly elegant nor relevant. Appropriate questions or statements for a yes-set largely depend on the situation and even on the local or business culture.

If you combine giving compliments with yes-setting and positive suggestions, you put a turbo on your cooperation booster, and as you might guess, this can have magical effects on the course of the conversation.

See how this can work in a business context. At the beginning of a meeting you could say:

"Hello, everyone, thank you for coming on time (compliment). It's Monday morning again (yes), the beginning of a new week (yes). Everybody received the documents on Friday (yes). Now that everyone is here (yes) and the meeting has started (yes) we can begin with our agenda. We will take a break at eleven o'clock (yes) and continue until lunch (yes). I want to thank Mary for preparing the documents thoroughly and, as always, on time (compliment). I know this team will all have looked at the documents (compliment) and formed a critical opinion about them that will be useful later on (compliment and suggestion)."

This way, the team is encouraged to think positively and expect positive results from the meeting.

Step 2: contextualizing

Nothing in life works in a vacuum, and likewise in business we don't operate in a vacuum. Everything that we encounter, we encounter in a specific context. To a great extent, this context determines, or at least greatly influences, how we perceive things.

Here is a simple example from daily life. When you are in a very busy period of your working life, with lots of things at stake, you can find yourself not paying enough attention to your loved ones. When a fight breaks out between you and your partner, prompted by a certain lack of attention, you probably can't dissipate this brawl by means of a quick "yes but I do love you" pacifier. Given the context of lack of attention, this little phrase — however heart-felt it might be — will not have the same effect as when you say it in the right context. A more appropriate context for the "I love you" formula is when there is wine, chandeliers, roses and, especially, some time.

An extreme business example will clarify the importance of context further. Imagine a company celebrating its tenth anniversary. They are planning a big party for all employees, clients, and suppliers to be celebrated the following week. In the week before the party takes place, an accident happens in production and two people lose their lives. Would this be the appropriate context for having the party anyway? Would you cancel this party or at least convert it into an entirely different occasion? Of course you would. It would be very disrespectful to act as if nothing had happened, as if that accident were merely a minor detail in the context of the life of the company and its staff.

So if it is true that the context (or circumstances) play a big role in whatever happens, then context deserves our appropriate attention. The importance of context is extremely simple because it is so obvious, and yet at the same time it is very complex since so many factors contribute to our circumstances, most of which we can hardly influence. Let's have a look at how you can deal with context in the best possible way.

When you are confronted with a problem, it's important to have a very close look at the context in which this problem occurs. The same goes for any situation you encounter in your corporate life. If you get an assignment to work with a new team, for example, you want to get to know this team and its different players, and you want to get to know the circumstances in which they operate. If your company is moving into a new business, you will take great time and effort to explore that new context before making any decisions.

If you also work as an internal coach or mentor, you can imagine employees coming to you for coaching because they sense that they are not moving in the right direction with their work. You will be much more effective as a coach if you first take the time to ask about the context of an employee and their work. You could ask something along the following lines: "Very nice of you to come to talk to me about your work. Let's not make the mistake of thinking that, since I work here too, I know everything about you and your job. Allow me to ask you some questions first. So, before we start working on your challenges, tell me something about yourself. How long have you been working here? What is it exactly that you do in our company? How has your career developed and what are your strong points? Do you think it is appropriate to tell me something about your personal life?"

Even if you have been working with these people for a long time, you should still ask these questions for the simple reason that — if you are honest to yourself and them — you probably do not know them that well. It's a strange paradox in corporate life that you work together with people on a daily basis for years and grow to think that you know them very well, and at the same time you haven't got a clue as to who they really are as (private) individuals. This is also why it is much easier if you start out by developing a good working relationship through socializing sufficiently (see step 1).

Context questions show the person who steps into your office that you are more interested in them as a person than you are interested in their problems. This in itself shows the people you are working with that you respect and appreciate them. Rest assured, this is a powerful intervention — on an emotional level as well as in terms of getting and giving those pieces of information that will point you in the direction of solutions.

Exploring and clarifying the context of the conversations you have with your staff also keeps you talking, listening and relating to them. You are provided with a wonderful opportunity to work on the quality of your relationship!

Step 3: goal-setting

For soccer players, the way to win a game is to be able to get the ball in the net of the opponent's side just once more often than getting the same ball in your own net. This so important that they use the same name for what they want to achieve (scoring goals) as for the strange contraptions that are built on both ends of the playing field.

The lesson here is something that every manager and business person should keep in mind.

> **TIP**
>
> Without a goal you can't score.

Setting the right goals and finding ways to help your staff set the right goals is a crucial task for a manager. Goals are the signposts that direct all the activities of your staff. Messy and unclear signposts lead you astray and certainly are no help in achieving your goals via the shortest path.

Clear, concrete, and realistic goals that are important to whomever you are talking to lead a conversation to swift and lasting results. The single most useful question here is what we call the "goal-setting" question: *"What should we discuss in this meeting so that this conversation will be useful to you (and the company)?"* This question is a powerful tool for initiating goal-setting. You can use this question at the start of every meeting in order to get focused on goals and avoid talking about trivial topics.

Goal-setting is an interactive activity that doesn't happen in a single shot. On the contrary, goal-setting is a continuous process. Every time a (partial) goal is reached or failed, the next line of goals is adapted according to this new information. The idea of goal-setting as a continuous process is important because it helps us not to fall into the trap of thinking that once a goal is set, it's there to stay forever. Business life is too volatile and flexible for that!

Let us first take a close look at all elements that play a part in this crucial step.

Goal-setting in business: the basic rules

1. The goals of the company come first

Economic reality tells you that the goals of the company have higher priority than your personal goals. It is obviously counterproductive to work on goals that only serve you personally (or your team) and that don't fit with the overarching goals of your company. One of your tasks as a manager is to see the big picture of where the company is heading and subsequently orient your goals towards the goals of the company. Have a look at this example.

A multinational manufacturer of industrial valves decides that one of their subsidiaries needs downsizing. In the process, they will have to reduce personnel by fifteen percent in all departments of that subsidiary. Shortly after the publication of this decision, Jeffrey, the chief engineer of the subsidiary concerned, sends a long memo to headquarters. In this memo, he argues that his engineering department is vital to the company, as are all his teammates in the engineering department — not one single person is dispensable and can be laid off. His memo contains an alternative downsizing plan. In it, Jeffrey describes in detail the people he thinks are superfluous in all other departments of the company. His personal goal is to keep his team intact and untouched by the downsizing. For his teammates in engineering, Jeffrey is the hero of the day. But guess who is not amused — Julian, CEO of the subsidiary. Jeff had not told Julian about it, so when headquarters informs Julian, he is taken by surprise. Julian is flabbergasted, and his first impulse is to fire Jeffrey on the spot.

Knowing from experience — he has learned the hard way — that impulsive reactions are counterproductive more often than not, he calls for a meeting with Jeffrey. While waiting for Jeffrey, Julian reminisces about his early days in the company.

In the beginning of his own career as a young engineer, and driven by ambition, he had made similar mistakes. So he decides to listen to what Jeffrey has to say first. In their meeting, it soon becomes clear that Jeffrey acted out of genuine concern for his team and for the company. Julian tells Jeffrey that he appreciates his concern for the engineering department but that bypassing him as CEO is totally unacceptable. Julian points out that the downsizing will have to be executed in all departments, engineering included, and that the future of the subsidiary depends on their cutting cost. He offers Jeffrey a choice, to defend and maintain his views as described in the memo and leave the company or to cooperate with the downsizing exercise and work out an optimal solution for all parties concerned. Jeffrey starts understanding the overarching implications of his behavior and realizes that he has made a big mistake. He opts for staying on board and supporting the downsizing plan. At the end of the conversation, Julian asks Jeffrey to withdraw his memo to HQ and invites Jeffrey to draft a plan on how he thinks the engineering department can be downsized without losing its edge. Julian also proposes an outplacement program for those who no longer fit in the company. The result of this incident is that Jeffrey's goals very soon line up with the goals of his company.

If you want to move up the ladder faster, align your own professional goals with the company's goals.

2. Respect the individual and his or her goals

Companies consist of people and machines operated by people. Even in the most capital-intensive corporations where most of the money is locked up in hardware and investments, a big part of the company's capital are the employees. If you consider your workforce to be an important investment and you are interested in a good return on investment, then showing them due respect is simply natural.

Some hard-boiled, cynical managers live and work under the assumption that everybody goes to work to merely do the utter minimum and try to get away with their salary without headaches. This category of managers is not the most successful when it comes to managing people. Their distrust keeps them from seeing the potential of their staff, and they miss a lot of opportunities.

In contrast to these kind of managers, solution-focused managers assume that everybody tries to do his or her utter best until proven otherwise. Mind you, this is no naive assumption made by naive managers. The catch is in the "until proven otherwise." Measuring effort and controlling efficiency remains one of the manager's key tasks.

Treating your employees and teams with respect means that you accept their values, beliefs, and opinions even if you don't share them (and as long as they don't impede your team's success). Rejecting or refuting the beliefs of others generally produces tension and is counterproductive. For example, individuals who are sensitive to stress are often perceived as weak, particularly in the business world. However, these individuals are often the most sensitive to what is happening in the company. Therefore, if you respect their hypersensitivity and ask them for information sensitively, they can often teach you quite a bit about the company. Respecting harmless oddities of employees doesn't cost you anything but always yields a dividend.

Make sure your interventions are focused on the wellbeing of the employees. Power games, Machiavellian machinations and the like are, unfortunately, part of everyday human existence. They also occur in the jungle of business. If you want to learn how to deal with them, we refer you to chapter 6 for possible answers. For now, suffice it to say that solution-focused management has a strong set of ethics. Don't do anything that can harm the individual employee.

Successful solution-focused management always strives to improve every aspect of life and work in a company and the employees subsequently benefit from this. This ethical approach is, at the same time, also very pragmatic — happy, or at least content, employees contribute more and do so with pleasure, to the wellbeing of their company. A balanced ecology in which the whole takes care of the parts and the parts take care of the whole maximizes the value of the parts and the whole. We've come up with a neologism for this combination of ethics and pragmatics, **"pragmethics."**

Here is a dramatic example:

The employees of a large industrial contractor were required to travel frequently because many of the company's yards were located abroad. This was very difficult on the employees and their families, who were often separated for months at a time. Above-average salaries helped to compensate for this. Nevertheless, the owner of the company was well aware of the fact that the demands placed on the employees and their families were high.

When the seventeen-year-old daughter of one of the company's employees got burned badly during a family barbecue and was rushed to hospital, the owner relieved the employee from projects requiring travel for the duration of his daughter's stay at the hospital. He even suggested that the employee work part-time until his daughter's health had stabilized. After the daughter's long recovery process, there was still a massive amount of work to be done by the plastic surgeon. Through a foundation, the owner anonymously paid for the surgery. The employee nearly fainted when they told him that the bills had been paid. He suspected that his boss had paid them and decided to ask him, but the owner denied that he had anything to do with it. The employee talked to his colleagues about this and they too suspected ... but the owner kept denying it.

A couple of years later, one of the company's main clients went bankrupt, causing the company itself to teeter on the edge of bankruptcy. In response to the crisis, all three hundred employees spontaneously agreed to accept a postponement of payment of thirty percent of their salary. It took six months to get over the crisis, but the company survived — one of the main factors in the survival being the postponement of paychecks.

If the company takes good care of its employees, the employees will take good care of the company.

Useful goals

If you want to obtain maximum results with minimal effort, then we recommend that you use the following criteria when setting goals. (If however, for some obscure reasons, you prefer maximum effort with minimal results, feel free to do the opposite!)

1. Goals must be realistic and achievable

This point is fairly obvious. However, in business it is often overlooked. The myths of "more is better," "the harder to get, the better it is" are a good way to overstretch and thus overstress yourself and others. However, even the strongest elastic breaks when overstretched. As solution-focused managers we are always on the lookout for ambitious goals that can be reached with the resources of the company. Why try and bring down the moon when you can work on good quarterly results?

William (twenty-nine) has been promoted twice during the last couple of years. He has a PhD in economics and is labeled as a "high potential" within his company. He is the assistant to Tom, the Vice President of a soft drinks production plant. William's job is to control production planning. A minor heart problem forced Tom to stay home for some weeks, and William was asked to take over Tom's position temporarily. Top management said to William: "If you manage this well, you are on your way up the corporate ladder." William tackled his new task like the proverbial bull in the china shop and his over-enthusiasm showed in his behavior: "eyes-wide-shut and full speed ahead." He jumped into the task feet first. With a lot of theoretical knowledge but little workfloor experience, he started ordering others around. Feeling justified by the top manager's remark, he started to overstretch himself by introducing all kinds of changes in the production planning. He started acting like a newly appointed crisis manager and was talking about wonderful new goals for the production department. "If we really set our mind to this, this production plant can become the world's top. We can double production, lower personnel cost, we can even give a lot of advice to mar-keting and sales since they hardly know anything of the production possibilities we have." In short, William got carried away by aspiring to unrealistic and unachievable goals. Along the way, he also forgot to con-nect to the reality of life "in the trenches" and he lost the connection with his team. William was quickly overwhelmed. The unions were on his back, and his co-workers didn't like having an "upstart" as a boss. Within two weeks, William's position became untenable. Top manage-ment considered removing him from the position. Fortunately, from his sickbed Tom showed more wisdom than anyone else. He wrote an email to the management, to William, and to the workers on the production floor: "Give William a fair chance. Let him take on tasks that he is capa-ble of fulfilling, and use your years of experience to get us through the peak season. I will coach William from behind the scenes as much as I can given my health situation. Please continue to do what all of you have been doing for years now: take care of the company." The gist of this email was practical. It said to management: "Don't overestimate William by expecting things from him that he can't handle." The message for the people on the shop floor was: "Don't underestimate him and write him off, either." In the following weeks, Tom invited William to his house twice a week to coach him on his management methods and to soften him up. William accepted the fact that he needed more guidance. The co-workers became much less critical and more understanding. Positive changes were soon underway.

So what is the moral of this tale? If you introduce unrealistic and unachievable goals and start to act like these goals are the only measur-ing posts, then failure is imminent. It really does not matter whether you burden yourself or someone else with these unrealistic and unachievable goals, the end result is always the same: failure. Now let's state that more positively — choosing and designing your goals in terms of realism and achievability greatly enhances your chances of obtaining good results.

2. Concrete goals can be described in terms of observable behavior

When goals are not translated into concrete, clearly defined and visible behaviors, they remain vague and unclear. Consider these goals: "You should work harder," "You must be more motivated," "Try to get your results faster," "Strive for more cooperation in your team," and, "Loosen up in your social contacts." These goals are vague because everybody will have his or her own interpretation of what "working harder" or "being more motivated" etc. means. This often leads to time-consuming debates about the how and when of what should be achieved. It is easy to see why such goals are hard to achieve — you have no clearly visible sign that tells you when you have reached them. In such situations it can seem like it is up to the whim of the boss whether something is rated OK or not!

If you translate these goals into exact and observable behavior, it becomes much easier to be successful in reaching them as progress can be measured. "Be on time" turns into "Start at eight o'clock." "Work overtime to finish that project" turns into "Go home when the job is done. Make sure to finalize that project by the end of this week." "Loosen up at the office" becomes "When you enter your office, say good morning to everybody, and go out for lunch with your colleagues." When goals are stated in terms of concrete desired behavior, it is much easier to know what one should be striving for. These behaviors act like signposts on your way to the goal. Stated simply, the more concretely you describe your goals — "What do I want to be doing to obtain my goals? What do others need to see me doing?" the easier the road to achievement becomes.

Let's take a business example that you might recognize — how to translate rather abstract ideas about quality into concrete behavioral guidelines. (When you read this, you should be able to imagine all kinds of rather abstract managerial topics. You will see how they get lost in the mist of managerial babble when one fails to translate them into concrete behavior.)

The Tooltech Company is a multinational conglomerate that designs and builds machinery for refineries. They are preparing for an ISO 9001 quality certification in all subsidiaries for which they have specialists available with particular knowledge of ISO 9001 procedures. The standard operating procedure is that the local company prepares the first draft of the quality handbook. Then the specialists from the group step in to help with the implementation of the project. Yvonne is the quality specialist assigned to Tooltech. After months of preparation, the general manager of one of the subsidiaries sends Yvonne a three-hundred-page quality handbook. As Yvonne studies the book, it soon becomes clear that it only contains very theoretical views. It is full of highly technical details but it says next to nothing about what actually has to be done. It appears to her that the local quality team has written a "Proustian trilogy on quality" instead of an ISO 9001 manual! Knowing how much time and energy this draft must have cost them, Yvonne compliments them on the job they have done. She tells them that their draft is the perfect starting point for a much more practical version of the handbook and sends them examples of how this can be done. The local manager and his team accept both the compliments and the advice. With help from Yvonne, they translate their initial draft into a thirty-six-page booklet filled with procedural rules.

This little booklet is filled to the brim with very practical what-to-do topics that help people write and act according to the most powerful quality rule: "Take note of examples of best practice, write down what you do that works fine and then follow these procedures." This way, quality management goals are translated into concrete behaviors that will themselves result in quality.

3. Start out with small goals and work your way up to big goals

Success breeds success. Setting a string of small consecutive goals towards your bigger goal makes it easier to achieve the big goal. Taking small steps instead of giant leaps is often the most useful and reliable way to get what you want. Small victories create an ideal breeding ground for further and bigger successes.

In addition, while defining these small steps towards the bigger goal, you also automatically define what you should avoid doing. This saves you a lot of energy.

Two major banks plan to merge. A taskforce is set up to streamline this merging process, chaired by Linda. The big goal for this taskforce is obvious — make this merger a success. From previous experiences, Linda knows that mergers are delicate to handle. So she starts by asking the key people of both companies what is working so well in their respective companies that it should be transferred to the merged company. The question serves to show the key persons that Linda will respect their strengths and reassures them. She then maps out the similarities and the differences of both companies. Together with her colleagues in the taskforce, Linda designs a program that will help smooth out the unavoidable difficulties inherent to all mergers, and calls it the "Best of Both" program. The goal of the "Best of Both" program is to avoid the classical fight in mergers about who will set the tone in the resulting company. There are, of course, many differences between the companies that have to be dealt with. The taskforce's next step is to determine the order in which these differences will be tackled over the next six months. They make sure that the (apparently) small matters are handled immediately, such as a direct telephone line between both locations, connecting the intranet systems, and the distribution of a list of the names and positions of all employees. Linda and her team organize dozens of short seminars under the label of the "Best of Both" program. Apart from offering information about the proceedings of the merger, the main goal of these seminars is to give people from all levels of the companies the opportunity to get to know each other.

Checklist for useful goals

When you are aiming for optimal efficiency as a manager, mentor or coach, you can use the following checklist to make sure that the goals you set for yourself, your co-workers or your company are geared towards success.

Useful goals are:

1. Realistic and achievable
2. Concrete, i.e. stated in terms of observable behavior
3. Preferably from small goals to big ones

Common mistakes in goal-setting

If the saying that we all can learn from our mistakes is true, then the moment has come to profit from the lessons that can be drawn from this saying. All of us make the mistakes that are described below. Being aware of these all too common mistakes can protect us against making the same mistake over and over.

1. Icarus, or the setting of self-destructive goals

Goal-setting is a basic managerial task. On your way up the hierarchical ladder, you will have done this many, many times. To get to your current position you must have been successful in hitting the mark on a regular basis. But who hasn't overstretched him- or herself by setting over-ambitious goals? Are you sure you never set goals that involved too many people and demanded changes that were too vast? Did you never indulge in goals that would have such an enormous impact on the market that they would bring your competitors to their knees? Dare you say that you have never chased impossible goals? Of course not, you are a manager. Managers do set these kinds of unreachable goals. If they hit, they hit big. But experience tells you that these types of goals usually aren't achieved. Usually such ambitions peter out, embarrassing you or causing a rough spot in your career. Even worse, the higher you are on the corporate ladder, the more means and resources you can put into chasing unreachable goals. And sometimes, this causes the downfall of the company you work(ed) for. Checking your goals for the risks they involve is a very wise move.

Think of the story of Icarus — if you want to fly towards the sun, don't make wings that are held together with wax. For that matter, don't try flying towards the sun at all — if you do succeed, you can be certain that success will kill you.

2. Unclear goals paralyze you

You often hear comments like: "It's not going well; we aren't making any progress; there is too much to do; there isn't enough time." These comments are the direct consequence of unclear goals — your employees aren't sure what it is they are working on, much less how they should be working on it. If the goals are not clear, they will by definition be harder to accomplish. Consequently, it becomes extremely difficult to determine how (or whether!) progress is being made. Since it's not clear where you are going, you simply don't know what your next step must be. Working on vague and unclear goals makes one insecure, and in turn insecurity causes your interventions to become even more vague. Your employees also become insecure, act accordingly and mutual dissatisfaction arises.

Visionary goals: I have a dream

What do Martin Luther King Jr., Mahatma Gandhi, Nelson Mandela and other great leaders have in common apart from the fact that they had a great impact on human society? They all had visionary goals, which from the moment they were conceived served as beacons for an extremely ambitious and an almost inconceivable yet possible future. Martin Luther King's famous "I have a dream" speech called for a world that was almost unthinkable at the time the speech was given. A young Nelson Mandela expressed hope that one day he would be the first black South African president. He then spent thirty years in prison. Chasing a dream (sometimes) makes the impossible come true.

However, contrary to common romantic thinking, the biographies of these great men teach us that their road to ultimately reaching their goals was very long, winding, tedious, difficult, and occasionally life-threatening. It also took them many years and thousands upon thousands of little steps towards small goals, one step at a time.

We do want to encourage managers to create visionary goals — and to actually achieve them, but remember, it is better to take one little step at a time. What also really helps is keeping your feet on the ground. Not everybody must or even needs to be the next Bill Gates. If instead you look beyond everyday work and you follow your own personal ambition, constantly translating your high hopes into small, feasible steps, then you can be the Bill Gates of your team.

How does goal-setting work in reality?

You can choose any topic to demonstrate goal-setting, but maybe it would be nice to take a moment to apply it to yourself. How do you go about setting goals for yourself? Is it an informal thing or do you make the effort of sitting down and thinking? Reading the following example, you might apply the questions to your own situation and see where they lead you.

Imagine a manager, Douglas, and his team member Juan. They work in the administrative division of a pharmaceutical company. Juan is the recently appointed office manager of a team of nine persons. Douglas is his boss and supervisor. They are having a meeting to streamline some of the problems that Juan has been reporting.

Now, let's see what a goal-setting conversation might look like. (See if you recognize steps 1 and 2 from the seven-step dance.)

Douglas: "Hi Juan, nice of you to call this meeting. Before we start, could you update me a little on how things are going in your division. How long have you been in your new role now?"

Juan: "About six months. But it is not until recently that I have really found my way around things."

Douglas: "Good. It's pretty normal that one needs some time to acclimatize. Now, you wanted to talk to me about certain issues. What do we have to talk about so that this meeting will be useful for you and your team?"

Juan: "I think you are aware of the fact that not only I am new to this function of office manager as a person but that the role itself has recently been created in our company, and it is certainly quite new to the team I am managing."

Douglas: "Yes, we all are well aware of this. And as far as I can tell, you are doing a fine job."

Juan: "Thanks. Still there are some questions that still puzzle me. Two big questions actually and that's why I am happy that we are having his meeting today."

Douglas: "Very well, let's tackle your questions. What do you want to start with? And maybe it's useful if you explain a little of the context of your questions first, so that I understand your concerns better."

Juan: "It's nothing complicated, you know. The problem consists of two elements that interconnect, of course. Since I am new in my role, I would like to know how my team sees my contribution and what I could do in addition to what I am doing now. On the other hand, this team has been used to a pretty, well I wouldn't say sloppy organization ... but I think you could say that there is almost no organization. They all do their best and work hard, but there is no clear or shared description of tasks and responsibilities. There is little or no control — and nobody gets real feedback even when they are under-performing. Since I am new, I am a bit reluctant to jump in with all kinds of new stuff that they are not used to. They might take it personally, or it might put me in a difficult position."

Douglas: "Well, seems like you've got your finger on the pulse of your team. You mention several elements that you might be able to improve. The team is hard-working, so that's a good start. The fact that you as "new kid on the block" are careful not to stampede your way in shows your common sense as a manager. That's a good start, too. Now, let's consider the topics that you mention: your own contribution, putting in place some form of feedback, starting out with some kind of agreement on tasks and responsibilities. What would be the smallest step forward?"

Juan: "If I could find a way to take the lead in getting them to work with me on the task descriptions. For the moment, I am pretty convinced that some of them are working on things that are already being worked on by others because they are not communicating — and they are too busy anyhow."

Douglas: "You have already mentioned an elegant method to get them to cooperate. As office manager you oversee all tasks in your team and from your standpoint you can help them to free up some time by ensuring that they avoid doing things twice. I am pretty sure that will be appreciated."

Juan: "True. And that would be a nice way to get them to collaborate on the task descriptions, wouldn't it?"

Douglas: "I think so, yes. How long do you think you will need to get this job done with your team with good results and without disturbing the daily work?"

Juan: "I think this job and the changes that will come with it can be done in three weeks. And then we only have to implement the changes and see how we'll keep adapting from there."

Douglas: "Very good. If you coordinate this project, would that be a good way of showing your added value to your team?"

Juan: "If I go about it slowly and carefully, yes."

Douglas: "OK, that answers your first question and gets us to your first goal, namely knowing your contribution to the team. You might simply ask your team members for feedback on how they think you are doing in helping them."

Juan: "*Will do. That leaves me with the feedback goal. But as we are talking, I can already see that feedback can easily be made part of the task description project. It is obvious that we will need feedback on the results of the task redistribution. After all, we are doing this to become more effective, meaning to be able to do more as a team with less effort. Everybody will be interested in finding out if the project helps them in their daily work or not. As office manager, I could try and find a way of measuring the progress. I need to think this over but I will find a way to make it work.*"

Douglas: "*Very good. I am sure you will succeed with the project. Is there anything that you would like to discuss further for the moment?*"

Juan: "*No. This is enough for now. My goals are clear and I know how to go about sharing my goals with my team members. Thanks.*"

Self-test for useful goals

Consider some of the goals that you have been working on during the last few months. Now compare those goals to the elements in the checklist.

If you consider which goals that you have been working on were reached in the end, it is highly probable that they were defined along the lines of the left column. It is also likely that the characteristics of the goals that you did not meet correspond to the criteria in the right column of the checklist.

Every one of us is working daily to achieve goals. So it might be useful to take a few minutes to list the goals that you are working on now and check their characteristics. If you find out that your present goals belong to the left column, you may give yourself a big compliment because chances are high that you will be successful. If you discover that you have phrased them in terms of the right column, congratulations also. All is not lost, you are just in time to rephrase them in terms of the left column.

Step 4: Uncovering resources

Classical problem-oriented management models run on the basic assumption that problems arise due to the deficiency of the staff and/or the lack of resources. Or in other words, when problems arise, they always arise from some kind of deficit — the person is not capable (enough), there is not enough willpower or entrepreneurial spirit, competition is too strong and we are too weak, etc.

The solution-focused model starts out from a totally different standpoint and assumes that every human system, be it an individual or a team, has resources at its disposal at all times, *even in times of trouble!* When problems occur, we see it as an indication that the concerned parties in the problem have momentarily lost confidence in their own solution-focused possibilities, simply because they have lost the access to their own resources. You might say that they have (temporarily) lost their personal manual on "how to use our resources."

The job of the solution-building manager is to help his or her staff (re)discover their "forgotten" resources and/or to give them new tools for building solutions. In this context, we define "resources" as "every available tool that can be used to create solutions." Resources can be very intangible, such as effort, motivation, loyalty to the company, team spirit, or expertise, but they also can be very concrete tools, such as communication skills, crisis and conflict management skills, procedures, business insights, technical tools, time, money, or attention. Sometimes what initially seems negative can be considered a positive thing. A crisis can become an opportunity — a setback in business opens your eyes, losing

clients may prompt you to pay more attention to them, complaints may encourage you to become more customer-oriented. In short, your company's weaknesses may be turned into opportunities for improvement, and threats can turn into chances.

We understand that this concept of resources might go against your intuition at first. If you have the bad luck of working for a cynical boss, and you think that your company and staff are different so that you can't possibly see what resources they might possess, please allow us some leniency. Although it might seem vague if you are in the middle of a struggle, the resource concept is not some kind of weird New Age "everybody-can-do-anything-if-only-you-put-your-mind-to-it-and-eat-lots-of-yoghurt" concept. On the contrary, if it is used to discover what you need to solve your problems and meet your challenges, it is a highly effective tool for change and maintenance.

The essence of resource orientation is that you turn your attention and the attention of your staff to everything that still goes well in spite of the problems you are facing. By focusing on what still works and on the available resources, you dispel the counterproductive problem trance and boost your possibilities for finding fitting solutions. So let's put on our detective hats and take out the magnifying glass to uncover the hiding places of your resources and those of your team.

Sleuth for resources

Isn't it remarkable that people tend to forget what they know when they are under pressure? And to make matters worse, the bigger you think your troubles are, the more you tend to think that your problem is omnipresent and will never ever go away. Of course, this is primarily just a perception and for that not a very useful one. Actually, concentrating on the perceived impossibility of a solution is a mistake. Pregnancy and death are problems without an exception but — as you will learn in the next chapter — these are not really problems but limitations.

The solution-focused resources orientation is a powerful antidote against the common problem poison. By asking the right solution-building questions, you can help your staff to uncover the resources that they don't think they have available. These resources can be found in places that are sometimes so obvious that one forgets to look there — let's examine these "hiding places" one by one.

1. Exceptions to the problem

There is not a single problem in the (business) world that is present all the time and with the same intensity. There are always exceptions to the problem that can be identified in moments and under circumstances when the problem occurs to a lesser degree or even not at all.

When you think about exceptions to the problem, and you have a close look at the circumstances in which these exceptions occur, you will become aware that your team is already using its resources and is already able to create partial solutions.

Exceptions and resources are two sides of the same coin.

Once you grasp the idea that exceptions to the problems point to partial solutions, you will be able to elaborate on them by using solution-building questions. This way, you promote gradual change towards more permanent solutions. The solution-focused manager concentrates on the "who, how, what, when, and where" of exceptions — the more details the better.

Think about a moment in which your own problems seemed so overwhelming that you were convinced that they were definitely here to stay, and you would simply have to live with them and suffer them. You can pick a problem from your private life, such as problems with your children, or a problem at work like a seemingly impossible conflict situation. Ask yourself some of the following questions and notice the difference.

- What did you do differently when your problem wasn't present?
- What did you do differently during the time when the problem could have occurred but somehow did not?
- Who in your team/your family did what differently when the problem wasn't as big as it is now?
- What worked best when you solved a similar problem in the past?
- What would your co-workers or family say you do differently when the problem is less intense?
- What worked best in a similar previous project (e.g. when you also thought that you would go over budget)?
- What were you doing differently during the last successful project?
- Which aspects of the project are still working well in spite of the fact that the project as a whole is stuck?

The answers to these solution-building questions are filled to the brim with resources.

When you systematically ask more and more details about the exceptions, you will find that these exceptions multiply. You facilitate the chain reaction of intensifying solutions, and chances are high that the problem will practically dissolve itself.

TIP

Each exception contains the beginning of a solution.

2. Solutions from another context

Resources can be found in solutions that have been applied in contexts other than the problem context. Staff members and employees (just like bosses and managers, by the way) have a life outside the problematic situation that they are encountering in their companies. Top managers are fathers, sons, wives, mothers, neighbors, friends, country club members, etc. The same goes for all of us. We all have different resources available in other contexts, and we tend to forget them when we are locked away in our corporate difficulties. Why don't companies tap into these resources? We all know colleagues who are grumpy at work but fun to be around at the yearly company barbecue. We all know colleagues who do not seem to be able to get themselves organized in their work and yet, if you asked them, they would tell you that they are single-handedly managing the upbringing of three kids at home.

Maybe you also know or recognize the persons in the following scenarios.

The chief engineer gives sharp presentations to his own team when it comes to technical matters. However, when he needs to do presentations for top executives, he tends to become insecure and loses himself in details. You can help this engineer with his presentation skills more effectively if you look at how he does it in front of his team than by asking why he under performs in front of his bosses. By looking at the presentation skills he uses in front of his team, he gains access to what he already knows how to do well, and he only needs some help on how to apply these skills in the more challenging environment of the meetings with top management.

An employee who suffers from fear of failure may seldom speak during meetings, but use every break to talk about his clever ideas. Unfortunately, most of his ideas cannot be used because he hasn't brought them up during the meeting. His interesting proposals in the breaks are pearls cast before swine, since he never dares to come back to them in the meeting, for fear of not being taken seriously. You can help that person, and your team, to profit from these useful ideas, if you look for a suitable moment during the meeting and then invite the employee to state his contributions on the spot.

3. Human resources

It is no coincidence that the personnel department of every company is now called the "Human Resources Department." As you know, humans are the single most important assets of every company. But you do not need an HR department to appreciate the importance of human resources, you only need common sense!

You can find many resources in the human characteristics of individual employees — intelligence, motivation, job experience, the ability of a person to smoothly switch between teams, critical thinking skills, etc. But resources can also be found in teams and in the organization as a whole — team cooperation, loyalty towards the company, group cohesion, market leadership, corporate culture, technical know-how, financial strength. You can also detect resources outside the organization — your private banker can be very useful if he or she hands out a cocktail of different finance techniques to help reduce loan costs; your most important supplier of software is willing to think along the lines of your own company; the government's continual changes in tax regulations stimulates fiscal creativity in your financial department. All these resources are available to you if you take the time and have the courage to look for them and utilize them.

4. Standard management techniques

Standard management techniques — ISO 9000, integral quality care (IQC), balanced scorecards, benchmarking, etc. — seem very problem-oriented at first. They seem to be trying to fill the gap between the current situation and the desired state, and they focus on what is lacking. However, when you apply them in a solution-focused manner, these standard management tools can be turned into fountains of resources. You simply have to switch the focus.

Most quality programs, for example, are geared towards erasing poor quality. With a small twist, your quality programs can be turned into the ongoing search for constantly improving quality. Instead of staying focused on the removal of poor quality, the focus is moved to sustainable technology that keeps on producing good quality.

Here is another example. By benchmarking your own company with the best common practice in the field, you are then more focused on introducing techniques that work well for others rather than just removing under-performance in your company.

5. Solutions hiding between the folds of the problem

The solution-focused manager trains him- or herself to detect the resources that hide between the folds of the problem. Here is an example of how that can be achieved.

The regulations department of a high-tech multinational corporation was under great stress from a reorganization exercise that had swept through the whole corporation. They were forced to lay off many of their highly trained technicians. Before the restructuring, the regulations department had been responsible for the regulation of services all over the company. They created, controlled, and monitored procurement of all the company's products. This ranged from the exact dimensions of pins in a socket to the density of the foam used in headphones. It's evident that they had a lot of work and a lot of power. Nobody could start production without approval. However, this all changed radically after reorganization, when the regulation task was decentralized. Every department was required to set its own regulations and the original regulations department's task was reduced to overseeing and ensuring that these standards were communicated throughout the consortium. The only instances in which they still executed their technical specialization were when products needed to be manufactured in different parts of the company and then needed assembling. In such cases they still had the overall responsibility.

On top of this, every department, including regulations, was converted into an independent business unit with its own income responsibility. The result was that the remaining employees of the regulations department, who once were the cream of the crop when it came to technical skill and responsibility, now had a very reduced turnover due to their limited tasks. The remaining staff members were living under the constant threat of not making their budgeted turnover, and the likely consequences. This led them to exert their influence by using their regulations stamp whenever possible. The result was that lots of interdepartmental regulations were painstakingly slow, overly precise, and, therefore, overpriced, sometimes to the client's great dissatisfaction. The self-protective response of the regulations department, or more precisely of what was left of it, was very counterproductive as they were serving themselves instead of their clients.

Before the situation spiraled out of control and debilitated the whole company, the director of the regulations department decided to organize a two-day seminar to which she invited the complete team to consider the following topic: "Let's go with the flow by using what we know."

Readers who have gone through a similar reorganization process will know from experience how the first hours of this seminar went — whining, complaining, telling war stories from the good old days, more whining. After a while of this, there almost always comes a moment in which the team members come to the conclusion that more whining isn't going to help them get ahead. At precisely that moment, their manager asked them to sit in small groups and to discuss their true skills and specialties and how these could be used in the future. They soon found out that their know-how on technical procedures would be a perfect fit for the ongoing corporate-wide quality program. After all, developing, controlling, and securing technical procedures is what they knew best. In addition they had in-depth knowledge of communication procedures that streamline implementation processes in a large company. They decided to become service providers to the corporate-wide quality program and offer the specialized technical support that currently had to be purchased from outside suppliers. The seminar ended with a detailed proposition for the vice president of operations. All went well and a few months later, the regulations department had a steady income from this new project on top of their specific regulations work.

This example shows you how you can detect resources by looking into the folds of the problem. The department looked at its own resources and this helped it generate ideas about what it could do with these resources to solve its problem. Thinking out of the box can help you to uncover resources you had previously not been aware of.

Techniques for finding resources

1. Constant resource awareness

Developing a keen eye for resources is like developing a keen eye when you are harvesting mushrooms in the wild. The untrained eye sees nothing whereas the trained eye finds lots of them. Once you know what to look for, it's fairly simple to find more. In terms of business, you don't need to wait for a problem to occur to start looking for resources. Be on the lookout for whatever your staff is doing well and then comment positively on it all the time. Be on watch for every possible aspect of your employees' behavior and focus on whatever goes well in spite of the problems.

> Develop your resource radar and resources will pop up everywhere.

2. Execute repetitive resource audits

Instead of auditing your company or team for problems, why not try auditing for resources? A great way to do this is to encourage everybody, you included, to take some time to write down everything that goes well in the company or team, and to make notes on all the resources that you have been or are using when dealing with work. Take care to concentrate on resources that you use in circumstances other than just your company or team. Then sit together with your team and share everything you've learned. You will find that this exercise will heighten your resource awareness.

If you do this exercise regularly, it will have the same effect as going to the gym on a regular basis — you will give your solution-building muscles a good workout and help them develop.

3. Develop a healthy resource obsession

It is natural for managers to occupy themselves with analyzing problems all day long because most think that that's what they are paid for. Actually, managers are really paid to help others find solutions. From this perspective, the most useful occupation is to be obsessed with detecting resources and exceptions in the doings of your staff. This utterly healthy obsession always creates a productive atmosphere that is a driver for success within your organization.

Resource obsession is more useful than problem obsession.

What to do with resources once you have found them

So what do you do after you've found (or created) resources? You put the spotlight on them! Use simple phrases like "fantastic!", "wow," "excellent," "great" or "congratulations!" Never hesitate to express your appreciation loud and clear and as quickly and directly as possible. It is amazing how quickly employees and teams will pick up on this, and use their resources once they have been pointed out to them. In this way a solution-focused manager helps employees to help themselves and each other by creating their own resources and exceptions.

In short, bombard your employees with their own (rediscovered) resources and give them all the credit. You will learn more about the art of giving compliments in step 5 of the solution tango (page 77).

How does uncovering resources work in reality?

The following conversation goes on between a sales manager and a staff member. The reason for the conversation is that the junior salesman, Felix, has just lost a promising big account and is very unhappy about it. He needs some support from his boss.

Junior salesman Felix: "Thanks for seeing me at such short notice. I really need to talk to you about losing that big account — it should never have happened and I am afraid that I have lost my touch as a salesperson."

Sales manager Shirley: "Not so fast, slow down. Before you undermine yourself, please explain what happened."

Felix: "Well, you remember I told you that I have been trying to win that big account for over three months now. I got an email late last night that bluntly states that they have chosen another supplier. That's it. No explanation, nothing. First thing this morning I called my contact, but she had nothing to add except that the board had decided to go for the competition. When I called someone else at the company, he told me that it has nothing to do with price or service. 'Just a freak decision,' he said, 'nothing you can do.' Well, that doesn't help me at all. I sent them an email in which I asked for more information on the decision, I also made it clear to them that we are still up for negotiating a better deal. The only response was 'maybe next time.' I am completely stumped."

Shirley: "I can understand. On the other hand, was there anything that you should or could have done differently?"

Felix: "I don't think so, but you never know. I spent all night going through this thing in my mind and trying to figure out what could have gone wrong. This was such a big opportunity to boost my sales figures, the deal would have made my year. Now, I've got nothing."

Shirley: "Hold on, not so fast. You are tossing out the baby with the bathwater. Try not to throw out the bathtub and the bathroom, too! I completely understand that this loss hits you hard. Indeed, this single deal would have catapulted your sales figures way over your trimester budget. But you've still got a lot of deals going on apart from this one."

Felix: "Yeah, well. I know that's true but it's no consolation at the moment. I'm really disappointed in myself. I shouldn't be telling you this, but it is gnawing on my self-confidence."

Shirley: "I am glad you are so open with me. All of us encounter disappointments, and doubting oneself is pretty normal. As long as you don't allow your doubt to choke you, it keeps you alert. Try looking at it from another point of view: I greatly admire your persistence in how you dealt with the client, and you didn't let go easily — that's always a sign of a good salesman. Now let me ask you some questions. This is probably not the first deal you lost, and it will not be the last deal that you will lose in your career. How did you cope with deals that you lost in the past? What is it that helped you get over it and continue?"

Felix: "Oh, it has happened a lot, especially when I started in sales."

Shirley: "How did you deal with setbacks then?"

Felix: "At first, I got the impression that I was not made for sales, but at the time, I talked it through with my manager. He taught me to focus on the next possible deal instead of lingering on the lost one. He was very encouraging, and I learned from all my beginner's mistakes."

Shirley: *"So you were persistent from the beginning. Good. Now what could you learn from this situation?"*

Felix: *"Maybe not to focus on the loss too long and put my mind on the next possibility. It's like when I play tennis. In the beginning when I played competition, I regularly lost simply because I could not get my mind off a bad ball. I kept thinking about it, and of course, the next ball also went astray. When I became aware of this, I started winning more."*

Shirley: *"So, how did you learn to become a winner in tennis?"*

Felix: *"Once I had understood that lingering on a bad ball is useless, I trained myself to use the mantra 'next ball'. That got me going. I no longer lost energy on bad balls but concentrated on the next ball."*

Shirley: *"So tennis can teach us stuff that we can use in business, can't it?"*

Felix: *"Yes — you are so right. Actually, my client did say in that last email 'maybe next time'. So, I'm going to concentrate on the next big account. Thank you so much for talking to me."*

Step 5: the art of giving compliments

How do you feel when you get an email from your boss saying that he or she really appreciated your contributions in the last meeting? How does your staff respond when you congratulate them on their nice presentation? How does your supplier react when you compliment her on her good services towards your company? How do you react when someone

gives you a compliment about a job well done? It makes you feel good. Is that important in business life? Yes, it definitely is. When you feel good because other people make you feel good, you perform better in whatever it is you are doing.

In contrast to this scenario, if people are grumpy to you, snap at you at all occasions, constantly point out in great detail what you are doing wrong or — maybe worse — simply ignore you, how does that make you feel? How is that helping you do a better job? There is a lot of talk about retention management — however, countless people leave their jobs because they feel misjudged, never receive compliments, or no longer "feel at home."

Of course, a seasoned manager like you realizes how sensitive people are to the way they are treated. You know that showing respect and acknowledging people are the most powerful management tools you've got. You also know that one of the most powerful ways of doing this is by giving compliments to people.

Typology of compliments: general and functional

It's important to be aware that there are two main categories of compliments which are useful in different circumstances: *general* compliments and *functional* compliments.

General compliments

What you have learned in step 4 (page 67) on resources is useful when it comes to *general* compliments. Great people managers have a keen eye for resources in their staff. Your well-trained eyes and ears see and hear resources everywhere, and that gives you ample opportunity for giving compliments to everybody you're working with.

The hiding places of resources are possibilities for *general* complimenting:

1. exceptions to the problem
2. solutions from another context
3. characteristics of your employees
4. standard management techniques
5. between the folds of the problem

Ample use of these general compliments is a great cooperation enhancer. By using this category on a regular basis, you create a very nice place to work. However, there is more to complimenting than this — you can achieve even more by using another form of compliment which we call "functional compliments."

Functional compliments

Functional compliments are used to reinforce aspects of your staff's behavior that you would like to see happening more often. It is actually very simple: if an employee does something useful that is beneficial to him- or herself, the team and the company, give them a compliment on it. "Thanks for staying late and helping your colleague out when his planning program crashed yesterday. Without your expert knowledge of the system he would certainly not have been able to get production planning running by the time the factory started up early this morning. Congratulations on your expertise and team spirit." A compliment can be about anything useful — on someone's good memos, clear information, sharp analysis of a certain case, punctuality (or, if the person is habitually late, conscientiousness in always letting you know), firm convictions (or open-mindedness), etc.

What's the benefit of giving compliments?

Complimenting is so much more than just being friendly and trying to garner approval from your colleagues. Effective managers don't waste their energy on trying to be seen as "Mister Nice Guy." On the contrary, giving compliments is an important tool in establishing and then developing your working relationships. In that respect, dance step 5 of giving compliments ties in with the very first step of our solution tango, namely socializing. Functional compliments show your staff that you notice their contributions and that you make an effort to say something about them. These functional compliments are good reinforcers of useful behavior.

So the benefits of giving compliments are multiple.

- You build a cooperative working relationship because your staff notice that you make the effort of being attentive to what they do well.
- Your compliments on what your staff do well enhances their self-confidence.
- Complimenting your employees on their resources turns their noses in the direction of possible solutions instead of staying fixated on the problem.
- Complimenting results in an ever-growing atmosphere of trust and cooperation that will support and increase the possibility of and desire for change.
- Perhaps most importantly, your *functional* compliments are a powerful confirmation of the useful behavior of your employees, they help them to do more of what works.

Giving compliments: a neglected skill

Don't you find it strange that so few people are aware of the power of giving compliments? Speculation about why this is so is rather futile — yet we do observe, quite often, that people don't compliment one another enough. Giving compliments seems to be an art that most people lose when they enter adult life. In addition, giving compliments seems to be a skill that is left behind in the parking lot of most corporate buildings. All too often this skill is not picked up again when those managers go home in the evening.

This is a sad state of affairs, especially when you realize the beneficial influence that giving compliments has on human performance. Have you ever run a marathon? Well, I personally haven't, but even for much shorter runs, I know from personal experience that encouragement and compliments on your effort makes you run that extra mile.

Some people have a natural talent for giving compliments, but for most people it isn't quite so easy. That is not a problem at all. Giving compliments is not something genetic or inborn that only an elite part of the general population can do, it is a skill that you can learn or rediscover. To become convinced of the utility of compliments, you need only have an open mind and notice the positive influence that compliments have on yourself.

A word of warning may be appropriate here. You will probably run into macho manager types who will deny categorically that giving or receiving compliments has any benefit whatsoever. These self-proclaimed iron men of corporate life call people management a game for softies, just like they tend to define complimenting as an action that is reserved for wimps. Our advice is to ignore these remarks. When it comes to these people, let us ask just one question. Do you really consider people who talk like that to be good managers? Are they successful when it comes to dealing with their colleagues? You already know the answer ... discussion closed.

In the long run, even hard-boiled managers will succumb to the usefulness of giving compliments once they realize that complimenting staff (or anybody for that matter) will encourage them to do more of what works.

Giving compliments is not flattery, and being critical is a must

It is important to note that giving compliments has nothing to do with a badly misunderstood and overcooked "New Ageism" ("Hi, nice to meet you, miss you already") nor with feigned or exaggerated optimism ("Wow, you look good for a dying person," ... "Good for you, be happy, your bankruptcy really gives you a new start and a clean slate from which you will conquer the world.") This type of communication is off-putting and always counterproductive.

Solution-focused management is not about making a dismal reality look good and denying the suffering and the difficulties. Solution-focused management is a way of getting **out** of these difficult situations, and finding a way of dealing with them.

Giving compliments is not the same as flattering someone. Flattery is about fake behavior, about buttering people up and treating them in a superficial way. Flattery is utterly counterproductive because it reinforces the wrong behavior and does not let people know what the standards and goals in the organization are.

Compliments also do not preclude criticism. Solution-focused managers are not softies, who agree with everything — they give criticism, react, complain, confront, put colleagues in their place, respond promptly and if necessary in a sharp fashion. In short, they do what is necessary to get the job done. However, they do it in a respectful way that does not endanger their working relationship with other employees.

Misunderstandings about complimenting

Misunderstandings that occur in the world of business need to be cleared up or they remain unnecessary roadblocks on the route to greater efficiency. Maybe these misunderstandings stem from the popular myth of a heroic, untouchable and ever-strong manager who has everything, his own emotions included, perfectly under control and who never wavers under stress. Such individuals simply do not exist, and I do hope that you will grant us permission to refrain from endorsing this kind of fantasy.

Instead, we will outline a few of the most popular misunderstandings about giving compliments, so that those readers who are still struggling with the importance of giving compliments can see the benefits. If you know which kind of misunderstandings are around, it is much easier to deal with them.

- Many managers in the harsh world of business are afraid of being considered "soft" or "wimpy" if they are merely friendly and open with their employees, and are certainly not prepared to give compliments. They are scared of losing their cool image. However, being friendly and open does not mean that you let everything slide and that you fail to set standards and boundaries.
- One of the biggest misconceptions in contemporary management is that the middle/top manager must know best, if not know everything,

and that they must act accordingly, meaning giving orders in a firm way without a shadow of a doubt. Now, it is obvious that someone who puts himself (or is put on) the "I-know-everything-because-that-is-what-I-am-supposed-to-know" chair has no latitude to compliment anybody else. He/she is supposed to know it all and tends to reserve the compliments for him/herself, and take all the credit. Today, corporations need to retain, empower, and use all the talent in their organization — if you can make your team more than the sum of the individuals by creating a great spirit through complimenting, that's worth more than being recognized as the specialist in a small area of expertise.

- "But I have never been in the habit of giving compliments. I don't see how I can start now if I haven't been giving my staff compliments from the beginning. Besides, if I start now, won't my employees think that there is something wrong?" There is a simple way around this if you just admit that you haven't said it before. You could say something like: "I don't think I ever told you this before but actually I think you are doing a great job — especially that last report on project X, which was really useful. Congratulations."

- "Yeah, complimenting is an idea, but will this not open a Pandora's box where my staff see opportunities everywhere to start asking for all kinds of favors from me? Such as 'you gave me a compliment, now give me more money'." By the way, compliments need not be complemented with money!

- "Giving compliments is too complicated for me. When I don't take care to distribute the compliments very evenly among my staff, some will feel excluded and others might become jealous." This misconception comes from the utterly strange idea that a) employees are like children who all want the same amount of candy and b) that compliments are a rare commodity of which the supply is limited. And of course, this is not true — once you start, you will find that there is more to compliment on than you can say in one day.

- "Why should I bother to give compliments to my staff when they are doing a good job? They are very well paid to do their job and that should be enough." At the end of the day, however important money is, there is far more at stake. Money is an expensive incentive while compliments are a free reward — and a high motivation of your staff will pay big dividends in the long run.

- "When I give a compliment to someone, I am afraid that they will not believe me. On the contrary, they might think that I am exaggerating and become suspicious of me. They might doubt my honesty." Well, congratulations, your statement proves that you are already handing out compliments. Now you just need a little help with how to do it in such a way that you become self-confident in giving compliments. Please read on, help is at hand.

- "In our (corporate or national) culture, people are not used to getting compliments and therefore it is not appropriate to give them compliments." I remember a story from a good friend who is a specialist in intercultural management. She was sent out to a Central Asian country to do a change management project with a large bank. Before leaving, she double-checked all the handbooks on intercultural management and communication, and she triple-checked with a local specialist. The advice was: "Do not compliment Central Asian managers too openly." Being convinced of the power of compliments, she did the contrary, and gave them lots of compliments on what they did well in spite of their difficult situation. She got only enthusiastic reactions and the change management project went smoothly. During her farewell party, the biggest compliment that she got in return came from one of the local top managers. In his speech to the whole team he said: "When we knew you were coming for this change project, we told each other that we had survived communism, we survived capitalism and we will survive that western consultant. There was no need to survive you! On the contrary, thanks for all your help." The efficiency of complimenting is not dependent on culture — **how** you compliment is.

Beginner's guide to giving compliments

If you are not accustomed to giving compliments or if you would like to learn how to do more complimenting, we have designed a few helpful techniques.

When you are not used to giving or receiving compliments, it can feel a little awkward in the beginning. You might think: "I can't do that; I have never talked like that to my staff. What will they think? How will they react?" In this case we advise you to "test the water." Start with a small and inconspicuous compliment, and see/feel how people react. When you gain some confidence from their reactions, you can slowly work yourself up towards bigger and more important compliments on bigger and more important aspects of the work of your staff. And with gained self-confidence and positive reactions, you can slowly increase the frequency.

When you use the tool of giving compliments, you will probably encounter a situation where the reaction of the subject startles you. Maybe the compliment came out a little too abruptly or maybe the moment was ill-chosen. This is a crucial moment in your learning process.

At this point, many beginning "'complimenters" give up: "See, it's not working." Knowing this will happen and having a deep-rooted memory of a compliment that worked perfectly is the best preparation for such a moment.

Once you get through the initial stages, it's boomerang time. When you show respect, you receive respect, and the same goes for compliments: when you give compliments, you are bound to receive compliments in return. These return compliments can be words of thanks or just seeing that the person you complimented "grows" as a person. The boomerang effect of compliments can very soon become a positive cycle that will enforce your use of them. This will make your (working) life a lot easier, more pleasant and a whole lot more effective.

With further practice, the skill of giving compliments becomes an attitude. When that attitude becomes second nature, you have become a master in the art of giving compliments.

Every compliment yields a dividend!

When it comes to complimenting, there is one and only one law that everybody should know — complimenting always has a positive effect. Giving compliments is like putting money in a safe investment — you always get a dividend. Well-delivered compliments are never a waste of time or useless.

What you should notice almost immediately is the positive effect that giving compliments has on your working relationship with your staff. And if you do not see an immediate positive response, you can be sure that sooner or later, especially when you become a chronic giver of compliments, you will reap the rewards.

Because of the primary importance of this law and because it is so nice to see it in big print, please humor us here:

Every compliment yields a dividend

Important prerequisites for giving compliments

If you want your compliments to be useful, there are three conditions that you absolutely need to meet. When you sin against one, two or — heaven forbid — all of these prerequisites, your compliment will miss its target completely, and that will have bad consequences. Worse, you will lose face, validity, and credibility — which is why we urge you to take extremely good care that these conditions are met.

1. Compliments must be genuine, authentic, and sincere

In brief: If you don't really mean what you say, say nothing.

By the way, if you do not have a clue what genuine, authentic and sincere mean in real life, you are in big trouble!

2. Compliments must be appropriate to the situation and based on reality

When not appropriate, your compliment will be accepted but it will make no difference whatsoever because it will not have the desired effect of reinforcing behavior that you would like to encourage. On the contrary, it might have a downgrading effect. For example, when you conduct an appraisal, it's hardly appropriate to compliment your employee on his well-shined shoes or on her nicely manicured fingernails (unless of course you are the manager of a shoe shop or nail salon).

The compliments you give should be based on reality. Don't compliment someone on a presentation that hasn't been given yet. Saying that you think it's fantastic that someone comes to work every day is not a compliment, but telling them that you appreciate their punctuality is.

3. Exaggerating is never good

Tailor your compliment to the situation and the person you're dealing with. You don't have to throw your arms around your secretary's neck when she finishes a report on time, and you don't have to nominate the accountant for the Nobel Prize when she suggests a favorable fiscal plan.

When it comes to complimenting, more is certainly not better. On the contrary, less is more, especially if the "less" is well designed.

How do you deliver a compliment?

Solution-focused managers always seize the opportunity to congratulate their boss, employees, clients, or suppliers. Commonly used words are: good! wow! excellent! great! well done! terrific! congratulations! fantastic! Allow us to give you a little advice here, and that is to use only expressions that you yourself are comfortable with. If saying "wonderful" feels awkward when the word leaves your mouth, simply stick to "OK."

Shake people's hands or pat them on the back to let them know you are genuinely impressed. Your facial expression is also important — it underscores your words and body language. Don't worry too much about it, though. If you are authentic about your compliments, and it is really a behavior you want more of, your body language will naturally be appropriate.

Don't be afraid to send a "well done!" email or attach a Post-it note expressing your appreciation to an employee's computer screen (where everybody can see it). Written compliments are particularly useful because the receivers usually keep them and remember them. (But don't forget other employees in other departments!)

A very powerful method for delivering compliments is by doing it indirectly. Take the example of a young mother who is standing in line to pay in a shop. An elderly couple who are waiting in line behind her tap her on the shoulder and say, "Congratulations, you have a very beautiful baby." The young mother will love to hear such a compliment. Now imagine that the elderly couple do not tap the mother on the shoulder, but that they say to each other, just loud enough so that the young mother can hear it, "Have you seen what a beautiful baby she has?" Now, what would be the difference? Both compliments will work, of course, but which one do you think will be the more powerful? The indirect method probably will be more powerful for there is no resistance possible.

The indirect method of delivering compliments works equally well in business life. You can use this technique on the phone, for instance, when you are talking to someone from a different department and your assistant is within earshot: "Of course I can send you the documents. You know Sally, my assistant, always has everything at her fingertips, it is such a joy to work with such professional people!" This way you can compliment without seeming patronizing at all.

How does complimenting work in reality?

Step 5, giving compliments, should be used in conjunction with all the other steps in the solution tango. It's useless to only give compliments without dancing the other steps. Compliments are never given in a vacuum, and although step 5 is one of the most used and important steps in the dance, it is just a tool and not a goal in itself.

If you would like to see how giving compliments works in real life, we suggest that you leaf through this book. In the many business case examples you will almost always find evidence of compliments.

Step 6: offering differentiation by asking scaling questions

"Oh, it used to be perfect in our company but now, after the merger/take-over/reorganization/new boss, nothing works like it used to." Do you recognize this? When people are unhappy and frustrated, be it at home or at work, they sometimes have the slight tendency to think and talk in terms of black and white. They feel good or they feel bad. Something goes well or goes not at all. The company results are good or bad. The light is on or off.

This has happened to all of us, managers and staff alike, but when you realize what is going on, it is not too much of a problem. However, when your staff is not aware of their black-and-white *modus operandi*, two potential problems might impair their functioning.

First, when people are thinking in an undifferentiated mode, they run the risk of getting entrapped in "either-or" thinking, good *or* bad. If things are not very good, then they are very bad. This, of course, can't really be true, there are shades of gray, as we all know. They are far better off with the "and-and" notion combined with differentiated thinking: "Sometimes it's worse *and* sometimes it is better." This differentiated *modus* allows for a lot more freedom of thinking and acting.

Second, this black-and-white thinking will quickly trap your co-workers into believing that a problem isn't really solved until it is totally gone and everything is back to perfection again. We all have learned, most of us the hard way, that perfection in (business) life is an illusion. And, striving to fulfill an illusion is in itself an utterly frustrating activity that is doomed to fail.

With the exception of being dead or alive and being pregnant or not, most matters in life and in business aren't black and white. Step 6 of the solution dance is to help our personnel to perform optimally by inviting them to face reality as it shows itself in shades of gray (or even more accurately in color!). As a matter of fact, the range of gray is almost infinite, and our task is to help our employees think and act in a differentiated manner so that they have many more possibilities then just staying stuck in black and white.

How to offer differentiation

We have several methods to help our black-and-white thinkers to switch to a more differentiated and colorful mode.

It's always good to start with the most obvious method, common sense. You might try to challenge the black-and-white thinkers by pointing out that they are indeed thinking in black-and-white. "Oh, come on now, it's not that bad. It can't possibly be that everything is as black as you tell me." If this method works, you're done. But lots of people respond to this challenge by gearing up the arguments why it really, really is a total mess. If you encounter this response, you'd better drop this attempt because of tenet number three (see page 22): "If something you do does not work, stop doing it and do something else instead."

The next method you might try is asking solution-building questions that can elicit differentiation:

- Do you remember when it was not as bad as you say it is now?
- What was different then?
- What did you do differently?
- How did your colleagues behave differently?
- If I could ask your colleagues about times when it was not so bad as it is now, what would they tell me?
- Do you remember instances when it has been even worse than it is now? How did you cope then? What did you do to make it less bad?

The answers to these kinds of questions are bound to reflect some form of differentiation and provide useful information about positive differences that will show you how to proceed.

In the solution-focused model, there is an even more elegant way to dance the step of differentiation. You can use a ten-point scale to help to reveal these shades of gray. This technique is exceptionally useful in the business world, where people are used to working with numbers, and scales are readily accepted.

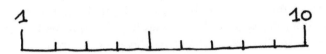

In the following paragraphs you will discover the elegance of asking scaling questions. We suggest that you think about how, and in which situations, you could use scaling. While you are reading this, specific situations might come to mind and you can try to ask yourself scaling questions in your mind. This is the best possible exercise to prepare you for real-life use. By the way, it's good to remember that scaling questions tie in to what you already know about asking solution-building questions in general (page 33).

Different types of scales

As you will discover, we have many different types of scales at our disposal. Actually, once you master the basic concept of scaling, you can tailor them to fit perfectly to any thinkable situation. Armed with the basics, you will learn to be creative and thus create an endless variety of possibilities. The better you fit the precise wording of the scaling questions to the specifics of the situation, the more useful the answers will be and the swifter your staff will make progress. Later in the chapter we outline a handy protocol to help you to use all types of scales, but first let's explore the topic further.

1. The scale of progress

This is the generic version of the scale of progress: "Can I ask you a question please? On a scale from zero to ten where the zero stands for 'the worst things have ever been' and the ten stands for 'OK, this is good enough, now I can cope and do my job in a satisfying manner', where are you now?"

The scale of progress probably is the most useful scale one can apply. It offers your staff a simple, elegant, and almost irrefutable opportunity to snap out of black and white and slide into differentiation.

Merely asking this question already installs the possibility of differentiation in your staff's minds. All of a sudden they are invited to think in shades of gray.

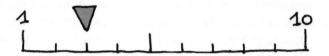

Your employee might respond by saying, "I am about a three."

This answer reflects how she assesses her situation with regard to the problem at hand. Besides the fact that this is useful information for you as manager and for your employee, this number indicates how she perceives the difference between how things are at zero and how they are now. In that respect, the given number is an indication of progress towards the ten on the scale. Your next questions will help your employee to explore what it is that she is already doing well.

You continue by asking, "OK, so you say you are on a three. Good, now what is already different so that you are able to give it a three?"

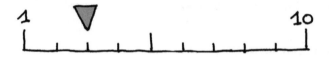

Your employee will now give you details of what she perceives to be different already. It is evident that there will be answers to this question, or she would not have chosen the number three. You accept the answers, and you invite her to give as detailed a description as possible of what she is already doing differently so that she is able to give herself a three. The best way to keep her answers flowing is by using the magical "What else?" questions (page 37).

When you notice that she has exhausted all possible details, you move to the next step in which you invite her to look in the direction of the ten. It's important not to ask her about what she intends to do to get to ten. If you ask about such a huge leap, or worse, request it, both of you would run the risk of failure. Just invite her to make the smallest step possible.

Just stick with the following question: "Good. You are very clear about what is in that three. Now starting from this three, what could be the smallest step that you could take? What would you need to do differently then?"

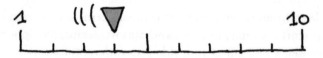

The answers you will get now are reflections of little steps for the better. You only have to acknowledge her answers on what she might do to make things better. Her answers are actually suggestions she is giving to herself. Your task now is to help your employee stick to feasible steps forward. You do that by paraphrasing what she says in terms of very concrete and doable behaviors on her part. At the same time, you protect her from taking steps that are too big and risky.

The art of using solution-building questions, here, is to accompany your employee so that she chooses little steps instead of giant leaps. The beauty lies in the fact that you as manager do not need to tell her what to do next. On the contrary, she discovers for herself what the next steps should be and, in that respect, she owns her own progress. Your task is to simply "lead from behind."

When you notice that she is getting a good grip on her answers, you congratulate her and ask the next question. "Very good! Now, if you are able to make these small steps ahead in the coming days or weeks, where would that take you on the scale?"

Your employee might say: "Then I would be on a five."

Now you can wrap up the scaling interview by inviting your employee to act out some of the things that she defined as little steps forward. "Would it be a good idea to try out some of the things you just told me in the coming days and weeks, and see for yourself what a difference that will make? You might even want to write down the number you have been on each day and add some details on what you did differently. We'll talk about your progress in a few weeks. Good work and good luck!"

At the next meeting, you again use the ten-point scale: "In our last meeting we worked with scales and you found many useful ways of making little steps forward. Where are you now on that same scale where zero stands for big trouble and ten stands for good enough?"

People will seldom say that they are at the same spot. This is easy to understand. She started out with what was already going well (the details of the three) and this gave her a head start. Nudged on gently by solution-building questions, it was the employee herself who — with a little help from her friend the manager — pointed out the next little steps towards the ten. For the simple and obvious reason that people very seldom lack motivation to try out things that they themselves suggested, chances are high that change will have occurred during this try-out phase. These differences are the topic of the second session, which should run along the same lines as the first one.

2. Scale of usefulness

A classical format of this scale might run like this: "OK, this meeting about our new investment project has been running for about an hour now, and I have heard some pretty constructive contributions from each of you. Allow me a question. On a scale where zero stands for 'we can talk all day but this will not be leading us anywhere' and ten stands for 'this is a very useful meeting,' where are we now?"

When you use this scale of usefulness, you invite staff to an open evaluation while at the same time you open space for differentiated answers. This greatly contrasts with the all too familiar lure of being overcritical in business meetings that smothers all constructive discussions. At the same time, anxiously avoiding all forms of evaluation is equally smothering, and that is where this usefulness scale comes in handy.

Openly asking this question gives everybody the opportunity to give feedback and adjust what is happening. Suppose the answer to the question is: "One big fat zero, this meeting is going nowhere," then your next question is simply, "OK, so what do we have to talk about *instead* so that this meeting *will* be useful?" If you get a higher number on the scale, let's say a three, then you continue with the question, "Good, what is it that we have already covered that means you can give this meeting a three?" The answers will be first steps on the road to solutions.

If you use this question with your team, it is only natural that not everybody is on the same number. You just have to give everybody the opportunity to say how he or she arrived at their personal number and what is in their personal number. This will give you a general feeling of where your team stands vis-à-vis the issues they are working on. Here is an example for using scaling questions with a group: "Hello — today we meet again as a quality project group. Let's say we were at zero two months ago when we started this project. Where would we be now on a scale from zero to ten, where zero stands for how it was two months ago and ten stands for achieving the ISO 9001?" Everyone is then asked to give his or her individual number. Some will choose a four, others a six, still others a mere two, and maybe you will hear a seven. Take your time to ask everybody for details about what is in his or her number. When this round is done, you invite the team as a whole to choose a number. "OK, so as a project group we are at a four. What does that four mean? What did you do to reach the four?" Let the group list what has been done to reach the four, and then continue with: "What needs to happen in order to reach a five within the next two weeks?" This helps them to map the gradual progress and ensures that progress is made in little steps, which makes failing less likely. This openness is likely to propel them towards the next steps.

The "usefulness question" can even be deployed without the scaling. In the middle of a conversation around a specific topic, you can ask your counterpart(s) the question: "Is this useful, the way we are talking now?" and you invite open feedback. The goal of this is not to get appreciation for yourself as the leader of the conversation but to direct your counterpart's attention towards the goals of the conversation. Whatever the answer is (yes or no), there is always a next step possible. If no: "What should we be talking about so that this meeting will be useful?"

If yes, you get room for compliments and might say something like: "Great, thanks, now what is it exactly that you find useful in our conversation?" The details you then get are again great starting points for further exploration of the road towards the solution.

Dear reader, you have now come to page 93 in your book. Congratulations. On a scale from ☹ ...... to ...... ☺ where ☹ stands for "I am wasting precious time" and ☺ stands for: "Reading this is very helpful to me," where are you now?

3. Scale of motivation

This is a standard format of the scale of motivation: "On a scale where zero stands for 'this is an impossible situation and we have no motivation whatsoever to try and do anything about it' and ten stands for 'we will do everything in our power to tackle this problem and solve it,' where are you now?"

In this case, the fact that managers and employees have a tendency to rate themselves highly on work motivation is a great asset. If they answer with a blunt zero, you know that as a manager you are facing a lot of work ahead. Whatever other number you get, you can always work from there. Whatever number other than a zero you get, compliment them on it, and ask what it is that gives them this level of motivation. And by the way, please ask for details, details, and more details. When you feel that the details of what already motivates the people are exhausted, you proceed with the next question: "Great, now what is it that you need to be able to notch up your motivation a little? What will you be doing differently when you notice your number going up?"

By asking these questions, acknowledging the answers, and encouraging them to make small steps, you encourage your personnel to move ahead. You are not dictating what they ought to try, their own answers will define what exactly it is that they will need to do in order to improve things. Hence you are not pulling at them but you give them a gentle push in the back so that they move in the desired direction. That is what leadership is all about.

Protocol for using scaling questions

When you read all the different examples of scaling questions throughout this book, you will notice that there is a hidden pattern that emerges. In order to make using scales easier for you, please feel free to use the following protocol and adapt it to your taste.

1. Prepare by asking permission to ask your counterpart a scaling question.
2. Offer a scale where zero equals the starting point of the scale, e.g. the most difficult moment or situation, and ten stands for "good enough."
3. Ask: "Where are you now?"
4. Accept whatever number you are given and ... offer a (small) compliment: "Good."
5. Ask: "What is it that you are already doing differently so that you can give yourself this X?"
6. Accept all answers, and repeat what is being said in order to emphasize the little change.
7. Ask: "What else?" to elicit more and more details.
8. Broaden the question by asking: "What would your colleagues, boss, partner, etc. tell me if I asked them this question?"
9. Ask: "What will be the next smallest step that you could take?"

Tips for the optimal use of scaling questions

1. React enthusiastically

No matter what number the employee chooses, always react enthusiastically. When your employee says she is at a one on a scale from zero to ten, you respond by saying: "Good, that is ten percent progress. What is in that one?" If at the next meeting she says one again, you can reply: "Good — despite the difficult situation, how did you manage to remain on that ten percent progress?" It may happen that she moves back on the scale and mentions a lower number in the next meeting. Don't worry about this and just accept it. "OK, last time you were at five and now you are at three. How come? What did you do differently so that you are at three again? How were you able to limit moving down so that you didn't end up at two? Is there anything you forgot to do that might get you back to five?"

2. First ask what is in the given number

Whatever number on the scale the employee chooses, first make inquiries about what she is already doing differently so that this allows her to choose a number higher than zero.

The answers will point out the resources and the exceptions to the problem that the employee is already using. "OK, so on a scale where zero stands for no progress at all and ten stands for reasonable progress, where are you now?" "I am on a seven." "Good. What progress have you already made so you can give it a seven." Asking information about what it is that she is already doing, and that allows her to mention the chosen number is failsafe, as it simply helps her phrase what she already knows. The more details you get as answers to this question, the more useful it is. Make abundant use of the question: "What else?" This information always contains solutions and pathways to coming solutions.

It's best to refrain from asking too quickly what the next higher number on the scale would mean, because colleagues often do not know how to answer. Once you have established what is in the current number, you should fight the urge to ask how they could move up to a ten. That would be too big a move. If someone is able to answer this question, they would have given you the ten from the beginning.

Go slow instead, and ask your employee what they could do differently in order to move a little higher on the scale. For example: "Now that you are at a six, how would you know that you had moved up a little? What would you do differently to get to six and a half?" Or you can even reverse this question: "You are now on a six. What will you be doing differently when you reach six and a half?" Small changes are much safer and more likely to happen than big changes.

Remember, evolution tops r-evolution.

3. The numbers on the scale are metaphors

People in business generally like numbers. Numbers in business very often refer to concrete facts. The number of "currency units" in your bank account is an objective representation of how well-off you are from a financial point of view. The exact number of machine parts in your warehouse is an objective indication of its worth.

However, when it comes to numbers on scaling questions, we enter an entirely different realm. The numbers you get when you ask a scaling question are not mathematical representations of the change involved.

These numbers are indicators, pointers, road signs, and not scores on an exam sheet. So it is helpful to bear in mind that these numbers are metaphors for change.

This has several consequences. First, you always accept the given number at face value and never question that number. Second, any given number does not serve as a baseline measurement — you cannot use the given number like a budget or a sales prognosis against which you match the coming results. This would only lead to rational arguments and stand in the way of progress. Third, when you conduct the next meeting and ask the scaling question again, you do not need to have the number from the previous session at hand in order to check factual progress or change. No, you merely continue asking them more solution-building questions and leave the responsibility of comparing numbers to your staff. Lastly, the content of what is in the number is far more important than the number itself. A three for Peter means something totally different than a three for Nancy. The given number is just a driver.

4. Involve other colleagues

"What would your boss say if we asked her where she thinks this team stands on a scale from zero to ten, where zero stands for 'the strategic plan is far from finished' and ten stands for 'we have a workable strategic plan that is ready to be implemented'?"

"You tell me that your division went up to a seven on the scale where zero stood for 'almost total lack of market drive' and ten stands for 'our operation is fully market-driven.' Great. Now, if I could ask your customers about the same scale, what would they answer?"

"Talking about the two new sales people in your team, can I come back to your scale where zero stood for 'brand new and they need to learn our products and market from scratch' and ten stands for 'they are fully equipped and can hit the road to our clients without any additional help.' You tell me that they moved up to eight over the last months. How did you notice? What are they doing differently so that both you as sales manager and they themselves were able to reach this eight? Where would their colleagues put them on the same scale? What number would their customers give them? What would the rest of the team say that the new sales people need to do differently or learn more about in order to move up to a nine?"

"Now that you have moved up to a five on the scale where zero stands for 'I don't feel accepted at all by this new team' and ten stands for 'I truly feel part of my new team,' how do your team mates notice this? What will they see you doing differently when you move to a six?"

These specially designed questions are called "triangular questions" — you ask your employee to enter the mind of his or her colleagues who are not present during the conversation. The virtual reality that pops up during the conversation becomes reality when your employee starts thinking about the implications that his or her answers have for others in real life.

So these triangular questions help the employee to see how his suggested solution affects the relevant people in his environment. The answers do not remain locked in the head of one person — they are broadened and gain more scope and reality.

5. The journey is more important than the destination

It is important to avoid fixating on the "final goal" — the ten. If we become obsessed with reaching a ten, we fall into solution fanaticism. Therefore, ten should never indicate perfection, as that would set you up for failure. The ten should be defined as a situation in which things are *good enough*. Beware of perfectionism since it is counter-productive!

There is a great quote from Steve de Shazer, one of the founding fathers of the solution-focused model, that fits very well here: "We can know what better is without knowing what good is."

What if you get a number off the scale?

Some employees are in such distress that they respond way off the scale: "I'm at minus thirty! It's hopeless. My team leader drives me crazy." What do you do then? Don't panic but gently accept this answer and ask: "How do you keep going? How do you manage to keep working when things are so bad?" We call these types of questions "coping questions." In itself this question is a compliment because you tell your staff member that, however difficult his or her situation might be, he or she is keeping up. Better yet, the answers to coping questions always contain information about resources and exceptions. "I keep going because my boss is frequently abroad and that's a big relief." Upon this exception we can build further: "Where are you on the scale when your team leader is out of town? How do you behave differently then? What would you need to change so that you can behave this way even when your team leader is around? If you were able to do that, then where would you be on the scale?" So, whenever your employee is so low on a scale that his hopelessness threatens to drag everyone down, immediately ask him how he is coping, and you will get information that will point you in the direction of possible solutions.

Summing up

Offering differentiation by using scales bypasses resistance, and your employees will accept the possibility of change in an almost unnoticeable way. In using scales, you implicitly assume:

- that change is possible,
- that small steps are more effective than giant leaps,
- and that not everything must (or even can) change in one step.

Step 7: future-orientation

Solution-focused managers are much more interested in the future than in the past. When we are interested in the past, it is in a very different way. Why?

The past is a limitation, which nothing can be done about. The past is over and it is a total waste of time and energy to try to change it.

Problems belong to the past while solutions belong to the future. Problems that we are not having now, but that we might encounter later, are not today's problems. When you face a problem today, then the

solution for it — by definition — belongs to the future. If we had the solution for this problem now, it would obviously not be a problem.

So what parts of the past are we interested in? First, the past is an important part of the context of today's problems (see step 2). Second, and most importantly, as you have learned in step 4, the past is a vast reservoir of resources and exceptions to the problems. In it you will find the tools to tackle your problems.

Still, solutions belong to the future, hence our future-orientation. By looking to the future, we act to bring the desired future into the realm of today. The future is not here yet, so how can we use this virtual reality in today's world? How can we help our employees to direct themselves to the future instead of remaining stuck in the past or in their search for causes for their problems?

Future-oriented questions

The easiest way to help your staff to look forward is to ask them the proper solution-building questions by which one can "retroject" possibilities for future solutions into today's realm. Here is a sample of useful questions:

- What do you want to see happening, and how will you know it has?
- What will be the first signs that you are making progress towards your goals?
- What will you be doing differently then?
- How will the other divisions notice that we have solved our problems?
- What will your team be doing differently when the problem is solved?
- What will the CEO see us doing differently when we have implemented the new organizational structure?
- When this merger is implemented, what will we be doing differently?
- What will be the first small sign that our team is sorting out its internal struggles?
- Imagine that we are one year on from now, and that we have survived the bid for the hostile take-over, how will we be working then?

The miracle question

Another tool used to elicit future-orientation was invented by Steve de Shazer and Insoo Kim Berg and is called "the miracle question." Conceived at the beginning of the eighties, their invention was the catalyst for a radically new and innovative method for dealing with human problems. Their solution-focused model is now one of the leading models in psychotherapy, and it is still spreading!

The miracle question introduces a radical new way of looking at problems and of creating alternative solution possibilities. Of course, one always has to be very circumspect when applying insights from one field to another, especially if the application jumps from the world of psychotherapy to the world of business. It would be too simplistic to say that business and therapy are the same, simply because both fields have to do with human interaction. In order to profit from the richness of the miracle question when you apply it to business, it's good to give it a business-like twist.

If at first sight the miracle question seems a little odd, it captures the essence of the solution-focused model, and offers a true innovation to the world of management. In that sense, the miracle question is a hologram of the solution-focused model.

Offer yourself a little miracle!

You have been reading this book, hopefully enjoying it, and occasionally being stretched by your effort to digest some of its ideas. Having come this far in the book, you have already been working very hard. Now we would like to invite you to offer yourself a miracle. To grant yourself this pleasure, please take a (little) problem you are struggling with in your mind. This can be something about work or it can be something from your personal life — you decide for yourself what you would profit the most from at this moment in time. Now read your personal miracle question and take some time to reflect on the answers that come to mind. You might like to write down some of the answers for future use! Here is the "light" version of your miracle question.

While you are reading this book, you are sitting somewhere comfortable. After putting it down, you go about doing things that you will do today. The day goes on and eventually you get tired and go to sleep. Suppose that while you are asleep, it is as if a miracle happens. In that miracle, the problem you have on your mind is solved to the extent that it no longer bothers you so much. But since you are sound asleep, you do not know that this miracle has happened. Tomorrow morning, you wake up not knowing that this miracle has happened to you. How would you notice that a miracle has happened for you? What will you be doing differently now that this miracle has happened? Will you be getting up in a slightly different way than usual? What would be different about your breakfast? How would your partner at home notice that this miracle has happened? Would you go to work in a slightly different manner? What could that be? When you come into your office, what would be different? How will you behave differently at the office? How would your employees notice that a miracle has happened?

This is the basic version of the miracle question and, as you will see when you read on, there are myriad ways to phrase this wonderful question so that it becomes a question full of wonders.

How does the miracle question work in reality?

Jonathan, an experienced salesman, who had previously been working for a company's competitor, is hired to head the sales department. In his career to date he has always worked exclusively as a salesman and has never had to manage other people. Jonathan did well during his training period, but once he was up-and-running in his position as sales manager, problems soon arose. Having no experience as a manager, he was uncertain what to do — so he jumped in, feet first. The first thing he did was to visit lots of customers with his salesmen. This, of course, provided a perfect introduction, but during many of these joint visits, he behaved like a salesman and took the lead in the meetings with the customers. His salesmen did not appreciate this, especially since Jonathan sometimes corrected them in front of the customer. In the car back to the office, Jonathan, in a well-intended attempt to help, always lectured his colleagues on what they should or shouldn't do or say; and told endless stories about his successes as a salesman. Although well meant, these lectures showed more of his uncertainty than anything else. The ensuing conversations led to a lot of arguments between Jonathan and his team members. Jonathan felt that his colleagues did not accept him and the team accused him of not sufficiently assisting and supporting them.

After a few weeks, this situation was no longer bearable and the sales team jointly asked for a meeting with George, the general manager. The team made it very clear that they understood Jonathan's well-meant efforts but that they were fed up with him treating them like beginners. "We know he's just insecure in his new job as sales manager but he won't listen to us."

George sets up a meeting with Jonathan. After listening to Jonathan's version of the facts, George asks him the miracle question. "Jonathan, after a long day of hard work, you will go to sleep tonight. While you are asleep, suppose a miracle happens in which all the problems you are having in the team today are sufficiently solved so that you are no longer bothered by them. Once you wake up tomorrow morning, how will you discover that this miracle has happened?" Jonathan replies, "All my colleagues would accept all my proposals, and they would do what I tell them to do."

In its initial form, Jonathan's answer is useless. Still, George accepts it without arguing and continues. "Not so fast, Jonathan, you are lying in your bed, you open your eyes and wham, you notice that something special has happened but you don't know that your miracle happened. What would you be doing differently when you get up in the morning?"

Jonathan answers: "When I wake up in the morning after this miracle, I will be in a better mood and feel a little more self-confident. I probably wouldn't go to work whistling, but still, I would be more at ease."

George: "Great. What difference would there be when you enter the office?"

Jonathan: "At work, instead of running around and trying to talk to as many people as possible within the first half hour, I just would say hello and start with my emails. When my emails are done, I would walk around to see if something special has come up, and then I would retreat into my office for an hour or so just to think."

George: "Interesting. What will be your next small step?"

Jonathan: "'Maybe I need to start out from what I know best."

George: "That's a good idea. Would you mind explaining this to me? How will this help you?"

Jonathan: "I realize that I might have been overstressing my new role as sales manager. If I try to walk a mile in my sales people's shoes, maybe I can come up with things that will help them to accept me better. I could do this by writing down the things that helped me the most when I was a salesman."

George asks: "Good, what else would you do differently?"

Jonathan: "Come to think of it, I realize that my former sales manager in my previous job was a great help to me."

George: "In what respect?"

Jonathan: "He hardly ever told me what I should do. He was always asking questions about my work, about customers, about my planning. I might do the same."

George: "Very good. What else?"

Jonathan: "Instead of going along to see customers all the time, I would try to design an action plan based on the sales budget. Yes, I could think about which actions could be taken at short notice. Out of that I could distill a proposal for my colleagues."

Just by giving these answers, Jonathan is starting to think in a different way about his job as sales manager. Now the time is right to help Jonathan expand his ideas from actions to interactions.

George: "If I could ask your staff what changes they will notice about you after the miracle, what would they say?"

Jonathan: "They would probably tell you I am much less pushy and more easy going. I hope they won't start taking advantage of me, though."

George asks another solution-building question: "Well, nobody likes being taken advantage of. If they try it on, you will know immediately. How would you react then?"

Jonathan: "Well becoming pushy again certainly wouldn't help. On the contrary. Actually, I don't expect them to do so. Why should they? They know their job better then I do."

George: "Do you think it would be helpful if you show them how you appreciate their professionalism? How could you combine this with the next little step of the miracle? How would you act differently towards your colleagues, Jonathan?"

Jonathan: "Yes, I could slip in some compliments about how they do their jobs instead of just proposing ready-made plans that they are not likely to accept."

George: "Now, how would you do that?"

Jonathan: "When my proposal is ready, instead of just presenting it to them, I would ask one of my salesmen to go through it with me. I would ask him what has worked best for him in the past and would integrate these ideas in the final proposal. I would also ask him what should be in it so that it will be accepted more easily by his colleagues."

George: "Very good, Jonathan. What would you need to be able to put into action what you have just told me?"

Jonathan: "I just need to do it."

What does this dialogue reveal? Instead of remaining trapped in arguments about who is right or wrong, Jonathan is able to look at his problem from the angle of a possible solution. George doesn't respond to Jonathan's solution ("All my colleagues would accept all my proposals, and they would do what I tell them to do") because that would have to be a real miracle, which is of course highly unlikely.

When George urges Jonathan to go slowly, useful answers promptly follow.

With the follow-up questions, Jonathan is invited to expand his growing feeling of confidence and translate this into actions at the office. Continuously asking for little steps invites Jonathan to concentrate on what he needs to do in order to mentally move away from the problem and direct himself towards possible solutions. Jonathan then chooses to talk about step 4, resources and exceptions, spontaneously. He instantly gives himself feedback about tenet 3: "If something you do doesn't work, stop doing it and do something else instead" (page 23). This gets him thinking about a strategy for enhancing cooperation between himself and his team. In his description of how he could shape his problem into a possible solution, Jonathan prescribes himself a possible solution.

How does the miracle question work magic?

In other words, what are the operative components in this seemingly naive question? Let's list a few:

- The "suppose" component of the question allows your employees to step outside their purely rational thinking and to let go of entrenched thinking patterns which concentrate on the problem. The word "miracle" gives your counterpart permission to think about the widest spectrum of possibilities. After all, a miracle doesn't have any boundaries or rules. Therefore, the staff member is prompted to think broadly.
- The question circumvents resistance: because the answer does not need to be part of the "rational" world, there is no need to use rational counterarguments.
- The miracle question is future-oriented. The answers are connected to a future in which problems are no longer problems. The miracle question de-emphasizes the problems of today and yesterday and refocuses the staff's attention toward a possible future in which more satisfactory solutions are at hand.
- It is an elegant way to elicit clear, future-oriented objectives and goals from your staff. Finding solutions becomes much easier once clear goals have been set.
- By follow-up questioning, you elicit detailed and comprehensive information about solutions your employee probably would not have come up with had he or she been thinking only rationally.
- The ongoing questions, by which you help your employees to formulate possibilities of how the future might look after the problem is solved, offer them little steps towards that preferred and wished-for future.
- The appropriate series of solution-building questions builds a map that unveils the road towards solutions.
- The detailed description of concrete and feasible little steps towards the wished-for future works as a prescription.

The miracle question without the word "miracle"

Let's be frank, the word "miracle" is not always acceptable in corporate environments, especially not when you are "talking business." And since we are great believers in the adage "Speak the language of the people you are working with," we propose that you skip the word "miracle" when you feel or think that the word in itself might endanger the exercise.

As you will learn from further examples, you can capture the future-orientation with or without using the M-word, and you will still find that the essential ingredients of the miracle question are operational. How do you do this? You simply use the magical word "suppose," and you have a miracle-like question. Instead of saying: "Imagine a miracle happens overnight and all your problems are solved…", you simply say "Suppose all your problems with… are solved…"

Using future-orientation when working with teams and large groups

The miracle question works for individual employees, teams, and even very large groups. The condition is, of course, that you prepare the question well so that the method becomes understandable and acceptable. You can adjust the exact words of the miracle question according to the situation.

*"Ladies and gentlemen, we are here together today as a steering committee to implement project X. **Suppose** that on Monday morning we come back to the office after a refreshing weekend. Now just **suppose** that during the weekend all the problems we are dealing with today have been solved just enough that we can easily make progress in the implementation of our project. What will make you realize this on Monday? What would you, as a project group, do differently? What would be the smallest step forward then?"*

The following example shows how the miracle question can be used successfully with a large group:

A transport company was working on the implementation of an ISO 9002 quality system. The director-owner had already used solution-focused techniques in other projects, and ten employees from every hierarchical level of the company had been trained in the technique of using the miracle question. During the next phase of this quality project, a one-day workshop was organized for the entire personnel of the company. All the truck drivers, the middle management, the dispatchers, and the directors were present. After a short introduction, the director asked all one hundred people the following question. "I would like you to think about what would happen if during the night all the current problems we are dealing with were solved to such an extent that they wouldn't bother *us anymore. Let's **suppose** this happens and tomorrow we all come back to work. What would the management, your colleagues, and you be doing differently? What would be different within the company?" Then the group was divided into small groups, each of which was directed by someone who had been trained in asking the follow-up questions to this miracle opener. Many people were surprised by the question. As is common in large groups, a few jokers tried to sabotage the process. The director invited these individuals to join him in his group. During the course of the day, many relevant propositions and insights came up, convincing the director that the miracle question was indeed speeding up the implementation of the ISO 9002.*

Protocol for using the miracle question

When you read the specific phrasing of the various cases presented here, you will notice that there is a pattern hidden in the way the miracle question is asked. Since this miracle question is a simple yet not-so-easy tool, we offer you a step-by-step protocol to enable you to use this tool with maximum efficiency. Of course, as always in this book, we suggest that you experiment with your own way of applying the method.

The consecutive steps for using the miracle question and the follow-up questions

1. Ask permission to ask a "strange and remarkable" question.
2. Make use of a yes-set (see page 50) to prepare the ground.
3. Ask the miracle question.
4. While asking the miracle question, be sure to define what happens during the miracle.
5. Accept all the answers you get without discussion, even if they do not seem useful at first.
6. Assist your interviewee(s) by asking questions about what he/she would do differently.
7. Elicit more and more details by asking: "What else?"
8. Ask your interviewee(s) how people from their relevant context would notice that the miracle has happened.
9. Give compliments with every useful answer. ("Usefulness" here refers to those answers in which the interviewee describes the different behavior he/she would show instead of the problematic behavior.) Repeat in your words what the interviewee has just said.

If we now convert these consecutive steps into everyday language, you get the following *generic* version of the miracle question.

1. Can I ask you a strange question?
2. Today it is Thursday (yes), it is eleven o'clock (yes), we are sitting in your office for this meeting (yes), tonight after work you'll go home (yes), in the evening you will do whatever needs to be done (yes), and then you'll go to sleep (yes).
3. Now *suppose* that while you sleep, a miracle happens. But you don't know that since you are sound asleep.
4. In this miracle, all the issues that you have problems with are sufficiently solved that they no longer bother you. Tomorrow morning, you wake up without knowing that this miracle has happened. How would you know this miracle happened? What would you do differently?
5. Interviewee: "I would..." (Describes what would be different after the miracle happened.)
6. Good. What is it that *you* would do differently now that this miracle has happened?
7. What else?
8. How would your colleagues (partner, co-workers, manager, boss...) know that this miracle has happened for you? What will they see that you do differently? What else would they notice?
9. Great. So now that this (miracle) has happened, you would... (Repeat what interviewee just said.) Very good!

Tips for optimal use of the miracle question

1. Make it acceptable

Make this somewhat odd question acceptable for your staff by putting the question tactfully. Ask your staff member if you can ask him or her a strange, surprising question, or, even better, explain the question. "What I'm about to ask you will sound very strange. But when you think about it, you will notice that it will help you to think differently about your situation." You can even embed the miracle question in a little story.

Suppose, Elizabeth, that after our conversation you go back to your office. You do the things you still have to do for today and then you go home. At home you will probably have lots of things to do — maybe you need to cook or work on some household chores. Maybe you even take some work home. Later on you watch television with your family until it's time for bed. You go to bed and fall into a nice, deep sleep. While you are sleeping, let us suppose that your patron saint is playing cards with her colleagues. Suddenly Saint Elizabeth says: "You know what, I feel like performing a miracle this evening, it's been a while since the last one." She looks down through the clouds and sees your house passing under her cloud. "There we are," she says to herself, "a namesake is sleeping there. I might as well perform a miracle for her." You, of course, don't realize what is happening because you are sound asleep. Then you wake up in the morning. What would make you realize that the miracle has happened? What would you do differently?

When your counterpart reacts stubbornly by replying that she doesn't believe in miracles, you can side-step this obstacle easily by saying: "Neither do I. Of course miracles don't exist, but suppose for a moment that they do. What would you do differently when you wake up?"

2. Avoid perfectionism

It is better not to ask about what needs to happen in the miracle to make everything perfect. Just as miracles are very rare, perfection is plainly impossible in business life. So striving towards perfectionism is counterproductive. The miracle question is intended to help you discover what small changes are needed to make the current problem less of a problem. The outcome of the miracle or the miracle-like question is best phrased in terms of "good enough." And it is better that the follow-up questions ask for the smallest differences that you would notice after waking up. This questioning strategy makes your intervention as failsafe as possible.

3. Listen to every answer you get

Even if an answer doesn't seem useful at first, it may contain important information that you would normally never get. The first answers are often something like: "The market for our product would get larger," "The margin would improve" or "The competition would go bankrupt." Although these answers are not useful in their present form, they can become useful with questions like, "Imagine that the market does indeed get larger. How would you react to that?" or "What would it take to improve the margin?" or "How would your company take advantage of the fact that the competition has gone bankrupt?" The answers to these questions often contain ideas that can be translated to reality. Following this line of questioning will increase your chances of creating new openings from which the conversation can continue in a constructive direction.

4. Concentrate on your staff's own actions

At first, employees tend to give answers in which only other people act differently. You will get answers like: "My boss would get off my back and let me do my job," "My colleagues would treat me with the respect I deserve." You may accept these answers initially but it is important to then move beyond them. Get to the very core of the matter. It is about the behavior of the employee him- or herself. In the follow-up questions, you try to elicit answers in which the employee acts differently by asking: "What would *you* do differently? What would you as a team do differently?"

5. Ask for details

Don't be satisfied with general answers such as "I would feel better" or "My boss would give me more responsibility" or "I would win the lottery and stop working for this company" or even "We would have better coffee." Your follow-up questions will help your employee to come up with more concrete and therefore more useful answers.

For example, you could ask: "Suppose you were to start feeling better, what would you do differently?" or "Suppose your boss did give you more responsibility, what would be the first thing you would change?" or "If you did win the lottery and quit this job, what would you do then?" or even "Suppose your office got nicer coffee, what would you do then differently as opposed to what you are doing now?"

Details, details, and even more details, that is what matters. It's by going into the details of the miracle that resources, exceptions to the problem, and solutions are found.

Go slowly by encouraging your employees to describe step by step what they would do differently after the miracle. Don't allow them to envision the results of the miracle as a still photograph, because this will provide only static data. Process their description as if it is a movie that you analyze frame by frame. Have them break it down into small steps and invite them to describe active details. If you do this you will extract useful details that can be expanded into ever-growing steps towards solutions.

Co-create a new reality

As you know very well by now, questions shape the answers you get and vice versa (page 33). By asking and answering all kinds of future-oriented questions, new possibilities for solutions emerge. The outcome of such a cooperative dialogue is the co-creation of a new reality. This concept of co-creation runs counter to the preposterously false idea that, in business and human affairs, one person possesses ready-made solutions. In ancient Greece, this was called "hubris," and the Greek gods were swift with their punishments, resulting in impossible but eternal ordeals. They made you roll a big stone to the top of a hill and with your success came your failure — it rolled down the other side of the hill — pretty tiring and boring!

So if you want to avoid eternally tiring and boring repetitive ordeals, you'd better stick to the T.E.A.M adage — *together everybody achieves more*.

In the back-and-forth movement of the dialogue, you can easily facilitate cooperation by repeating what your employee has said in your own words. This allows you to give it a little twist and ask the next question. This back-and-forth movement guides the conversation towards optimal results and newly found solutions.

Conclusion of the seven-step dance

This chapter has taught you all the steps of the solution dance. From inviting your personnel into a conversation and a clarification of the relevant context, you proceeded to goal-setting. Keeping a keen eye on the resources of your staff gave you room for compliments, while offering a differentiated view on what is happening helped you to dance towards a new future. So now you know what to do and how to interact in the simplest possible way with your staff so that together you achieve the best possible results for your company.

The beauty of the solution dance is that there are almost endless combinations of these seven steps. And, as with all dances, the elegance lies in the fact that you can dance in all directions thinkable. You can even dance backwards without retracing your steps.

When you take your time to practice the solution dance, you will notice that not every situation requires the use of all seven steps. In fact, the fewer steps towards solutions, the better!

Before you move to the next chapter, we would like you to take a few minutes to consider the following questions:

- Which steps fit the best with your personal characteristics as manager?
- Which steps would you like to practice more so that you can add new skills to your repertoire?
- In what situations do you feel confident enough to allow yourself to put this solution dance into practice?

To help you grasp the seven steps quickly, we propose that you list all seven steps on a piece of paper. Then make a scale for each of the seven steps where zero stands for: "This is not (yet) my piece of cake" and ten stands for: "I master this step fully." Now start practicing the steps in your daily job and after a week or so, set yourself the same scales. See how the numbers have changed and reflect on what you are doing differently when you have moved up a notch. Have fun!

Now that you have learned *what* you need to do, you can move to the next chapter where you will learn *when* to do what.

Chapter 4

Flowchart

Introduction

While the chapter on the seven-step dance to solutions showed you the "what to do," this chapter will teach you "when to do it." In business, just like in show business, timing is always important, sometimes crucial, and occasionally vital. This chapter will present you with a tool to help you with the timing of your interventions. This tool comes in the form of a flowchart: a decision tree that will guide you through the jungle of business problems towards the land of solutions in the quickest and safest way possible. Learning to use this flowchart will enable you to become even more efficient in your managing of people.

Occam's razor

Management is the art of getting things done through people. Evidently, for this, you need to develop a relationship of some kind with these people. The act of leadership is through the interaction with your employees (page 27) so you need more specific knowledge about the type of relationship that you have with your employees at any given moment in time. The flowchart gives you a simple tool to assess the quality of this relationship on a continuous basis. The quality of this working relationship determines what kind of mandate to intervene you get. This allows you to decide what will be the most useful interventions that fit with the current type of relationship.

How does this work? Faced with the complexity of life (and business), as solution-focused managers we choose to make our lives as simple as possible. With William of Occam's statement *"Entia non sunt multiplicanda praeter necessitatem"* (Matters should not be made more complicated than necessary) in mind, we have formulated four fundamental questions intended to simplify life. These questions function like Occam's razor — they remove the needless and superfluous issues of (business) life without compromising its complexity and richness.

Since these questions deal with fundamental distinctions, four of them suffice. The answer to each question guides you to a certain position on the flowchart. For each position on the flowchart, we have designed specific interventions.

The limited set of questions

Given any relationship that you are in with your staff, you only need to ask yourself the following questions:

1. Is it a problem or is it a limitation?
2. Is there a request for help?
3. Is this request for help workable?
4. Can my staff use their resources?

As you can see in the flowchart diagram on page 115, the answer to each question guides you to a certain position on the flowchart. Question 1 helps you to draw a fundamental distinction that is the basis for all the other questions. Questions 2, 3 and 4 point to four different relationship types (the names in parenthesis below are useful reminders):

- The *non-committal* relationship with members of staff who have not requested help (the "passers-by").
- The *searching* relationship with members of staff who *have* asked for help but who present their problems in an unworkable manner (the "searchers").
- The *consulting* relationship with employees whose problems are presented in a workable form but who are not capable of accessing their own resources or tools (the "buyers").
- The *co-expert* relationship with employees who present their problems in workable form and *are* capable of using their resources and tools (The "co-experts").

For each position on the flowchart, there are specific interventions that will help you to obtain maximum results with minimal effort. The correct use of this flowchart will help you to figure out what you should and shouldn't do — after all, doing the right things is as important as doing things right.

To get the best out of the flowchart tool, you should follow this sequence: situation at hand → question 1: distinction between problem and limitation → answer → question 2, 3 and 4 → relationship type → specific intervention.

Once again, we trust that this visual aid will facilitate your learning of the different layers that are hidden in the book and that it adds to the fun of reading.

Combining the flowchart with the other tools of the solution-focused model (the seven-step dance and solution talk), and adding this skill set to what you are already doing that works well for you, will turn you into the most efficient manager thinkable! You will become a master in the art of "less is more."

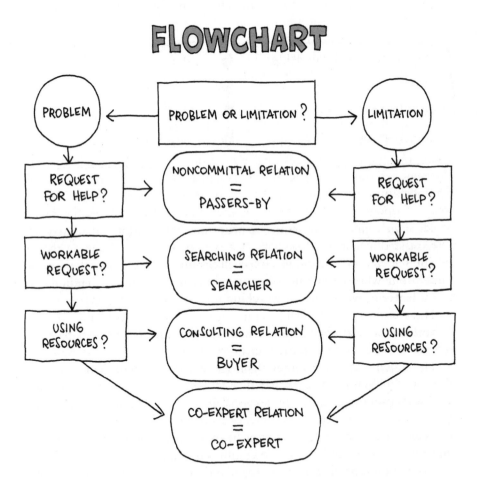

Preliminary remarks

The relationship types describe the working relationship between you and your staff at that particular moment and in that particular context.

They do *not* refer to intrinsic characteristics of the respective staff member(s) but are strictly indicators of the type of *relationship* that exists at the moment. That is why we use the terms non-committal relationship, searching relationship, consulting relationship and co-expert relationship. However, we will also use the terms passer-by, searcher, buyer and co-expert, for short. Please keep in mind that the category of passer-by doesn't describe the intrinsic characteristics of the person involved, but talks about a non-committal working relationship between you and that employee. For your convenience, remember the following chart:

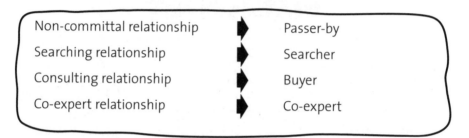

Non-committal relationship	➤	Passer-by
Searching relationship	➤	Searcher
Consulting relationship	➤	Buyer
Co-expert relationship	➤	Co-expert

The position on the flowchart has no qualitative appreciation to it. It's just a "topographical location" of the relationship type on the flowchart, which guides you to the appropriate interventions. In that way, you could think of the flowchart as a type of compass. Thinking that a position lower on the flowchart is necessarily better than the higher ones is a misunderstanding. For example, a non-committal relationship is not better or worse than a searching relationship. Each position just is what it is.

Reality and relationships are dynamic, not static. The same is true for the position on the flowchart: over time, the working relationship moves up and down over the different positions on the flowchart. This constant flux can happen during one specific conversation as well as throughout an intervention over different sessions. In addition, your working relationship with your employees can vary according to the topic that you are working on. On topic A, you might be in a consulting relationship while on topic B you might be in a non-committal relationship.

It is a counterproductive misunderstanding to think that the solution-focused manager's task is to help staff get as low as possible on the flowchart. The task of the solution-focused manager is to assist the staff to get to the position that is most useful for achieving the goals of the parties concerned and the company.

Is it a problem or a limitation?

Distinction: problem or limitation

God, grant me the serenity to accept the things I cannot change, the courage to change the things that I can change, and the wisdom to know the difference.

Serenity Prayer

When faced with any type of situation, it is useful to ask yourself the first and most fundamental question: "Are we dealing with a *problem* or a *limitation?*"

A *limitation* is defined as something you can't change — something for which no solution is possible. Everything that happened in the past, physical losses, laws and legal prohibitions, market forces and macro-economic circumstances are examples of limitations. If you have lost both your legs in a car accident, you will never get them back, no matter what you do; if you made a bad investment for your company last year, you can't go back in time and change it. The only thing you can and need to do with limitations is to acknowledge and accept that they are indeed limitations that you can't change.

Consider the example of a company where a fire takes the lives of several employees and totally destroys the production capacity. If you try to provide guidance with the assumption that this situation is a problem, you will be making a serious mistake. The trauma, the loss of lives, and the company's economic devastation are of the realm of facts and limitations. Pretending that these are problems that can be solved by rebuilding the company and hiring replacements is counterproductive. The fire can't be undone, the dead employees stay dead. However, learning to accept the tragedy and dealing with the consequences is the problem, and there are solutions possible here. Once the company and its employees have found ways of accepting and "processing" the incident, everybody can start rebuilding. Out of that acceptance new possibilities for the company can emerge. The company may change its strategic course, use the need for reinvestment to make leaps forward, change the organization according to lessons learned, etc. The common mourning process can bring employees closer together.

A *problem* is defined by the fact that a solution is thinkable and doable. A company's past bad investment may be a limitation, but the current situation that stems from this bad decision is a problem. There are many ways to deal with the ramifications of the bad investment, from drawing up a rescue plan to preparing for bankruptcy.

The *rule of thumb* is to remember that something is a problem if a solution is possible. If no solution is possible or even thinkable, then you are dealing with a limitation. It is vital to make the correct distinction between problems and limitations for (at least) two reasons.

1. If you treat a limitation as a problem, you are doomed to fail. No matter how great your arsenal of techniques, you will never solve an impossible situation. Remarkably enough, people quite often refuse or are unable to see that certain matters can't be changed. This overzealousness keeps them investing time, money and energy while it is obvious that this will lead nowhere, except straight towards frustration and burnout.

2. It is less common but just as futile to treat problems as if they are limitations. How many times do you hear something like: "No use trying to get that guy motivated, impossible" or "I have tried everything but those people are impossible to work with" or even "Half of my team are morons so trying to get some action out of them will never work." It all leads to the same point — problems are mistakenly regarded as limitations. Only cynicism will emerge from this, and cynicism is neither very helpful nor constructive in business. We propose possible ways to stay out of these (and other) traps in chapter 6 on frequently asked questions.

It is remarkable what this distinction between problems and limitations illustrates, namely that problems are in fact defined by their solutions! After all, if a solution isn't possible, then it's not a problem; it's a limitation. Put another way, there is a potential solution for every problem or it would not be a problem! For limitations in themselves, there are no solutions; but for dealing with the consequences of a limitation there are solutions, namely accepting the limitation and learning how to deal with its consequences. This is a positive and hopeful insight because the feeling of impossibility no longer crushes us. And there is more to limitations then just accepting them. Often, once you accept a limitation for what it is, new possibilities open up.

Interventions

Once the question of whether the situation is a problem or limitation has been addressed, four basic interventions can be applied.

1. Differentiate between problems and limitations

Make the distinction! Situations in which the difference between problems and limitations is clear are easy. However, most situations are a mixture of problems and limitations. If a company is about to go bankrupt because its sources of credit have been withdrawn, and the creditors won't allow further payment postponements, the company faces both problems and limitations. We must try to recognize which elements of the situation can and which cannot be solved.

2. Accept the limitations

Accept the limitations for what they are. A cancelled source of credit will remain cancelled, but you can find a solution in other credit sources. If a company is bankrupt, fighting that bankruptcy will be a waste of time and energy. You must accept the situation and find a way to move on. After all, there is life after failure.

3. Concentrate on the consequences of the limitation

Instead of staying fixated on the limitation, it is much more useful to concentrate on the consequences of the limitation and to learn how to deal with them appropriately. The consequences of a limitation are often problems for which solutions are possible. Your company went bankrupt. What actions can be taken to limit the damage? What can be done to avoid personal liability? How can the failure be managed on a personal level? How can you prepare for the next part of your life in business?

4. New possibilities emerge from accepting

In life we sometimes have to endure difficult things without being able to do anything except to go through them. This is a harsh fact of life, yet human beings are resilient creatures.

Once you accept the inevitable, once you stop trying to change what can't be changed, once you stop trying to find a door in that brick wall, once you accept a limitation, all the energy you were wasting in vain becomes available — and you start looking around and you see lots of opportunities where you weren't looking before.

Allow us a tragic example: when you lose a loved one, this is a crushing emotional experience. Yet, the world keeps spinning around and with time and emotional effort most humans are able to somehow process this loss. Grieving for your loss, cherishing sweet memories, being grateful for what you had together, thriving on the love that the lost person had for you, will help you to accept the loss sooner or later. All of this will probably change the person you are and you might gain a softer perspective on life. In short, the loss will stay with you forever, but you can learn to accept the loss, pick up your life, and move on.

The limitations that we encounter in business life are luckily much more mundane. This does not mean at all that we should take limitations in business life too lightly, for they can have great impact on lots of people. But, dealt with in the right way, handling limitations in business life can open new opportunities. Some examples will clarify this:

- A multinational closes one of its local plants. The community is hit hard because over two thousand jobs are lost. The government decides to invest money for the reconstruction and turn-around of the local economy.
- Due to a major reorganization, a division is dissolved. Some of the employees are sent off to other departments, some get a golden hand-shake and have to leave the company. All of them face a new future.
- Your temporary assignment is not extended, let alone turned into a definite contract. You have to leave but you take the experience with you.
- You are a small entrepreneur and have invested a lot of time and money in developing a novel product. Patents are pending. Six months after launching it into the market, you become aware that a big foreign company markets an eerily similar product but they have the capability to do it on a massive scale and at prices that will kill your business. You try to fight them in court, but you can't afford lengthy procedures. Angry and disappointed that your brainchild is stolen, you realize that you are fighting a lost fight. Once you decide to sell your company with all your knowledge to the foreign competitor, you have the money and resources to move on to a new business venture.

A word of caution and understanding: this plea for accepting limitations in the best constructive way possible is no badly understood "New Ageism"! On the contrary, acknowledging and accepting limitations, dealing with the consequences and looking for possible new opportunities that open up from this is hard work. It is "real politics." We are not trying to make the terrible look good — we are trying to encourage you to face realities and to use all the opportunities that you have.

So what is our task in this? It is simple but not always easy: our task is to make the correct distinction, first ourself, and then to help our employees to acknowledge and accept any limitations for what they are. From that point onwards, our next task is to help our employees deal with the limitations in the best possible manner. This will reduce the chance that our employees waste time and energy while, at the same time, we can help them to open up to new possibilities.

> If you treat a limitation as a problem, you will fail. If you treat a problem as a limitation, you will become desperate.

The non-committal relationship: the employee with no request for help

Definition

Once the distinction between limitations and problems has been made clear, you can ask yourself the second fundamental question: "Does my employee have a demand for help at this moment?" When the answer to this question is "No," you can see on your flowchart that we are dealing with the non-committal relationship type. The employee has made no request for help concerning the topic at hand. You remember from the chart on page 115 that we also use the term "passer-by" for the employee without a request for help. It is obvious that someone who has no request for help will not commit him- or herself to working on that topic. In this non-committal relationship, you are not granted a mandate to intervene on the problematic issue. In a "passer-by" relationship, you are dealing with someone who walks down a street lined with solution shops but shows little interest in what is offered in the shop windows. These people just pass by.

Different categories of passers-by

Passers-by usually fall into one of two groups: passers-by who say they don't have a problem themselves but that someone else thinks they have a problem, and passers-by who admit they have a problem but believe they don't need our help.

As solution-focused managers, you are likely to come into contact with the *first* type of passer-by because he or she is referred to you. They do not recognize or acknowledge that they have a problem but they say that someone else has a problem with them, and therefore, they are forced to come to talk to us. The following statements are typical of passers-by: "My boss ordered me to talk with you about my leadership style, but it's only because she doesn't know how to deal with people herself" or "I don't have a communication problem, but my colleagues don't know how to consult" or "My co-workers say that I don't function well, but it's because of the politics of the whole organization" or "I'd probably benefit from a time management course, but they won't give me time to take it." In extreme cases you'll hear a passer-by say: "I'm here because I was forced to come."

The *second* group of passers-by consists of people who admit that they have a problem but believe they don't need your help for solving it. They only come to tell you that you are not the right person to help them. This type of passer-by will say things like: "I don't know if you as an HR manager will be able to help me because my problems are caused by the recent reorganization" or "I can't get my division to buy into the new ERP software package because no one really backs it, you as a manager can't really do anything" or "I don't understand why my boss thinks I have to talk with you about this project management course. Sure, our three last projects were a bit late, but that was obviously the fault of the subcontractors and definitely not mine. So there is nothing you can do for me."

Passers-by aren't always just individuals. An entire department can take a passer-by approach and get caught in a non-committal working relationship. You might recognize the following classic example.

A breakdown in communication occurs between a company's sales department and the research and development department. Actually, they are in an open fight. Neither department recognizes that their lack of cooperation is perpetuating their problems. The research and development department claims that the sales department is selling the clients tailor-made products they can't possible produce within their project plan. The sales department claims that the research and development department sticks to making standard products they can't possibly sell and that therefore they have to sell tailor-made products. Neither department asks for or wants help for itself, they both believe that they are doing what they are supposed to do. The awkward situation is seen as the other department's fault and responsibility. Both claim that the other department must make the changes.

Little note to avoid misunderstandings

Employees or teams who don't ask for help are often rejected with a parting comment like: "He doesn't want to be helped" or "If she doesn't know what she wants she shouldn't bother me" or "I have better things to do than waste my time with his negativity." This blaming attitude toward staff does not fit the solution-focused model nor is it very helpful!

Please remember our comment on the nature of the four positions (page 116) — just because an employee has no request for help does not mean that that person is a "bad and unmotivated employee." There is nothing wrong with these people! This is just the relationship type at the given moment.

That, of course, does not imply that we merely accept their non-commitment and leave it there. On the contrary, we accept their non-commitment for what it is, without blaming. However, at the same time we evaluate their non-commitment to work with us on the specific topic at hand, and see what we can do to get them committed to something else that will be beneficial to themselves, their team, and the company.

Our task and responsibility as manager-coach is to work on the relationship to see if it can be changed into a more beneficial relationship for all parties concerned.

If, however, the non-commitment is deliberate, stems from ill-will and is done on purpose to create counterproductive or negative effects for the company, then we enter an entirely different ball game. This kind of behavior is sabotage and has nothing to do with a non-committal relationship as we define it here. Then the time has come to act as the manager-leader. See page 209 where we talk about how to handle corporate terrorism.

Moreover, when your employees act as passers-by and they do not commit themselves by asking for your help on a specific issue, this does not diminish their involvement in the company. The fact that they do not ask you for help on the topic at hand does not mean that they are not willing to do anything. If that were the case, they would be behaving obstructively, which in turn would force you as manager-leader to intervene differently. Then you would not be in a non-committal relationship but in an obstructive relationship, which is not acceptable within a company. In such a case it is important to take a much more formal stance and use your authority instead of coaching. Rest assured that nearly a hundred percent of your employees are aware that obstinate obstruction or blunt refusal to cooperate prompts dismissal. But for now, let's put corporate sabotage and unwillingness aside, and work from the belief that everybody is doing their utter best until proven otherwise.

When your employees show no request for help, they still show involvement towards the organization. This is the platform from which you can reach out to them in a non-obtrusive manner by using the following string of four interventions.

Interventions for passers-by

Contrary to the classical management models that have a tendency to consider employees without a request for help as a liability, solution-focused managers view working with passers-by as an exciting challenge.

And indeed, a challenge it is! In a non-committal relationship, you get the opportunity to test your management skills to the maximum. Employees who have no request for help surely have a reason for this. Maybe they do not understand, maybe they don't believe that something needs to change or even can change, maybe they are simply not focused on the issue at hand. Actually the "why" is not so important for two reasons. First, most answers to a "why" question lead quickly to a "who is to blame?" (page 37) and we definitely want to avoid that. Second, even if your employees have no request for your help at this moment, you have probably offered help in a gentle and subtle way in the recent past. This did not work, so it is time to do something else instead.

Here is a string of interventions very suited for dealing with these difficult non-committal relationships, and later on you will read how this works in a real case. The four elements of the intervention are closely linked to each other!

1. Refrain from force-feeding your help

This first part is simple yet very difficult for most managers — if your employee does not ask for help, do not offer help. You know how the saying goes: If you insist, I will resist. So instead of force-feeding your help, quickly move to the next part of the intervention.

TIP

You can't help anyone against his or her will.

2. Show your appreciation

In step 1 of the solution dance (page 47), you learned that a good working relationship is the motor for change. In order to shift the present non-committal relationship towards a more productive collaboration between you and your employees, it is advisable to further develop the basis of that relationship. Fortunately, this is not complicated! You only need to show genuine respect and appreciation for your employees. There are many ways to do this, and you can pick whatever suits your own personality the best from the following list:

- Assume good intentions behind their lack of enthusiasm for change and lack of interest in innovations for the topic at hand.
- Show your staff that you respect their experiences, insights, and beliefs.

- Be friendly and courteous.
- Openly appreciate whatever can be appreciated in your employee and tell them you do.

In short, do not focus yourself on the fact that they have no request for help at this moment and/or for this specific topic. Instead, do focus on whatever you staff has been or is doing for which you can give positive and appreciative comments. If you need a little help on how to do that, please go back to the chapter on the seven-step dance and look at the paragraphs on socializing and complimenting, starting on pages 47 and 77.

When you have done this, you will feel the tension ease, both within yourself and in your staff. This more easy-going feeling between you indicates that you can now move to the next phase of the intervention for passers-by.

3. Offer additional information

Sometimes employees have no request for help for the simple reason that they are convinced that help is not possible. This conviction may originate from lack of confidence, lack of information or most often a combination of both. In those cases, offering information may help them to open up to the idea that changes are indeed possible. If they can rely on this additional information, people may just muster the courage to take small steps towards developing a request for help.

Most of us can remember the time when the computer became a standard tool in the office. If so you can probably also remember those elderly employees who refused, or were certainly very reluctant, to start using the computer. You may remember the arguments for this: "I have been doing my work for so many years now without this contraption. There is no way I will waste my precious time trying to learn to handle it since I will not be able to use the computer efficiently anyhow." Forcing those elderly (and by now extinct) employees into using the computer very often had counterproductive results. Giving them information on how to use the "contraption" and especially demonstrating to them how they would profit from this step by step got most of them over the line. Now, this example may seem a little historic but when you have to introduce a new update for your accounting system, you might encounter something similar once again.

4. Find an alternative problem that is acceptable

After you have shown interest and appreciation for your employee, even if he has no request for help on the topic at hand, you can look for alternative problems on which he might be willing to work. This gracious yet tenacious method sometimes helps your employee to open up so that you can proceed. If this intervention works, you obtain a mandate to work on other issues than the ones that started the intervention in the first place. From there on it may become possible to deal with these initial issues later.

What is most important here is that you keep the responsibility of acting where it actually resides — within the employee him- or herself. Waiting until the rest of the world changes is often futile. It is far better to help employees in a non-committal relationship to search for what it is that they themselves can do.

What is the goal of these interventions?

To summarize, the goal of these interconnected interventions is to offer your employee the opportunity to work on developing some kind of request for help.

- If they accept, they assume their own responsibility, which is always the key to useful behavior and that is what kick starts cooperation. From that point on, you move down to the next level on the flow-chart.
- If they do not accept, then at least you have worked on the quality of your relationship. Then it is up to them to face the consequences of their non-commitment. In any case, your appreciative attitude did not block the relationship and eventually a request for help on their part may emerge later.

How does it work in real life?

The HR manager gets an urgent phone call from one of the production managers who says: "Look, can you do me a favor? I have this guy Eric in my team who is driving me crazy. I feel that he is constantly trying to undermine my authority within the team. We have just had a big fight and I told him to go and talk to you to get himself straightened out. I also told him that this was his last chance. If he doesn't stop his subversive behavior right now, I will kick him out. Can you talk to the guy right now, please? He is on his way to your office."

HR manager: "Is this guy good at his job? Do you really want to get rid of him or is he otherwise a valuable asset in your team?"

Production manager (taken aback a little by this question): "Well, he is very good at his job. The best there is. The problem is that he knows it, and he feels protected by it. But this time I mean it — get him to shape up or I will ship him out."

HR manager: "No promises from me but I will talk to him and see what can be done."

Eric storms into the office of the HR manager: "I have to come and see you because my boss told me to. He accuses me of undermining his authority within the team behind his back. But that's a lie. It's simply not true. He got so angry that he ordered me to come and see you or he would kick me out. I think the guy has just lost his marbles. That's it, I have nothing more to say — it should be him who needs the shrink."

HR manager: "What a mess! Sit down and let's see what can be done. Tell me what happened, please."

Eric tells a long and winding story that can be summarized as an avalanche of mutual misunderstandings.

After a while, the HR manager says: "OK, Eric, I see your point. I don't feel like getting into all kinds of rationalizations about who is right and who is wrong. You're only talking to me because you have to. And it is my job to talk to you. It is clear that your boss is upset with you. But look at the positive side of this: he sends you to come and talk to me, which means that he still sees a chance to get out of this mess. Otherwise, he wouldn't make the effort of referring you to me. Now, let me ask you a more useful question. What do you need to do differently with your boss to get him off your back?"

It is clear that Eric has no request for help whatsoever on the topic that his boss raises, i.e. his presumed subversive behavior. Therefore the HR manager decides not to delve into a fruitless search and analysis about the truth: is Eric acting subversively, yes or no? Such an intervention would lead nowhere except towards more trouble. The HR manager points out that the boss, even though he is cross with Eric, still has a positive reason for his referral. This probably has a soothing effect. The HR manager's last question then helps Eric to think about an alternative problem — what does Eric need to do differently so that he no longer has the boss on his back? Now that is a problem for which Eric might have a request for help. From that point, a useful conversation can take place, and Eric starts talking about what he could do differently to make his dealings with his boss easier.

Metaphor: selling a freezer to an Eskimo

In order to make this intervention more clear, have a think about the following metaphor. Imagine you are a salesman selling deep freezers and your sales region is the Arctic. You might not be able to sell a deep freezer to an Eskimo but he might be interested in an ordinary closet that at least allows him to store his food hygienically. In other words, the Eskimo hasn't asked for help in keeping his food frozen but by showing interest in his environment and not forcing your product on him, you may be able to sell him an alternative product — a machine that will protect his food against vermin. Even if you don't make the sale this year, if you behave in an appropriate, friendly and respectful way, you can at least come back the following year when you have a more fitting product.

Training uninterested people

For the trainers among our readers, or for those of you who have to teach or inform your staff regularly, here's another classic example.

Many people in management-training programs are made to participate by their bosses. Some of these individuals tend to behave in a way that non solution-focused thinkers would call obstructive — they show no interest; on the contrary, they rebel. If you respond to this resistant behavior by trying to get them interested in the program, you will probably only be met with greater resistance. If, however, you accept their negative attitude, and try to build a good relationship with them in spite of it, chances are high that you will be able to negotiate with them about participating in the training with a different goal. For example, you could agree that they will participate in such a way that they experience the least amount of irritation, try not to bother the trainer or disturb the other participants, satisfy the company that sent them, etc.

The "blame it on the subcontractors" case

Bill, a facilities manager responsible for the coordination of technical building projects in an oil refinery, is constantly frustrated. He complains to his employees that the contractors, and particularly their respective subcontractors, are not keeping their promises. Consequently, the building projects are chronically behind schedule. From fear of losing face, he doesn't talk to his boss about these problems. The problem comes to a head when the works on a special production unit doesn't finish in time, causing the whole production line to be stopped with big financial losses as a consequence. At that point, Bill is put on the spot by the management. The production manager and the financial manager are furious. They order Bill into their office: "What the %&$*!* is happening, Bill? You never tell us anything. We just have to guess how things are going in your part of the organization. And now you shut down production without warning us. This can't go on any longer." When Bill tries to defend *himself by blaming the contractors, the management reminds him that he is the one who is paid to get things done on time. The management agrees to give him another chance. They appoint Bruce, an experienced project manager, as Bill's supervisor. "You seem not to be able to get things straightened out on your own, Bill. You have been working hard in the past, that's why we aren't firing you on the spot. But our patience is up. We no longer accept that you keep us uninformed about progress. You accept help now or you are out." It should be no surprise that Bill doesn't welcome this move from the management, but he has no choice but to accept.*

In their first meeting, Bill tells Bruce: "I don't see why my management is after me like that. I have been working extremely hard and have done everything possible. To me, the fact that they're forcing you upon me seems more like a punishment than support. Mind you, I have nothing against you — you are just following orders. I don't see what you can do for me unless you have a magic trick to make sure that the contractors get their work done on time."

Bruce is immediately aware that Bill is not asking for help on how he can proceed differently to appease the management and accepts that Bill is stuck in his focus on the unwilling contractors. This is clearly a non-committal relationship. Bruce realizes that entering a discussion is useless so instead, he decides to give Bill the chance to vent some of his frustrations.

Bruce: "OK, Bill, you and me are not going to change the world, let alone the contractor's behavior. Why don't you first explain your viewpoint to me, then we can look into how you can use your skills to improve your management."

Bill relaxes a bit and, insisting that it wasn't his fault that the projects were behind schedule, he offers a litany of explanations and excuses. "I have done everything in my power to make the contractors do their work on time. You surely agree that I can't go after them with an Uzi. Constantly yelling at them doesn't work either. That just invites them to make up even more lame excuses that would cause even more problems for our company. The contracts I give them are already as clear and as strict as legally possible. In this business, you have to understand, Bruce, that you need to give people some leeway or you find nobody who is willing to accept the job. Whenever I finally contract a certain party that will do the job, I just don't have the time to sit down with them and talk it through with them. Once they take a job, the contractors are on their own — it is their responsibility to do a good job, not mine."

Bruce: "How do you communicate with your management during these processes?"

Bill: "Are you kidding? I don't even have time to talk to the contractors, let alone time to talk to the management about how I proceed. I leave them alone and they leave me alone — everyone to their own work."

Bruce: "So, if I understand correctly, what you are telling me is that, once the contracts are drawn up, you have blind faith in the outcome."

Bill: "Well, basically that's it, yes. Isn't that normal? I mean, when I say that I will do something, I just do it. I don't see why my contractors shouldn't behave in the same way. And I totally do not see why my management wouldn't trust me on this. But apparently they don't trust me or we wouldn't be talking now."

Bruce now goes for the second (appreciative) part of the intervention: "There is a lot that is still going well, Bill, in spite of the problems. You have earned a good reputation within this company. Most of your projects are on time, even if it's often a close shave. The fact that your management is worried and sent me over to work with you intrinsically means that they don't want to lose you. Plus, in the midst of storms, you have been able to maintain a positive attitude toward your contractors. However difficult your job is, you keep going at it."

Feeling supported, Bill relaxes some more and becomes a little less defensive. Then Bruce goes for the third part of the intervention: "What is it that you could do differently so that your management no longer feels that you and I need to talk about this?"

Bill: "If I could get all my contractors to do as they promise, I wouldn't have to talk to anybody at all. But I guess that's a fairy tale."

Bruce: "Correct, and fairy tales sometimes happen but it is best not to count on them happening. What about your management? What could you do differently, so that they would no longer be breathing down your neck?"

Bill: "Well, maybe I should cover my back a little bit more. As it goes now, I only do my best to get the contractors aligned, but there will never be a full guarantee there. Up to now, I have only taken care of putting the entire project into the planning software so that the contractors have an overview. I will of course keep doing that but maybe it would be good if I gave more feedback to my management about what's going on in the process. If things spin out of control, then they at least know this straightaway. What do you think, Bruce?"

Bruce: "Seems like a good idea. Any thoughts on how you could combine that with giving/getting more feedback to and from your contractors? It would be nice to kill two birds with one stone, don't you think?"

Bill: "That would be perfect but how on earth could that be done?"

*Bruce: "It is obvious that you haven't much time, yet you will proba-
bly need to make some time to get more time. I know that your
department is using planning software. Do you see any possibility of putting together reports from this software?"*

*Bill: "Sure, whatever you put in can be shuffled into almost any report
one can think of. Ah, it's dawning! Since I put every assignment into this
planning software, I can easily create two different reports from it. One
could serve as an implementation guide for the contractors and another
could go to management so that they can follow what is happening."*

*Bruce: "Excellent idea, Bill, excellent. Would it be feasible to take your
idea one little step further? When you assign a contract, might it be a
good idea to fix a meeting with the contractor and go through your
implementation plan step by step? That way you can involve the contractor from the very beginning. The report of this meeting then can be sent
to your management and at the same time it can be used as a continuation protocol."*

*Bill: "That's it. I can use that continuation protocol — have to find a
better name though — to satisfy my management, it keeps them in the
loop. At the same time, it obliges me to talk more to the contractors.
Although I have little time, this will save me a lot of time in the long run."*

Bruce: "Congrats. Go for it."

*The result of this intervention is that Bill finds a different way to deal
with his own management and that he develops an alternative method for
dealing with the contractors.*

In short: checklist for dealing with a non-committal relationship

1. When your staff has no request for help, you simply don't offer help,
   let alone force help on them.
2. Develop as positive a working relationship as possible.
3. Offer additional information.
4. See if an alternative request for help can be developed.

The searching relationship: the employee with an unworkable request for help

Definition

If the employee *has* a request for help, we ask ourselves the third fundamental question — is this request for help workable? When the answer to
this question is no, this indicates that, although they're asking for help,

your employees don't see what they themselves could do to find a solution. Therefore they expect someone else to solve their problem on their behalf. In other words, they give you the mandate to do the work on their behalf. We call this a searching relationship — they enter our little shop of solutions, put their problem on our desk and wait for us to give them a solution to their problem. It is not that they are not willing to work on their problem, on the contrary. They are looking for help, but they are looking in the wrong place instead of where help really can be found, within themselves.

Metaphor for the searching relationship

The searcher behaves like my neighbor John. After a meeting at the office that lasted longer than foreseen, he and his colleagues went for a drink that turned into a party. So John comes home in the middle of the night, slightly tipsy, not to say downright drunk. As quietly as possible, he tries to unlock his front door but the key slips out of his hands. A few minutes later, I arrive home very late after working too long in the office and see John crawling on hands and knees under the streetlamp across the street from his home. I walk up to him and ask: "Hi John, what's the matter? Need some help?" Slurring his words, John answers: "I lost my key at the front door." "So why are you looking for it under the streetlamp then?" John: "Because this is the only place where there is light."

Different categories of searchers

The four categories of searchers all share the same common denominator: they want help, but have no clue as to what they could do themselves. It is highly likely that you will recognize most of the following categories. Sometimes, you encounter a combination of categories which adds to your challenge as a manager whose basic task it is to help your employee change their own perspective. In the following pages, we will first describe the categories and then give you some possible interventions for dealing with each of them.

1. It's not me, it's them!

When you work with searchers, you will hear things like: "If my colleagues did what they have to do, I would be able to finish my reports on time" or "As long as top management doesn't show more interest in what we do, how can they expect us to show more motivation?" or "My salesmen can only fail if production stays behind schedule" or "I can only perform better if the others work harder" or "As long as the management doesn't give me the power to do something about the counterproductive atmosphere in our department, I don't see what I could do differently to make things better" or even plainly "If the other (colleague, boss, co-worker, partner…) doesn't change, then there is nothing I can do."

This type of searcher is probably the most common "subspecies." We all recognize this way of thinking within some of our employees and we ourselves have probably thought along the same lines at some point. This "it's not me, it's the herd" attitude is very recognizable. To be frank, who has never played with this way of thinking to get away with difficult situations where one felt powerless? The searcher acts like a victim of his or her circumstances or someone else's whims or lack of cooperation. The help that a searcher expects from you is that you as the manager change the others.

2. Cloud-like goals

You also enter a searching relationship when your employees ask you to help them to work on vague and/or poorly defined goals. This type of searcher makes comments like: "We are not communicating well lately," "I can't bring it up anymore," "We don't click anymore," "The atmosphere is negative," "Business is slack," "I have no energy left and I feel bad and insecure at work" or "I wish this company was the same as it used to be." When you ask them what they specifically mean by these expressions, you get answers like: "Well, you know, that's hard to put into words," "I don't know how to state it more specifically," "It is just a general feeling" or plainly "If I could answer that question, the problem would be solved." It is obvious that achieving goals that are so vague and poorly defined is nearly impossible.

3. Goal overload

If you are the lucky manager who has the honor of leading a team of overzealous employees, then you might end up with the next subspecies of searcher. This type poses so many different requests for help, on so many different issues at the same time, that the whole becomes unworkable.

You might, for example, run into someone who goes: "I am in the middle of the appraisal interviews with my staff, and I still have to talk to nine people this week. The budget also needs to be finalized as soon as possible, and approved by top management because it will have big repercussions on our investments. Plus, I am still in the middle of negotiations about the exact layout of the new production line, but I need to take more time to prepare the overall investment package that this will require, otherwise top management will not go along with it. Business is going so well that I urgently need a new engineer and I need to talk with our headhunter to get the exact profile out. On top of all this, I wonder how and when I will find time to prepare my workshop for our internal conference next week. I've been so busy lately that I seem to get nothing done, and I seem to have lost my concentration. Could you help me, please?"

It is evident that this superman of an employee takes on a workload that far exceeds his, or indeed anybody's, means.

4. I would like to … but I can't

Employees with self-annihilating requests for help present themselves as being in a Catch-22 situation: "I would like to … but that is impossible because …". They might say things like: "I would like to consult more but I can't, because being an engineer, I'm too introverted" or "I would like to introduce project management into our company but our organization is too messy to even try to structure it" or (an extreme example) "If the economy doesn't improve I won't be able to motivate my people" or (even more extreme) "If our prices don't improve it's useless spending time on bidding for new contracts." In short, it's like saying: "If only I had enough time, then I would follow a course on time management." These searchers tend to nip every possible solution in the bud or simply don't think about alternatives.

Interventions for searchers

The general way of dealing with searchers is to help them to express their problems in a more workable form, so that they regain the trust that they can do something themselves.

As you read through the interventions for helping searchers in the upcoming paragraphs, you will notice that three main strategies are always in the background. Strategy one is that you ask solution-building questions (see page 33) to help your employees reformulate their unworkable request into useful goals. For a reminder of the definition of useful goals, please have a quick look at the checklist in step 3 of chapter 3 (page 62).

The second strategy is that you use solution-building questions, but this time to facilitate a shift in their perspective so that they regain faith in their own possibilities for inducing change.

The third strategy is to make smart use of the seven steps of the solution dance that you have learned in chapter 3.

Although the strategies don't follow a sequence that is set in stone, keeping them in mind helps. You will learn several new techniques that you can add to your growing arsenal of solution-building interventions. Here is a list illustrating how these interventions work:

1. It's good that you are persistent in your search for solutions despite your lack of time. (Positively supporting)
2. What is it that you could do differently yourself?
3. What aspects are still going well enough to make you want to keep them? (Attention to what is going well)
4. Let's find out together if we can make things more concrete. (Make problems more concrete and/or prioritize them)
5. In which circumstances does the problem not bother you or bother you less, and what do you do differently then? (Search for exceptions)

1. Positively support the search

However inefficient their efforts might be, searchers are at least motivated to work on something. So, it is good to acknowledge and support their search and show appreciation for their efforts.

Your task is to help staff channel their energy in a different way, so that they are no longer trying to eat soup with a fork. How is this done? You give them compliments on their efforts: "You've told me you are getting frustrated because you are working so hard with no sign of success. But I have to congratulate on your untiring efforts. Would you be interested in trying to find another way so that your efforts become more effective?"

2. Keep the responsibility for change with the employee

An employee who does not believe he can change anything will give the following type of answer to the previous question: "I haven't got a clue what I can do differently if the others don't change," just as we said in the "It's not me, it's them!" section (page 132).

This conviction paralyzes your employee. If you try to convince your employee that his perspective is wrong, chances are high that the both of you will get lost in a sterile rational discussion that will have no beneficial effect on your working relationship. It is unlikely that something useful will come out of this.

But, there is another way. By asking the right questions, you can gently invite your employees to look at their frozen convictions from another perspective. Let's investigate how you can do this and, please, feel free to experiment with additional questions.

- Conviction: "If my colleagues did what they have to do, I would be able to finish my reports on time." *Question*: "What is it that you can still do without waiting for your colleagues' information and help?"
- Conviction: "As long as top management doesn't show more interest in what we do, how can they expect us to show more motivation?" *Question*: "Even if you do not feel the support from top management, what are the small things that you can do differently to help you work with a little more gusto?"
- Conviction: "My salesmen will fail if production stays behind schedule." *Question*: "How do you manage to keep your sales crew motivated? What aspects of their sales work are they still performing well?"
- Conviction: "I can only perform better if the others work harder." *Question*: "What might be the smallest step towards improvement that you are willing to try, even if you feel that the others won't follow?"

Even if your employees are not yet able or willing to act differently, then at least you have planted the idea in their minds that they can take responsibility.

3. What is going well in spite of the problems?

With this question you teach your employees that there is much more going on in their working life than the problems they come to talk to you about. This intervention helps them to look way beyond the scope of the problem at hand. This is nothing new — in step 4 (resources) of the solution dance, you have already learned the importance of uncovering your employees' resources. You can refer back to page 68 for a quick review of techniques and solution-building questions that you could use at this point.

In addition, we would like to offer you another elegantly simple yet powerful intervention, both in the form of a question and in the form of an assignment. This intervention is very well suited when working with a searching relationship but can also be applied to all other types of working relationships.

THE CONTINUATION QUESTION

The continuation question goes like this: "What do you think is important and valuable enough in your (personal and/or business) life that you really want to keep it like it is?" You can also ask the question directly: "What do you want to keep the way it is now?"

The continuation question can be about things that people want to keep going on a personal level but also about what they want to keep going within the team, department, company, position on the market, in cooperation with other departments, etc.

"In order to get a better idea of what has to change in your team, we must first know what *does* work well in spite of the problems. After all, we can't throw out the baby with the bathwater. Before the next meeting, take some time to observe what things within the team you definitely want to keep as they are."

"No matter how difficult you might find your job, I would like you to think about the things in your job that you find valuable enough to keep. These things can be important, like your health insurance plan, salary, or relationship with your colleagues, but they can also be small, like your cappuccino during lunch or the company subscription to the newspaper."

THE CONTINUATION ASSIGNMENT

An interesting variation of the continuation question comes in the form of an *assignment*. You ask your employee to point out the small things that are going well on a regular basis: "If you agree, I would like you to take some time every day between now and our next meeting — perhaps just before you go home — to go over your day and write down the things that happened that day that you would like to keep happening."

By asking the employees to write these things down "so that we can discuss them in detail next time," you turn these points into a concrete reality. The assignment invites your employees to really put their minds to this line of thought. Their focus then shifts from an exclusive fascination with their problem to a broader perspective.

WHY IS THIS CONTINUATION INTERVENTION USEFUL?

This technique is useful for two reasons. *First*, and maybe most importantly, is that that the intervention makes the employee focus on the things that are still working well in spite of the problems. Why else would one want to keep those things? Nevertheless, employees who are searchers have the impression that nothing is going well. Taking time to note the things that make you happy and functional can put your problems into perspective. This simple task is not always easy, but it is usually useful.

Second, the technique helps the employee to point their nose in the direction of solutions. No matter how small, the things that go well often contain elements of solutions that, once you notice them, can easily lead to bigger solutions. Whatever answers your employees give, they always create a platform from which you can build further. When asked what it is that she certainly would like to keep, the employee who complains that her colleagues load too much work on her may answer that she likes her work, likes to work for this company, thinks the pay is good, and is pleased that most of her colleagues say thank you when she has helped them. These answers can be starting points to help her overcome her complaints and do something differently.

A LITTLE DO-IT-YOURSELF PROPOSAL

In order to get a feel of the power of this question, we would like you to apply the assignment to yourself:

- What do you think is important and valuable enough in your business life that makes you really want to keep it?
- What do you think is important and valuable enough in your private life that makes you really want to keep it?

Jot down a few thoughts, let them rest, and notice the difference they make.

4. Make the problem concrete and prioritize

When you are in a searching relationship with employees who phrase their requests for help in a vague and poorly defined style (the cloud-like subspecies) or employees who suffer from an overload of simultaneous requests, then this is *the* intervention. It is probably the easiest and most straightforward way of helping your employees for the simple reason that this type of intervention is what managers specialize in.

However, we are not suggesting that you adopt the classical managerial style, where managers just tell people what to do and then expect people to do as they are told. As always, we prefer the indirect method of giving suggestions with a question mark at the end (page 149), or using of plenty of solution-building questions.

GOAL
SETTING

In step 3 (goal-setting, page 53) of the solution dance, you learned ways to translate general, vague, abstract and unclear problems into precise, well-described, concrete, and clear problems so that the road to solutions opens up.

Remember, useful goals are:

1. Realistic and achievable.
2. Concrete, i.e. stated in terms of observable behavior.
3. Preferably increasing from small to big.

Vague problems like: "It's not OK at the office, we should change things" or "I would like my employees to be happy on the job" or "We should all make an effort to be more ambitious" can easily be translated into a more workable form by asking: "What is the smallest thing that you could do differently to make things a little bit better at the office?" or "How would you notice that your employees are a little happier on the job? What is the smallest sign that would tell you that?" or "How would you define your ambition, what will you have concretely accomplished when you are further up on the ambition scale?"

The same goes for poorly defined goals like: "Our market penetration ought to be bigger" or "Our new mission statement must become sexier and flashier." Here you can use questions like: "What is our current market penetration, and what are the concrete steps we can take to increase it?" or "What could you phrase differently so that when you ask your employees to read your new mission statement, they will tell you it's more flashy and sexy?"

For "goal overload" problems, you can ask questions that help your employee define in what order they will tackle the pile. You could ask, for example: "Great to see you are taking on so many tasks at the same time. Now, if you list all your different tasks, would it be useful to organize them from small and easy to big and difficult? Or is it a better idea to put them in a grid with one side 'low to high priority' and on the other side 'low to high urgency'?"

The miracle question (see page 99) is an excellent translating tool, too. Describing how it will be after the miracle has happened is to portray the preferred future in vivid detail. Scaling questions (see page 86) can help to translate a set of blurred goals into small steps.

5. Hunt for exceptions to the problem

As already noted, all problems have exceptions (see page 69). But searchers rarely believe they are doing something to establish those exceptions. They assume that exceptions arise purely by coincidence and are independent of what they are doing. This mindset leads them to believe that they are powerless to create more exceptions to the problem. Our task as managers is to help these employees realize that there are many ways in which they can use exceptions to come to solutions. This allows them to regain hope — they regain trust in the possibility of change and that they can do something to make it happen.

You can do this by asking the appropriate solution-building questions. For example, when an employee complains that he can't do anything to ease the tension among his team members, you could ask: "During which moments in the recent past was the situation less tense? What did you do differently then, no matter how small?" or "When was the last time that you felt at ease in your team? What was different then? What did you do differently? What would your team members say that you do differently when things go a little bit better?" or "Last week when you all went to that product presentation meeting together, everything went well. How did you do that? What did you do differently to make sure your joint presentation was a success?"

To further enlarge your arsenal of solution-building techniques, have a look at these additional interventions.

THE OBSERVATION ASSIGNMENT

Giving employees an observation assignment is a very useful way of helping them to pinpoint the exceptions to the problem. Employees are asked to observe when, for example, the tension is less noticeable within the project team and to write down what everyone is doing differently. Or the entire team is asked to observe when the atmosphere is more relaxed during the next meeting and to note what they are doing differently during those moments. By giving this assignment you focus staff's attention toward more desired, useful behavior without telling them what they should do differently. This is a far more efficient way of enabling change, for the simple reason that your employees will be more motivated to behave in useful ways if they have discovered those behaviors themselves. If you experiment with this assignment, you will discover that employees are very creative in finding their own exceptions and therefore map out their own solutions.

THE PREDICTION ASSIGNMENT

It sometimes happens that employees just can't think of any exception that occurred in the past and pressing for an answer only makes things

FUTURE ORIENTATION

worse. So if looking into the past doesn't work, let's look to the future. How can you do this? You ask your staff to take time in the evening or in the morning, once a day or every two days, to predict their own behavior and the behavior of their colleagues. They are asked to make precise predictions about the intensity of the problem, the number of times it occurs, the degree of control they will have over it, which exceptions will occur, and how the problem will end. (Creative readers should feel free to vary the prediction assignment according to the situation.)

The scaling-prediction cocktail

Scales combined with the prediction assignment make up a strong cocktail. First you ask your employee a scale of progress (page 89): "Where are you on a scale where zero stands for 'no change at all, a total mess' and ten stands for 'this is good enough for the problems no longer to bother us'?" If your employee says three, you ask her what that three means in as vivid detail as possible. Then you combine this with the prediction assignment: "OK, you are now at a three on a scale from zero to ten. Good. I would like to ask you to take time every morning before you go to work during the coming week to predict where on the scale you will be that day. Write down that number, and in the evening go over the day and write down where you arrived on that scale. Observe what difference that will make." This assignment distracts staff from the problem and reorients their attention toward evaluating their prediction.

How is this seemingly odd assignment helpful? Of course, nobody in their right mind believes that people can predict the unpredictable. However, by focusing your staff's attention on exceptions (every number higher than zero), they create a solution-orientation. Moreover, by making predictions about the intensity and frequency of exceptions, the chance that exceptions will indeed occur is bigger. At any rate, the assignment will heighten the probability that your staff will look for exceptions in order to reach the predicted number. By predicting exceptions and then observing them, employees can't deny that change is possible. After all, they are the ones who created the self-fulfilling prophecy.

Case: corporate restructuring

Roberta is a commercial manager working for a large American multi-national company based in Detroit. She works from her office at home in Rome and is responsible for sales for a large part of Europe. She regularly gets into trouble because she has made agreements with some of her customers that were out of line with the general directives, especially on payment terms. Headquarters now insist that she follow the international guidelines on the collection of accounts receivable. The Detroit office has repeatedly told her that they would accept exceptions to those guidelines only after they had been consulted. Ensconced behind her desk and far from the main office, Roberta thinks this is nonsense. She is convinced that the people from headquarters have no idea about the way the European market, and especially the Italian market, functions. How on earth can she get the Italian customers to pay faster? She would lose the account! Moreover, her customers always pay their bills in the end, and she makes sure that the payments are protected by letters of credit. "So what's the problem in Detroit?" Knowing that she represents a large European turnover for the company, she feels rather at ease: "They won't come after me when I ignore their stupid headquarter inflexibility." Unfortunately, her director loses his patience. When Roberta again allows a customer to pay much later, he sends her a registered letter with the message that this is the last warning: "One more transgression and you will be fired on the spot." Such a formal warning is the last thing Roberta expects. Promptly Roberta calls Tom, the HR director and an old friend, for help: "Tom, could you help me, and try to explain to my director that the people in headquarters need to be more understanding about the different market situation in Europe and especially in Italy. It is absurd that I'm having this problem with HQ, because I do my best to sell as much as possible. They must acknowledge that I can only keep most of the Italian accounts because I give in to them over the payment issue."

After consulting with the director, the HR director gives Roberta some bad news: "Your director tells me that he really appreciates your work. You bring in a lot of turnover. But he is furious and fed up with the way you handle certain things, especially the way you keep overruling the policy on accounts receivable. HQ insists that you follow corporate directives. They urge you to stop making promises to your clients that you cannot keep, because they are against the international regulations. You have to stick to the corporate policy, end of story."

That message sends Roberta off the rails. For two weeks, she feels very insecure and is afraid when the phone rings in case it is one of her "unauthorized" customers. She considers sending in her resignation but decides that she loves the job; plus, as a single mother, giving up her job is not really possible. She is afraid to call some of her clients so she busies herself with a backlog of administration. After two weeks, she realizes that this can't go on forever and, in desperation, she contacts Tom again: "Tom, I need your help. I'm in a mess. I've been trying to find another way to work, but I just don't know. These clients are too used to my granting their wishes, I don't know what to do. Maybe I just have to throw in the towel and leave the company."

The HR director proposes a videoconference with her so they can look for a way out. It is clear to Tom that Roberta is a searcher: she has a strong demand for help but her goals are unworkable. The more she looks for a solution, the more she becomes stuck. During the first video conference, the HR director brings up every positive aspect of Roberta's work, talks about her successful track record in the company, and tells her that the company really is not out to get rid of her, far from it. Tom also stresses the fact that she has to find a way to get her "unauthorized" customers to accept the company rules on payments. He allows Roberta to vent her ideas and troubles and then asks her the following question: "Where are you on a scale from zero to ten, where zero stands for 'not having any hope at all for finding a solution to your problems' and ten stands for 'having enough hope of solving the problem'?"

Roberta answers: "A big fat zero."

Tom: "OK Roberta, what would be the smallest thing that has to change to get you to a one?"

Roberta: "To start again with full confidence instead of hiding behind my desk and hoping that particular clients don't call."

Tom: "Great, Roberta. That is a lot, maybe even too much. What else?"

Roberta: "You ask difficult questions. I don't know. Maybe I need to take another look at my travel schedule and call some clients — but only those who I know for sure are already following our standard payment requirements."

Tom: "Wonderful, Roberta. If you did that, where would you then be on a scale from zero to ten?"

Roberta: "Hmm. Maybe on a two but I don't know if I would get into trouble again. Sooner or later the unauthorized clients will call again, and I need them because they represent almost a third of my turnover."

Tom: "No problem, Roberta, take it easy. You don't need to address everything at the same time."

Then he gives Roberta the following assignment: "I would like to ask you to take time between today and our next meeting to look at each workday the night before and predict where you will be on this scale from zero to ten. Write that number down. The following evening you give yourself a number on that same scale that reflects how the day went. See if there is any difference between the number you predicted and the number you write at the end of the day. Also, jot down the things that you think are relevant in this respect. In three weeks, we will discuss this when I am in Italy. Good luck!"

Now that is a fairly vague assignment. The only goal is that there is a chance that it will help Roberta to look for changes in her behavior as she predicts different numbers. Maybe this will help her to broaden her attention to other things than just the one problem she is stuck with.

When after three weeks, they meet in Rome, Roberta is happy to tell her HR director that she feels a lot better. "After our call," she says, "I summed up all my courage and went to work full speed. I called almost all of my 'unspoiled' customers and I even made myself call prospective clients. It helped a lot."

In the last three weeks, she has made a good number of sales, all with the standard payment requirements. On top of this, she has also drawn up a proposal for the main office. The title alone is very promising: "Changes for the Improvement of our Client Relationship." In this proposal she has done a detailed and step-by-step analysis on how she will prepare for negotiations with each client in order to get them to pay according to the international guidelines. She clearly states that she will do her best to "sell" this to her "unauthorized" clients on the condition that the main office gives her a transition period. She also indicates the length of that transition period for each client. "That's all I can do," Roberta tells Tom. "Now it is up to the main office. If I lose turnover because of this, they have to guarantee that they won't blame me."

Tom compliments Roberta on her flexible attitude and creativity and promises her that he will do everything he can to support her proposal. He again asks Roberta the scale for hope. She is now at a five.

Some weeks pass. The main office studies her proposal, changes a few minor things, and approves. The director sends a fax to Roberta stating that he appreciates her attitude and that he will take responsibility for any lost clients.

In retrospect, three months later, only a few clients have been negative about Roberta's new approach, but even those clients appreciated the transition period. One client wrote to Roberta to say that he found it difficult to accept the changes but that he appreciated not being presented with a fait accompli, *which would have prompted him to pull out. Of course, some clients are still making special requests, but Roberta is now able to consult with the main office about this in an open way. She is certain to get permission for flexibility in some cases and the main office is confident that they remain in control.*

This intervention was designed in such a way that Roberta could learn not to fight a losing battle against company policy — she instead figured out a way to take the corporate rules into account without letting her clients down. The company learned that it is commercially useful to apply strict rules in a flexible way.

In short: checklist for dealing with a searching relationship

1. Positively support the search.
2. Offer help so that: "It's not me, it's them" becomes: "I can do something differently."
3. Pay attention to what goes well in spite of the problems: continuation question.
4. Rephrase the problem so that it is concrete.
5. Search for exceptions to the problem.

Don't give searchers the key; tell them how to look for it.

The consulting relationship: the employee without access to resources

Definition

Now let's turn to the fourth and final of the fundamental questions (page 114). Is the employee who comes to us with a workable request for help able to use his or her resources? If the answer is no, then we enter into a consulting relationship with these employees. They come to us for advice on how to use their resources and they are willing "to buy" what we offer them. In other words, once we enter a consulting relationship with our employees, they give us the mandate to help them to use their own resources.

As noted above (page 67) any tool that people can use to come to solutions is a resource. A tool is literally anything that can be used in a constructive way: insights, instincts, interpersonal skills, knowledge, exceptions to the problem, theory, experiences, help from the outside, tips and tricks, intelligence, etc. Sometimes our employees already have these resources available but they don't know how to make use of them. Sometimes they simply do not have or know about these tools, and then we offer information about these tools.

The case of Steve and Mike will illustrate the interventions that are appropriate when you deal with someone who clearly has a workable request for help. Steve, however, has no idea how to use his resources.

No time to make time

Steve is the manager-owner of a chain of real estate agencies. He built his company from scratch. Mike is a self-employed consultant and coach. They are both members of the same business club.

One day, Steve calls Mike: "Mike, I need to talk to you in private. I know you are coaching people for a living and I sure need help from a professional like you."

They meet in Steve's office. After some preamble, Steve explains why he wants to talk to Mike.

Steve: "I really think I need some help. I have postponed this for a long time now, but I can no longer cope. It has nothing to do with my business because that is running very smoothly. It has to do with me. I finally decided to call you for help because my wife urged me to. She is right, I do need help from someone to get another perspective. I am stuck."

Steve tells the long story of his business life. He remembers the days when he worked alone and had to do everything all by himself. With regret, Steve says: "Those were the days. I remember the pleasure and the thrill. I was lucky to start my company at a time when the real estate business was picking up, and I've been riding the waves since then. Sure I've had bad moments but all in all, everything has gone smoothly. Although I had to do literally everything myself, I feel that I had more time in those

GOAL
SETTING

days. Now I have several agencies and forty-five people working for me. I thought that having personnel to take care of the business would give me more freedom and time. Dead wrong! Nowadays I have no time for anything as I am always running behind."

Mike: "Great story. Congratulations on your success. You did a great job building this company. It's good to hear that your private life is a safe haven for you. Now, what should we talk about today so that this meeting will be helpful to you?"

Steve: "There is a lot, of course, but two things stand out at the moment, and they are interrelated. First, I don't have any time. I tried a time management course but that didn't work out. It was too complicated and besides, I don't have enough time to devote myself to really applying the techniques."

Mike: "No time to make time, that's an interesting paradox. What else?"

Steve: "I recently hired a sales manager. His job is to coach the sales team. I was hoping that this would save me some time so that I can do what I do best — making deals. I should coach him, of course, but up until now I haven't even found enough time to introduce him properly into my company. I sure tried and we set up many meetings but to no avail. It doesn't work. There is always some interference — a deal that only I can close, another meeting with a potential client that I simply cannot postpone. So instead of a solution, I have an additional problem."

Steve realizes that both his time management method and his way of coaching his personnel are very inefficient. His sales manager isn't too happy with the way it is working either. He tries his best but without vital information from Steve, he is only scratching the surface.

Steve has talked to his wife about this. She listened to her husband and offered good advice but to no avail. Steve keeps insisting that he has tried everything and still can't change the situation due to lack of time. He is constantly solving little things but never looking at the bigger picture. "I feel like a fireman, running around with buckets of water to kill every fire in every corner and yet the whole building is ablaze."

What can Steve do?

Even though resources are tools that are easy to use, it is not always easy to get buyers to use the tools in the right way. After all, they have made many failed attempts at solving their problem.

Usually this is because they don't have the right manual for the tools they use, or, they quit before they see results. ("I tried that time management thing for about two weeks but it didn't work.") Or they don't use them in the right way. ("In my job it isn't possible to set priorities because something else always comes up unexpectedly.") Or they jump too quickly from one tool to the next. ("I have tried everything from written reports I didn't really have time to write, to weekly meetings that never took place. Nothing works!") The examples show that they do have resources but they don't make use of them in the correct way.

It also happens that clients have no idea about the resources they have at their disposal. Some people have never heard of time-management, prioritizing, or an efficient way to share information via reports. You still (and maybe always will) meet teams that do not know how to have an efficient meeting. Then all you have to do is gently teach them these resources. But these cases are rare, especially in the sophisticated business environment you are working in.

The most important strategy we use to help buyers is to motivate and help them to (again) use their tools and resources correctly.

Metaphor for the consulting relationship

Employees who initiate a consulting relationship are like customers who are browsing the streets lined with solution shops. They enter our little shop of solutions with their requests. What they are out to buy are tools that will help them solve their problems themselves. Sometimes they already have these tools available but they have lost the manual on how to make the best use of their tools. Our role as solutions salesmen is to advise them on the best tools available and to offer them the correct manual so that they can help themselves.

Interventions for buyers

The basic intervention in the relationship is to create a context in which buyers learn how to (re-)use their resources in a more useful manner. As always, the solution-focused *modus operandi* of asking questions is a better way to build solutions then offering ready-made and off-the-shelf solutions.

All interventions for buyers share the following linked ingredients.

1. Analyze previous attempts at solutions

The question "What have you already tried that didn't work?" will clarify what your employee has tried without success. This will help you to save time and energy for the simple reason that if something does not work, you should stop doing it. The answers will also provide you information on how your employee thinks and works. In addition, this respectful question shows your employees that you are interested in their attempts at solving their problems themselves.

2. Find out about small harbingers of success

Find out which solutions were at least partially successful in the past. Here the question is: "What did you try that worked a little bit?" As noted earlier, most buyers have made many attempts to solve their problems but without success. By asking this question you will get information on partial successes. Frequently, buyers cut short their attempts because they don't get immediate results. They have a tendency to throw out the baby with the bathwater. Usually the methods they have tried can be made useful if you adjust them. It is often a matter of getting them to try things again, but to try using their resources more correctly.

Another useful question is: "What has been helpful with similar problems in the past?" From there, you can help them adapt the resources they used in the past to deal with similar problems, and apply these tools to the situation at hand.

3. Give advice preferably in the form of a question

Buyers are ready and prepared to accept help from someone else, and there is no reason we should withhold it. Here it becomes clear that the solution-focused model is a meta-model in which all the resources and techniques that stem from the vast body of common management knowledge find their place. All other management models and methods can be put to optimal use under the solution-focused umbrella.

The list of tools and resources you can tap into is endless: all possible management models and methods, scenario planning, organizational development, project planning, strategic business planning, common sense, delegating skills, crisis management, communication, financial management, budgeting. In other words, all the classic management tools, methods, techniques, and advice. The more knowledge, experience, insights and common sense you have available, the more helpful and efficient a manager you will be.

The most powerful way of offering advice is to put a question mark at the end of your advice. "Would you think that...?", "Might it be helpful to...?", "What if you tried...?" Giving advice by using questions avoids the trap of inducing resistance (If you insist, I will resist). On the contrary, by formulating your advice as questions, you offer the ownership and the responsibility of the advice to your employee. This works a lot better then just telling them what to do.

The "no time to make time" solution

Mike: "OK now, Steve, let's see what you can do differently. You told me you went to that time management course, tried out some of the techniques but in the end you just gave up. What is it exactly that you tried?"

Steve: "One of the things they taught me was to make lists of everything I had to do. I tried this. It gave me some overview of my work. Every day I sat down and made lists, but I gave up because I was drowning in these lists. Plus, nothing came out of it because I was almost never able to do what was on my list. At the end of each day I was even more frustrated because I was confronted with my failure. The only good thing was that I was pleased to see how much work I have."

Mike: "OK. So making these lists was a little bit helpful because it gave you an overview. Of course this is no instant cure. Would you be interested to learn a more useful way of making these lists?"

Steve: "Sure. Anything is better than what I am doing now."

Mike: "Maybe a little adjustment can help. I assume that you agree that working too hard is not always efficient but working smart is? To-do lists are, as you noticed yourself, particularly useful to get an overview. It is a frequent mistake to think that one actually needs to do everything on the list. People tend to put too strict a timing on all the actions, and that's where failure comes from. Of course you have so many things to do that you cannot possibly do them all. So it is useful to adapt these to-do lists."

Steve: "I'm curious."

Mike: "Would it be a good idea to differentiate between urgent and not urgent on the one hand, and important and less important on the other? That way your to-do list becomes a matrix, and you still have an overview. Would you be willing to try this in the coming weeks and see what a difference this makes?"

Steve: "Interesting concept. So you don't want me to put timing on this list? How will this be useful then? I still have to do all these things anyhow."

Mike: "Correct, no timing, just the overview matrix. Then you go about your business as usual. I wonder what you will discover when you do this exercise. By the way, this exercise works like jogging: there is no point in going out for a two-hour jog every three months — that is as dangerous as it is useless. The same applies for this exercise — it will only be useful if applied on a daily basis. You might even want to take some time every evening to reflect on what you have learned that day."

Steve: "I will give it a try. Like my father always said: 'If you don't shoot, you always miss." Now, what should I do about my sales manager? The few meetings we did have were very useful. If only we could meet more frequently, but there are not enough hours in the day. Even a week is gone in a blink."

Mike: "What did you try?"

Steve: "When he started working for me, we set up an ambitious plan. We agreed to meet for one hour every day. That went OK for two days but then I had to leave town for a few days, and we were never able to pick it up again. Mind you, it's not that we don't talk at all, we just don't talk enough. Lately I have been a bit worried about him. He has started complaining that I never make time for him. Last week he bluntly asked me if I am really sure that I want him as a sales manager!"

Mike: "Do you?"

Steve: "Sure. He is the right guy. He comes from the real estate business and has a lot of experience. I just need to give him enough inside information about my company. Plus, I want to know what he is doing all the time. He is a big investment, and I want to see results."

Mike: "Knowing what your personnel is doing all the time is a giant task. Maybe it's not possible or advisable."

Steve: "That's not what I mean. I have enough trust in my personnel to let them work in their own way. The same goes for my sales manager. But the way it's going now is wrong. We spend more time planning for meetings than actually having a meeting. We talk more about the fact that we should talk than anything else. It is frustrating."

Mike: "Good. At least this shows that you are motivated to meet with each other, no misunderstanding there. Would it be a good idea to decide first about what it exactly is that you want to tell him? And then decide what kind of information that you would like to get from him? Then think about the frequency and the method?"

Steve: "So you propose that instead of talking content we're better off taking some time to set up a structure?"

Mike: "Exactly. You could even ask your sales manager to draw up a proposal so that you don't have to spend time on it yourself. I am pretty sure that he will see this as a sign of trust from your side. You can always correct and fine-tune his initial proposal."

Steve: "OK. I will try it. This is bound to work better then what we are doing now. I just need to make a little time to make time. Let me work on this and let's meet again in a few weeks. Thanks for your advice, Mike."

Checklist interventions for Buyers

1. What did you try that didn't work?
2. What did work a little?
3. Offer advice in the form of a question.

Conclusion

There is nothing wrong with offering advice to your employees. You remember the fourth tenet (page 23): "If something works, learn from it or teach it to somebody else." There is only one strong prerequisite — that the employee must have a workable request for help. It is useless (and disrespectful) to give advice to someone who doesn't even ask you for help.

It is not just up to managers to offer advice. Employees swap knowledge, tips, techniques and advice amongst themselves. As managers, we want to encourage this sharing of expertise, especially in cases where your T.E.A.M. members are in a consulting relationship with each other so that *together each achieves more.*

Scientific work on Swarm Intelligence shows us that intelligence resides in the individual but, maybe more so, between the individuals of a collaborating group. If you promote the fourth tenet into the collaborative style of your company, and back it, your company might develop into a solution-focused swarm!

The co-expert relationship: the employee with access to resources

Definition

When the fourth fundamental question (Are they able to use their resources?) can be answered positively, you are entering a co-expert relationship, and we call this category of employees "co-experts." These employees have formulated a workable request for help, they have clear and feasible goals, and they know how to use the appropriate resources to solve their problems.

Different categories of co-experts

You meet employees in a co-expert relationship in the following circumstances.

The first situation is when you successfully move together through the different phases of the flowchart by cooperation with your employee on a specific topic. As you know, the position of your working relationship on the flowchart is in constant flux. By your managerial interventions, you help your employee to move from the non-committal stance, to searching, to the consulting position. In the ideal situation, you move to the co-expert position where your employees are in complete control of their own solution-creating skills. The principle in these cases is that you encourage your staff to: "Do more of what works!"

The second situation is when your employee isn't aware of the fact that they already have what it takes to come to good and lasting solutions. They know they are working well, but they need someone with expertise and authority to confirm this, and give them a little push in the right direction. The principle for these employees is: "Just do it!"

Thirdly, we meet co-experts when we are lucky enough to work with employees from whom we can learn as much as we can teach them.

Metaphor for co-expert relationships

Imagine yourself to be a mountaineering trainer. Once you get your trainees going on the mountain, you tell them that you will now adopt a very special training method. While you sit yourself in a comfortable chair, warmly dressed and equipped with a megaphone and binoculars, you tell your trainees to start climbing the next steep slope. By now, you know and trust that your trainees have sufficient mountaineering skills, and that you do not have to climb along with them. All you have to do is sit back, relax, and watch them carefully. Once in a while, you use your megaphone to caution them against loose rocks and paths that lead nowhere. The rest of the time, you simply suggest that they take the path of least resistance or even the chairlift towards the simplest possible solutions. It's only a matter of cheering them on.

Interventions for co-experts

When working with co-experts, your main task is to step aside, "applaud," and support your employees in doing more of what works. You should act as a sounding board and supervisor. On top of that, you have the opportunity to offer and add additional expertise from your own experience in business.

Interventions with co-experts are fast and successful. After all, these employees have learned how to solve their problems or, even better, have learned how to learn. With this skill in place, staff members will always find their way through the constantly shifting sands of business life. Working with co-experts is a great pleasure because seeing how people grow (professionally) is one of the most satisfying rewards you as a manager can get.

The intervention strategies for co-experts share the following ingredients.

1. Support "more of the same"

Support and help develop what your employee is already doing right. The mantra for all other positions on the flowchart is: "Do more of something else." The mantra for the co-expert is: "Do more of the same."

2. Discover your employees' strengths

Discover your employees' strengths, and help them to use these to compensate for their weaknesses. If we do a strengths–weaknesses analysis from the solution-focused point of view, we focus more on the strong sides and our sole interest in the weaker sides is to find out how to gradually turn them into strong sides.

3. Encourage your employees to use everything available

Encourage your staff member to use every possible technique, tip, trick, and tool that you can think of together. Together you design and develop interventions where the co-experts can make use of every skill and practice from the great body of management literature and experience. The most effective solutions will come from the co-experts themselves. They know the content side of their job the best and you are the expert in change processes. Most of the time, you will only act as a sounding board, and once in a while you will add new information or new ways of doing things.

4. Compliment them on what works

Step aside and compliment them on what they are already doing that works. By complimenting them on what they are doing well, you will boost their self-confidence to keep going.

5. Help employees to help themselves

In a nutshell, as a solution-focused manager, you help your staff to help themselves.

A co-expert case: leadership coaching

Bill works as head of the project management team in a bank. He is highly regarded by his colleagues and directors for his excellent work. However, when it comes to coaching his team, he has the feeling that he functions below par. He asks the HR department to help him with this. Denise is assigned to work with him on this topic. She is an expert on coaching individuals with high potential.

Denise calls Bill to make the first appointment and asks what he wants to work on. As an experienced coach, she immediately starts with a goal-setting question (page 53) during the phone call.

Bill: "When coaching my project managers through projects, especially when the going gets tough, I tend to get too involved and lose myself in details. Under time pressure it's very hard for me to refrain from taking over. In high-pressure situations, I simply don't feel confident enough to let them do it themselves and I take over and do the job myself. I lose a lot of time and energy by doing this. Plus, I realize that I don't give my colleagues the opportunity to prove to me that they can do it themselves. I know that they are able to do it themselves. They have proved that many times when I am not around. I realize my behavior is counterproductive. I want to learn to control myself so that I no longer allow myself to fall into this trap."

Denise: "Very good, Bill. That is a clear goal you have there. Can I ask you to make a little preparation for our meeting? That way we will be able to proceed fast."

Bill: "Sure. I expected something like that."

Denise: "I would like you to prepare an exhaustive list of what you think you are already doing right. Just take a few minutes a day and jot down what comes to mind. We will meet soon."

Bill says he will be happy to do this. In their first session, they go over this list together. It is clear to Denise that Bill has a lot of resources and tools available.

She compliments him on this and asks: "What do you think that your colleagues would put on this list if we asked them?"

Bill answers that they would put pretty much the same things on the list as he has done.

Denise: "Great. Now, Bill, let's find out what you think are your weaker points as a manager. If I were to ask your colleagues this, what would they say?"

Bill: "They would say that I tend to panic when I think there is a risk of the timing of a project getting out of control. Some of them would say that I should refrain from taking over their work when this happens. I think they're right, I do get very nervous sometimes and then I start doing their work myself."

With this in mind, Denise decides to ask for exceptions: "Bill, do you remember moments or situations when you were able to control your tendency to interfere?"

Bill: "Yes and no. Last week I learned something. We were in the last phase of the implementation project for the new resource-planning software. It was a complicated project for the bank. It was a thrill because at two o'clock in the morning we had to go offline for thirty minutes. All data communication had to be stopped in order to load the new software and transfer the old data across. Then our servers needed re-booting. Wow, it felt like doing a heart transplant. Anyhow, around one-thirty, it hit me again. I started running around, making hectic phone calls and demanding an update every five seconds. Suddenly, Peter, who is normally the calmest person in the world, exploded: 'You %&$*!* controlling %&$!*, stop it. You are doing it again. Get out of here and let us do our job.' Well, I can assure you that came as a shock. It felt like a slap in the face. I could understand Peter's point so I withdrew and let them get on with the proceedings. All went smoothly."*

Denise: "Wow, what a story! Now that's interesting. So, Bill, with a little help from your friends (laughs), you can do it. What did you learn from this so that you can use it in the future?"

Bill: "I can hardly expect to have Peter around to yell at me all the time (laughs). You know what, it sounds like a crazy idea but I'm going to put a little elastic band around my wrist and every time I feel the urge to take over, I will let it snap into my arm. That sounds stupid, doesn't it?"

Denise: "Not at all, Bill. It sure is a lot better then slapping yourself in the face (both laugh). What would you answer if I asked the miracle question?"

Bill is familiar with the miracle question technique. He smiles and says: "If a miracle happened, I would be able to say to myself in the morning, without snap or slap (laughs), 'Bill, today you will take care not to step into your little pitfall.' In the coming project meeting, I would be able to refrain from asking questions all the time. Instead I would feel confident and I would sit back and just listen to my team. I would just ask them if I could do anything to help, that's it."

Denise: "Wonderful, Bill. Now that would be a real miracle. But miracles do happen once in a while. (Both laugh.) I would like to ask you to do a strange thing. For the coming weeks, I would like you to pretend in the first hour of your working day that the miracle really has happened. Then see what it is that you are doing differently. Observe how your colleagues react differently. I wonder what difference that will make for you. Are you prepared to give this a try? When do you think we should hold our next meeting?"

Bill: "Give me three weeks. I have lots of work to do plus I really want time to experiment with this assignment."

In the next meeting, Bill takes the lead: "You remember that you asked me to act as if that miracle really happened? Well, I didn't do that. And I didn't use that stupid elastic band either. I just kept telling myself that it was all too normal that someone in my position occasionally feels insecure, especially when the going gets tough. Nothing wrong with that, is it?"

GOAL
SETTING

Denise: "Nothing at all, Bill. On the contrary, it keeps you focused. Go on."

Bill: "What helped me most was the fact that during the last few weeks I seem to have succeeded in just listening to my team instead of constantly being afraid that things might go wrong."

Denise: "How did you do that?"

Bill: "I designed a little scale which I use a lot. It works perfectly."

Denise: "Now you've got me curious, Bill. Tell me about it. I think I'm going to learn something here."

Bill: "*In the beginning of every project meeting I ask the team to choose a number between zero and ten where zero stands for 'we have no hope whatsoever that this project can possibly be done on time' and ten stands for 'we have a firm belief that this project will be on time'. If, during the start-up phase of a new project, their answer is zero, that means that they are convinced that they are heading for a failure and that we'd better cancel or postpone such a project. Luckily, I haven't been given a zero so far. Whatever other number they choose, e.g. a four, I accept it and ask them to explain what it is that they're already doing to get to that four. By doing this I force myself to just listen to them and they are invited to give me all the information that they've got on the project. After that, I ask them what needs to be done differently to get to a five. This helps them to work in small steps while it gives them confidence that they are in charge. I learned that is important to talk about small steps and not about giant leaps. Giant leaps got humankind to the moon but small steps got the rocket going. (Laughs.) And so we go on. It's very strange, you know, but this little scaling technique helps me to keep an overview on things without urging me to ask for details. I think my team likes this method too because I noticed that they started using similar scaling techniques amongst themselves.*"

Denise: "*Congratulations, Bill. I am convinced that, if you keep this up, you will gradually grow more and more confident.*"

Denise is very happy to see that Bill evolved into the co-expert position, and on top of that the team took the same position by using the scaling technique themselves. That provided a good opportunity to stop supervising and limit his intervention to just encouraging the do-more-of-the-same approach.

Do it yourself checklist for co-experts:

1. Do more of what works.
2. Exploit your resources.
3. Use goal-oriented assignments.
4. Give compliments.
5. Keep learning how to help yourself.

Tips to enhance the efficacy of the flowchart: more is less

Goethe said: "*In der Beschränkung zeigt sich erst der Meister.*" Or to paraphrase this in solution language, "Achieve more with less effort." The flowchart is a compass that shows you the shortest way towards a solution. Depending on the answers you get when you ask this limited set of four questions, you know what category your working relationship belongs in. Each category points you towards specific interventions. Thus, the compass helps you to limit the number of interventions you need to do in order to be of maximum use to your employees and the company.

1. Rule of thumb

The *rule of thumb* is used to determine, with accuracy, which category your working relationship with your employees belongs in. Once that's defined, you limit yourself to the interventions designed specifically for that category. If you misidentify an employee as being further along the flowchart than he or she actually is, you will encounter "resistance" and your interventions won't work. For example, with passers-by, it is useless to try and force them to accept your well-meant offer for help. These employees won't cooperate for the simple reason that they haven't asked for help. In the classic problem-oriented models, their behavior is labeled "resistant." From a solution-focused standpoint this is wrong — by their so called "resistance" the employee is letting you know, in every way they can, that your current behavior is not very helpful. It is your task to read these signs and act accordingly.

2. Rule of caution

The compass is also a tool to find out where you went astray. If you get the impression that your intervention is not working, you can use the compass to find out where it went wrong. Very soon you will find out that you are using interventions that don't fit the person's position on the flowchart. For this we have designed a "*rule of caution*" to maximize the chance that you do the right interventions or at least that you do not make too many mistakes.

If you are unsure about which position your working relationship with your staff is on, use the interventions for the position just behind the one you think is correct.

For example, if you think your relationship with your employee is in a buyer position but aren't completely sure, start by doing the interventions for the searcher position. This way you invite your employees to show you where they stand. The way in which the employee reacts will help you to figure out what you should do next.

TIP

One little step backwards helps you make a big leap forward.

Different positions on the flowchart

When you come to think of it, managers always function in a kind of triangular network of relationships and related mandates. As a manager you work with your employees, and you are an employee yourself who reports to someone higher up the hierarchy. When you are the top dog, you report to your board of directors. When you are the chairman of the board, you report to your shareholders. When you are an internal or external coach or consultant, you usually get your mandate to intervene from someone other than the actual person you are coaching or consulting. In these triangles, it is highly likely, especially at the beginning of an intervention, that all parties are not at the same position on the flowchart.

How can you understand situations with multiple positions on the flowchart and — especially — how do you deal with them?

We make a distinction between the principal "client" and the direct "client." The principal client is the one who has the final authority and who gives you the assignment. Your direct client is the one you are working with in the intervention itself. When, for example, you are a middle manager your principal "client" is your boss or even his boss and your direct "clients" are the employees you are working with.

If your direct client occupies a different position on the flowchart from that of your principal client, this means that they give you different mandates to intervene. If the principal client does not give you mandate, you simply will not be asked for help: you don't have the job. If the principal client has a request for help, they give you the mandate to help them. If they expect you to help them change others than themselves, then you have to find out if these others, your direct clients, have a (similar) request for help. If not, your direct clients do not give you the mandate to help them. But as you have seen, solution-focused managers have plenty of alternative methods at their disposal.

In the case of different positions on the flowchart and therefore different mandates, the following method yields the best results:

1. Define the flowchart category your principal client is situated in.
2. Define the flowchart category your direct clients are situated in.
3. First deliver interventions that fit the party in the least advanced category. In other words, start with the interventions appropriate for the client that is least ready for change, and who gives you the lesser mandate. They need the most attention in the beginning of the intervention.
4. Act with patience, respect, and diplomacy, but be persistent.
5. Both parties will eventually reach the same position on the flowchart and this will allow for more effective interventions.

If you neglect this basic method, you will most probably encounter resistance to change. The principal client becomes impatient and/or the direct client becomes more and more unwilling to follow you.

Differences in team coaching

When you do one-on-one coaching, you deal with one single employee. Here the position on the flowchart is transparent. When you work with a team — obviously — more people are involved. When you are managing a whole corporation, many parties are involved, some of whom you may not even know. Complexity grows. One cannot expect that your working relationship with everybody involved will be on the same level on the flowchart. This means that you get a different mandate to intervene from every party involved. Since this happens frequently, special attention is required.

When you work with a team where the different members are on different positions on the flowchart, it is similar to when they all have different numbers on a scale. Here is a little protocol explaining how you can handle this in the simplest way (although this is never easy).

1. Ask yourself where every single team member is on the flowchart.
2. Accept the differences without striving to level everybody.
3. Start out with the appropriate interventions for those team members who are offering the least mandate (and are therefore in the beginning positions on the flowchart).
4. Then apply the appropriate interventions for those team members who are further down the flowchart.
5. Make sure both parties do not enter a discussion (amongst themselves or between the different parties).

6. See if you can find common ground between the different parties, albeit on another topic.
7. Ask everybody a scaling question (page 86) and proceed with the appropriate intervention for each party involved by asking: "What could be your smallest step forward?"
8. Collect all this information and proceed with: "What will each of you do in the coming period, between today and our next meeting, that will help you make a little progress towards our common goal?"

The most important intervention in this protocol is that you accept the differences in your team and work from there.

Example: corporate restructuring

For strategic reasons, the board of directors of a large bank decides to merge two important departments, corporate banking and private banking, the reason being that they both tap into the same clientele and they need to offer an integrated service to this important niche market. Synergy is the magic word. Greater efficiency is needed in this lucrative segment of the market, and the merger will allow cost reductions. The strategic business plan has been in the making for months. The plans for budgeting decisions and marketing, along with the reorganization of personnel, are ready.

In a meeting with the directors of both departments, the chairman of the board informs them of the upcoming changes. The directors know from experience that, once the board has made up its mind, there is not much room left for negotiation, so they just listen carefully. The merger plans, however, come as a shock to them and they tell the chairman that they will have to consult the top personnel in their respective departments.

Since change is always difficult, it's no surprise that the two departments are not very willing to implement the changes. After consulting their departments, the directors argue that they have plenty of reasons to think this merger is not such a good idea. "The clientele of both departments is more diverse then you think, the subcultures of the departments are too different, the expected synergy is highly overrated," etc. In short, the directors and their specialists are convinced that the departments will function far better separately.

John is appointed as facilitator to help the implementation of the merger project. John is aware that the board and the departments are opposed concerning this project. John accepts the assignment to facilitate the merger of both departments on the condition that he get enough time to prepare both departments for the changes. It is clear to him that the directors of both departments, along with every employee working for them, are in the position of passers-by. They have no request for help. The board clearly has a workable request for help but they are not in the position to implement the merger themselves. The board is on the buyer position.

To all parties concerned, it is clear that a firm decision has been taken by the board: the merger will take place. So that is no problem but a limitation. Since change is always difficult for people, John knows that some employees in the departments are just scared about the consequences of this limitation.

John decides to take his time to do all the interventions suited for passers-by. Working towards a positive relationship, John gives everybody ample opportunity to describe what they feel is the biggest mistake the bank could do, i.e. to merge both departments. He lets them vent their concerns while listening for resources and exceptions. Soon he is able to give them compliments on their excellent track record as departments. He asks how they dealt with comparable big changes in the past and compliments them on how they realized those organizational rearrangements.

After a while, the intense resistance diminishes a little. The employees start to accept that nothing of what they say or do will make the board change its decision.

Meanwhile, the board keeps pushing John to speed up this process because they are in a hurry to get the merger going. After explaining his first interventions with the respective departments, John helps the board to accept that their classical "I insist"' will only lead to the equally classical "I resist." He then informs the board of the additional steps he needs to take with both the directors and their teams. The board now understands the process. They agree to give him more time. In that respect, the board moves to the co-expert level.

Soon afterwards, both directors tell John that they are now willing to take steps towards the merger, together with their employees. "But we need some help here. We don't have a clue as to how to do this without drowning in arguments and internal political debates." Coached by the respectful behavior of John, they are now in the buyer position: they have a request for help but don't know how to use their resources. This is the sign for John to initiate a project team that will work out all the details of the merger. Both directors agree to co-chair this task force and to get the cooperation of their employees. They ask John to coach them in this process.

Slowly both groups merge and during that process practically all the employees move to the buyer position: they willingly accept all kind of tools to make the merger process go smoothly.

Of course this merger process is still not easy, and some people resign because they can't accept the change — others are fired because they were openly sabotaging the change process. Yet, it is clear that without the solution-focused diplomacy that John used, the polarization between board and departments could have led to counterproductive behavior that would have cost a lot more time and money.

These kinds of triangles constantly occur in business life. Often the situation is even more complex, because there are more stakeholders concerned with different and even contradictory interests. The basic advice, however, always remains the same: keep the flowchart of the solution-focused manager in mind and act accordingly.

Closing remarks

In chapter 4 we have discussed the flowchart that serves as a manual for the things you should and shouldn't do. A correct assessment of the position on the flowchart guides you towards the most useful interventions.

Because of the constantly changing context in which we live and work, the changes in life we continuously encounter, and the complexity of our dynamic relationships with others, the position of your working relationships on the flowchart is in constant flux. Even within a single conversation, the position on the flowchart may vary, depending on the topic being discussed at each moment. This is perfectly normal. Accepting this flux as a given keeps you alert and creative.

Passers-by, searchers, and buyers need our help to stop doing what doesn't work and start doing what does work. Co-experts need our encouragement to do more of the same.

Constantly being in a solution-focused state is as difficult as reaching Buddhist enlightenment. Once you achieve it, you will lose it again — but that is not a problem, on the contrary: the essence of solution-focused management is *not to have arrived at our destination, but to be underway.*

Chapter 5

The Man in the Middle: A True Story

This story comes straight from life and illustrates all the conversational techniques covered in the previous chapters. Most likely you will recognize situations that you have also experienced in your own company.

The story is about an average manager — not a famous individual or a famous company, not a superman educated in an exclusive business school. It is about somebody like you and me. As the story unravels you will most likely be surprised and amazed by the power of words.

While reading, you will have your own ideas on how you would have handled the problems that come up. As the events unfold, you will notice many points in the story where it could have gone wrong.

For fun combined with accelerated learning, we suggest that you first read this chapter, skipping the paragraphs in italics. This quick run through will give you a feel for how the conversation runs. Then read it again, but in this second reading, you read the conversation and the italic paragraphs. For in-depth learning, you might even take the time to check the paragraphs cross-referenced in the story.

There we go. Have fun!

Background

Peter is a fifty-one-year-old petrochemical engineer. Having had a successful career in various other companies, Peter was hired by Solutions Focus Inc. and has been working with them for fifteen years. He is now vice-president of operations and he has the final word on a large number of projects. Peter's team consists of about fifty employees. The projects he manages are highly technical and often require additional help from external subcontractors. As a results-driven manager, like most managers, two major concerns are always on his mind: being on time and within budget. Although he likes working with people, Peter has little interest in the organizational and relational side of working on a project.

As an engineer, he sees the dynamics of human relations as a necessary evil. In fact, he calls it "too much political rubbish and window dressing." He does, however, enjoy the general spirit of cooperation within his team and department.

Top management has expectations of Peter that are slightly higher than his own. Isn't it a manager's job to do just that little bit more than he or she can? Peter in turn demands the same effort and results from his employees and from the external contractors. Typically, his project budgets are very finely cut and the time limits are always a bit too tight. The external contractors, who naturally also work for other companies, always try to stretch the limits of the contracts. After all, that is how the game is played.

Peter's team is not immune to the internal power struggles that often develop in such high-pressure environments. Up until now Peter has always been able to control these power struggles. As a veteran, Peter knows the rules of the game within Solutions Focus Inc., he has used those rules himself to move up to his current position.

For Peter, his home is a place free of tension and that is just how he wants it to be. He is happily married with two adolescent sons and a beautiful house in a residential neighborhood not far from the factory. He lives a healthy life, jogging and playing bridge with his wife and friends on Thursday nights. Except for the normal stresses that everyone encounters in a top management position, Peter has been enjoying a relatively peaceful life, until ...

Prelude

Last year, Solutions Focus Inc. merged with another company. Many of Peter's direct employees left, some voluntarily and some not. Peter's team underwent a major change — a significant part of his team is new. The style of the old company had been one of constant consultation and teamwork, of loyalty among employees and a sense of being at the service of the company. But with the new merger things have changed, job certainty has gone and so has the sense of teamwork.

Peter is confident in himself and his expertise. He never loses sleep over the fact that he, too, might have to leave with a golden handshake. During the merger process, Peter did his best to serve the new company. He worked hard to facilitate the amalgamation of the different "styles" of both companies.

From the beginning of the merger, Peter had to accept that someone from the other company would run the department. John, a thirty-seven-year-old engineer, became vice-president of operations — a fact that did-n't bother Peter that much.

Initially Peter got along well with John, but that soon changed. John is a man of the new company style. He has a bossy attitude and he doesn't socialize. His contacts are strictly businesslike, and he demands written reports on all possible issues. What annoys Peter most was that John didn't mind bypassing colleagues if it was convenient for him. John's style is to voice his opinion without worrying about what others think.

Two cliques soon form within the department. One consists of the employees who follow John's methods. Using the same bossy attitude, they push very hard to get their own way: team spirit is not their highest priority. When they are successful, John praises them and their success reflects well on him. The other clique consists of the old company's remaining employees, who keep to the "old style" of consulting and cooperating with each other.

Peter finds it hard to cope with the fact that things aren't going as well as they did "in the good old days." He has tried talking to John about this several times, but in vain. John plainly said that the good old days might have been golden but they now belong to the past: "If you can't adapt, Peter, you might have to think about finding another job. We don't have room for dinosaurs."

Peter has experienced one frustration after another. His secretary of many years took an extended sick leave and was not replaced. Peter was told to supervise a tiny project for several weeks. Peter sent a memo to John stating: "In my humble opinion, I believe I'm overqualified and way too expensive for this small project." John didn't even respond.

Over the course of the last few years, Peter had organized monthly meetings for every member of his department. These meetings were commonly known as "milestone meetings." The goal of these meetings was to provide an opportunity to all of his project teams to report on their work. Successes and mess-ups were openly discussed. Peter and everybody working in his team with him were convinced that these meetings were very useful for keeping an overall view on what was happening. When John took on his function as VP operations, he immediately abolished these meetings. He told Peter: "Your milestone meetings are an instrument of the past. They take up too much time, are too expensive, and I know that we can do without them." He replaced them with what he called a "real project-oriented approach." Each project team just had to consult internally and report to their project manager with written reports. Peter was on the copy list but John claimed the final decision: "I prefer to tell you upfront that when I think it is necessary, I reserve the right to talk to the project managers directly, even if this means bypassing you." Peter was obviously not very happy with John's sudden decision to cancel these "milestone meetings." One can easily imagine the atmosphere in the department.

John worked very hard to keep an overview of all the projects. He liked to call himself "the spider in the web." Everyone, even Peter, had to admit that he succeeded in keeping everything under control. John therefore was held in high regard by the top management, a fact he flaunted to all his colleagues and especially to Peter.

About six months after the merger, top management announced a major change in strategy. A substantial part of Solutions Focus Inc.'s traditional products would be discontinued and replaced by new products. This required building a new factory. This strategy change caused much tumult within the company: the large investments needed for this new factory were a heavy burden on the short-term financial forecast, the unions were worried about employment, and many of the old employees were afraid that they would be "removed" along with the old plant. For the operations department, this strategic turn meant a great deal of extra work. After all, it wasn't just the building of the new plant that needed to be managed — the old factory had to be dismantled, too. From a safety and environmental perspective, the dismantling of the old factory was a substantial and risk-bearing project. Top management asked Peter to head this dismantling project. John would have the overall supervision.

The conflict

The first open conflict erupted when John summoned Peter to his office. John boldly announced that he wasn't confident that Peter could carry out the project that the management had just appointed him to. John explicitly expressed his belief that Peter was too easy on his employees and especially on the external contractors. Peter was shocked when John haughtily remarked: "You have to understand, Peter, that at this point in my career I can't afford to have you mess things up while you are under my supervision."

John had never before criticized Peter's way of working, or his results, this harshly. Peter reacted with anger. He said that it was John who had ruined the atmosphere, that it was John's fault that some projects were delayed, and that he was sick and tired of the way in which John played the different project groups off against each other. He angrily slammed the door and went directly to Jeff, the CEO of Solutions Focus Inc., to complain. Jeff soothed Peter by promising that he would talk to John, but he never did.

In the weeks following the incident Peter avoided John at all costs. He was so angry that he started to talk to his senior project managers about the conflict. Tension between John and Peter mounted steadily. During the kick-off meeting for the dismantling project the bomb really exploded: John repeated his doubts about Peter's capabilities for the project in front of the entire team. Peter started cursing him. After a few minutes they were yelling at each other and the meeting had to be disbanded.

This caused major problems. John and Peter had been slated to work together on the new project of dismantling the production line, but it looked like the project would run into serious problems if Peter and John couldn't reconcile. Employees began gossiping about the "bad chemistry" between their two managers.

The fight kept Peter awake at night. He came to work tired and quick-tempered. For the first time in many years he complained to his wife about work. Peter told her: "Now I understand what the saying 'lonely at the top' means. It's no longer safe to talk to anybody about anything. I wonder if I should look around for a job somewhere else."

When the budgets for the dismantling project had to be presented to the top management, Peter refused to support John's budget proposal. In the middle of John's presentation Peter remarked bluntly: "This proposal is rubbish. I will not work in such an unprofessional way, and I will not take any responsibility for the safety of my people who have to dismantle the production line." John couldn't control himself any longer. In the middle of the meeting he called Peter "an incompetent, sneaky old pig."

The CEO was not amused. He adjourned the meeting and summoned both men to his office. A massive brawl broke out there. Jeff had to refrain himself from firing both of them on the spot. He realized the enormous strains that both managers were under. Jeff wanted to fire neither John nor Peter — they were both highly esteemed managers with proven track records. After explaining that Solutions Focus Inc. wasn't a playground where little boys could fight over a ball, the CEO told them that he refused to stoop to such childish matters. They had to clear it up themselves.

The CEO had no choice but to inform his board of directors who immediately invited John for a meeting. They explained to him that they saw Peter as the only manager within Solutions Focus Inc. capable of heading up this project. Peter had built the factory that had to be dismantled: "He knows the ins and outs of the place. For safety reasons, we are convinced that Peter is the only one who should take care of the dismantling project." John grumbled a bit (he even considered giving the management the ultimatum "Fire Peter or I will leave"), but, wisely, he kept quiet and decided to leave Peter alone. He even mailed Peter to explain the management's point of view and wished Peter — not without double meaning — "Good luck."

In the course of the following weeks John and Peter kept avoiding each other. However, it was clear that Peter had lost his old zest. He repeatedly expressed his doubts to his closest employees, had regular outbursts, and was late delivering project proposals. At home he also became more and more grumpy, slept very poorly, and lost some weight. He skipped his bridge evenings to work late at the office.

One day Peter was standing next to the coffee machine when the CEO walked in. Always keen on personal contact with his personnel, Jeff asked Peter how things were going. Peter blushed, started to sweat and stutter, and went to his office without the coffee. The CEO followed him, and prompted him about what was going on. Peter poured his heart out: "I can't do it anymore. Everyone is working against me. I don't believe that the new project will succeed. I am working my butt off without any results. Maybe I should resign." The CEO was shocked. He wasn't used to hearing Peter talk like that. And it certainly wasn't the kind of language used in the macho world of Solutions Focus Inc.

Jeff went back to his office to think about the situation. He immediately ruled out drastic changes: no one would get fired, promoted, or demoted. He still believed John and Peter were the right people in the right places for the company. But what should he do?

How would you deal with this situation? Jot down a couple of suggestions, think of a strategy — imagine that you are the CEO of Solutions Focus Inc.

- *Who would you involve?*
- *What would be your first step?*
- *Which positions on the flowchart (page 115) are you dealing with?*

The intervention

The CEO decided to ask Ronald for help. Ronald is vice-president of the sales department. He is known for his tenacious diplomatic skills that provided him with the nickname "the gentle pitbull." Ronald goes back a long time with Peter — so it will be no problem to get his help accepted by Peter. Jeff asks Ronald to coach Peter and John in order to:

- Put Peter back on the right track.
- Get the dismantling project on track.
- Improve the cooperation between John and Peter.
- Make sure that their team keeps its sharp edge.

How would you deal with this situation? Jot down a couple of suggestions, think of a strategy — imagine that you are Ronald.

Ronald sends the following email:

Highest priority
Strictly confidential

From: Ronald@solutionsfocus.inc
To: Peter@solutionsfocus.inc; John@solutionsfocus.inc
cc: Jeff@solutionsfocus.inc
Re: dismantling project plant

Peter,
John,

Jeff told me about the high-pressure situation surrounding the dismantling project. Jeff expressed his conviction that the two of you are the experts to handle this difficult project IF you cooperate. He asked me to help you steer away from counterproductivity. Jeff gave me the mandate to try and help you out. If this will not work, he will take it to the board.

I hope you both agree with this offer.

I will talk to you individually first and then I offer to coach Peter on the dismantling project.

I expect your go or no-go within 48 hours.

Strict confidentiality and discretion is vital. We will solve this problem before Solutions Focus Inc. suffers from it.

Hope to hear from you soon.

All emails on this topic must be copied to all parties concerned (no bcc's please). I will do the same.

Best regards,
Ronald, VP Sales.

John was the first to react. He emailed Ronald that it was OK for him. John sees the fact that "Peter needs a coach" as proof of the fact that he himself is "right." He then sent Peter a short memo in which he again — but now with an undertone of sarcasm — wishes Peter "the best of luck."

Peter took the full 48 hours to react. Then he called Ronald's secretary to make an appointment.

Ronald emails everybody involved to confirm that they are in the game. He will first talk to Peter.

Meeting 1

Ronald contacts Peter to make an appointment. Their first meeting is held in Peter's office. Peter has, of course, prepared for this meeting very well. He is determined to explain the "truth" about how the company's way of working has changed and especially about John. Peter rattles on about this for ten minutes.

Ronald makes sure that Peter feels at ease by allowing him to let off steam. Ronald simply listens because he knows from experience that arguing is counterproductive at this stage: people tend to cling even more tightly to their beliefs when they feel challenged. While Peter vents, Ronald concentrates on little exceptions in Peter's story about the quarrel. When he feels that Peter's arguments are losing momentum, Ronald seizes the opportunity to ask the goal-setting question that will help to point Peter's nose in a more constructive direction.

Ronald: "OK, Peter, you've made your point. What do you think we should discuss during this meeting so that it will be useful?"

Peter: "I don't know. That is something the management has to decide. Or John, for all I care. I am doing my job and that should be enough. If they aren't satisfied with my work, they shouldn't pay me. I don't know what they think is wrong with me. Haven't I proved in the past that I can handle my job? I don't understand why they don't trust me with the new project. I want to complete it successfully but they are working against me. Anyway, I don't know what I should do differently. They should tell me if they know."

Peter isn't answering the question. Ronald accepts this, knowing that the question will steer Peter toward solutions. Ronald isn't interested in delving into the underlying causes of the problem nor will he allow himself to be seduced into the battle of who was right or wrong. He doesn't react to

Peter's strange deduction that top management is opposing him. Thinking of the flowchart, Ronald judges that Peter is currently in the position of passer-by (see page 121). This means that Ronald's only job for the moment is to establish a positive relationship with Peter that will allow him to work on eliciting an alternative goal.

Ronald: "OK, that's clear. I can understand. I know that you have been doing the most difficult jobs within the department for years now. In the past few months, you have worked very hard to introduce the new employees to their jobs as smoothly and quickly as possible. Everyone admits that the past few months haven't been easy, especially not for you. Now, you know as well as I do that there are things that you, and I, can't change. All those changes within Solutions Focus Inc. belong to the world of limitations. We can only accept them and learn to deal with them in the best possible way. I have noticed that you handled all the changes in as positive a way as possible. How did you manage to cope with that?"

After complimenting him, Ronald subtly teaches Peter about the difference between problems and limitations (see page 117). He then uses a kind of "coping" question (see page 30). By asking Peter how he handled his problems in the past, Ronald implies that Peter has been successful in handling them. In itself, this question hides a compliment. This solution-building question gives Peter the opportunity to think, despite all the difficulties, about his strengths and resources.

Peter: "What a strange question. I was just doing my job, what else? I have never been the type that gives up. I have always kept my promises towards my employers. When I take on a job, I go for it. Up until now, I have never met a challenge that I couldn't handle. Mind you, I am no superman. I've had my share of difficulties but somehow I always coped."

Ronald: "Excellent. That's the go-getter I know. So I'll repeat my question: What do we have to discuss today so that our meeting will be useful to you?"

Ronald is trying to "join" with Peter in order to establish a cooperative relationship with him (see page 126). Peter reacts favorably to Ronald's authentic and respectful approach.

Peter: "If we were able to work together constructively like it used to be, everybody would make efforts to contribute to the greater cause of the company instead of just minding their own career. I would like to get the mandate to manage the dismantling of the old production line in my own manner. I am not a child who needs supervision. I want management to let me do my job without having to inform them about every little turn I take. I never had to do that in the past and things went fine then. But, I don't think they'll go for that, John doesn't trust me and the management doesn't support me. Since the merger everything has changed because a lot of new employees came along. I do want to give them proper training but I'm afraid they're only interested in advancing their own careers. So I could use your advice about what I need to do to get my team cooperating again."

The relationship between Ronald and Peter now develops into a searching relationship: Peter asks for help. He is asking for a mandate to handle the project in his way and, at the same time, he wants to rebuild the cooperative mood in the team. Although these answers are perfectly legitimate, they do not express his goals in a workable format (see checklist for workable goals on page 62). As we will soon see, Ronald can help Peter transform his goals by asking the right questions. As their working relationship is just moving into the searching mode, Ronald decides to take a little step back.

Ronald: "Excellent, Peter. That's a good start. Here we are, at your office on a Friday morning, we have only been talking for about half an hour about how we can solve your case, and you have already come up with very valuable ideas."

Ronald now uses the technique of yes-setting (see page 50 and gives compliments (see page 77) to increase the likelihood that Peter will continue to approach the situation positively. Ronald chooses to follow the solution-focused adage: "If in a hurry, go slow!" He decides to use a scaling question (see page 86).

Ronald: "Peter, before we go deeper into this, can I ask you a question? If we take a scale from zero to ten, where zero stands for the moment last week when you felt that it would be better to resign and ten stands for your belief that things might not be perfect but they are good enough for you to continue working, where are you now?"

Peter: "At a two."

Ronald: "Good. What does the two mean? What has changed in the past week to get you from a zero to a two?"

Peter: "The fact that you are talking to me about how we can solve this. Even though I still don't see what good could come out of this mess."

Ronald: "Excellent. What else?"

Peter: "Well, maybe also the fact that John mailed me that the management wants me to do the dismantling. Oh, and the fact that John sent me a memo to wish me 'the best' of luck — and especially that I haven't heard from him or seen him since."

Remembering James William's famous quote: "The art of being wise is the art of knowing what to overlook," Ronald does not react to Peter's slightly cynical remark. He accepts all Peter's answers even though some weren't useful. He keeps the questioning going.

Ronald: "Perfect. What would be the next small step forward?"

Peter: "I don't know. But I do know that you ask me a lot of questions."

Ronald: "Yes, I do and do you know why? Because the right questions bring out the solutions!"

Peter: "That's funny. I never thought of it like that, but I must admit you have a point. There is one more thing needed, however."

Ronald: "And that is?"

Peter: "You need to be able to listen to the answers."

With a seemingly casual remark, Ronald teaches Peter the art of solution-building questions (see page 33). Peter reacts favorably by going along with it. This strengthens the working relationship and introduces the solution-focused approach without their even having to talk about it.

Ronald: "You are getting there, Peter, congratulations. So, you're saying that the fact that John has at least left you alone, that the management has entrusted the dismantling to you, and that the two of us are now working on a constructive solution is worth a two. Excellent! I know the past few months have been difficult for everyone — no one has yet processed the merger fully, and there are still problems with the personnel changes. This hasn't made work easier. Nevertheless, I have to congratulate you on the fact that you have continued to work in your trusted and persistent way."

Peter is a bit overwhelmed by Ronald's consistently positive attitude, but he cannot deny the truth of Ronald's statements. You may have noticed that Ronald put the problem in a broader context: the merger has still not been processed completely, there have been many personnel shifts, the atmosphere and corporate identity have changed, John's management style, the general uncertainty within the entire company, and the fact that there were no clear responsibilities or authorities defined for the enormous dismantling project. Ronald doesn't view these elements as explanations for the problem but rather as tools that he will use in a later stage of the intervention to steer things toward a solution. In Ronald's approach there is no room for analyzing the root causes of the problem. Furthermore, Peter admits that he has made twenty percent progress compared to last week!

Ronald: "OK. It might be too early to find out what could be the next small step forward. Therefore, if you agree, I would like to give you an assignment you can think about in the coming week. You know that even in the midst of a mess, there are always things that still function well. Think about which aspects of the company, yourself, and your colleagues are so important to you that you would definitely want to keep them. Whatever you feel is still working, big or small, interests me. I would like you to write down those things. We'll discuss them in our next meeting."

The continuation question (see page 136) focuses Peter's attention on what still works in spite of the problem. It will probably help Peter to step out of his problem-oriented fixation. By indicating that even little details can be important, it is made clear to Peter that no major changes are demanded from him.

The assignment is failsafe: even if he does not do it, it is highly likely that he will think about it for some time.

As you have noticed during this first session, no emphasis at all is put on analyzing the causes of the problem or on trying to explain the solution-focused model. On the contrary, it's "just a conversation".

Ronald does not tell Peter what to do. On the contrary, the use of questions invites the gradual development of a different way of thinking about the problem. The sequence of the solution-building questions is carefully designed by Ronald. Peter's answers lay the foundations for alternative possibilities to come from him. This elegant and unobtrusive method directs Peter step by step towards the solution-focused approach. Ronald is leading Peter from behind.

Meeting 2

The second meeting with Peter has a very different atmosphere to it. Peter is more cheerful, has loosened up a bit, and even before the meeting starts, he mentions that he has made some progress in his plan for the dismantling project. These positive changes are not uncommon when you use the solution-focused method. Once people have been able to avert their fixation on problems, positive signs turn up (seemingly) automatically.

Ronald: "OK, Peter, according to what you just told me in the hallway, it looks like you have made a lot of progress. That's good. For a start, let me ask you a question: 'What have you done well and what was difficult?'"

*It is very useful to start second meetings in solution-focused coaching with this question. It is designed in a special way. In the first part you ask your client what it was that he or she actively **did** well. This implies that everything that went OK is the result of activity from the side of the client.*

The second part of the question is phrased as if the client just undergoes the difficult things, without being responsible for them.

This double-sided question gives your client the possibility to choose which part he wants to answer first. It shows the client that we allow him to talk about both positive and negative matters. Working solution-focused does not mean that we are problem-phobic! Whatever the client chooses, we accept and build upon it. When the client chooses to answer the second part, you let him talk and, by asking solution-building questions, see if you can find exceptions or resources in his answers. Then you move on to the first part of the question, which of course is a lot more interesting.

If the client prefers to first talk about the good things, you encourage him and expand on the positive things he tells you. It's useful to dig into the details of all the useful answers that you get. Often the client wants to talk about the second part and then you proceed as mentioned above. Sometimes, this question just sets the client in the solution-focused direction and you can quickly take the next step, as in the case of Peter.

Peter: "What I've done well? I don't know but I do know that this thing with John is still happening. He avoids me but at the same time I have the impression that he takes every opportunity to talk to my employees when I am not around. As for the rest, I told you, I decided not to bother too much about him. I keep myself focused on the preparation of the dismantling project. I must say I feel a lot better since I am back into such a big project. I was tired of having to bother with small insignificant ones."

Ronald: "Very good. How did the assignment go?"

Peter: "Well, I certainly would like to keep my job in this company. The work in the project department used to go smoothly and in the past we proved that we can be successful. Solutions Focus Inc. might not be the company it used to be, but in life things change. So it goes in our business."

Ronald is pleased with these answers. They indicate that Peter sees exceptions to the problem and that he accepts that limitations exist for which no solution is feasible. Peter also expresses his commitment to the company. Ronald, of course, doesn't begin jumping up and down with joy — this answer isn't the ultimate solution. It is, however, the start of solution-orientation in Peter.

Ronald: "Perfect. Where are you now on the same scale from zero to ten where zero stands for 'this won't work' and ten stands for 'I am convinced that this will turn out well'?"

Notice that, despite the words "the same," this scale is actually different from the first one! The current scale has more to do with the belief that positive change is possible than with assessing how things are now.

Peter: "I think I am at a four. I have made a lot of progress with the preparation of the dismantling. John called me just yesterday to hear how things are going and, miracle of miracles, he just listened without criticizing! By the way, last Monday night our team went out for drinks because it was someone's birthday. We hadn't done that for a long time and it was very pleasant. Even the newcomers went along and it was just fun. We should do it more often."
    Ronald: "Very good. What else?"
    Peter: "Nothing. There are still a lot of times when I have doubts and think it will never work out. I am afraid that this improvement is just a temporary thing."

Ronald doesn't ask about the meaning of the four but simply allows Peter to explain about the change. Ronald goes on with the "what else" question that is useful for eliciting more details (see page 37). Nothing interesting follows and Ronald does not insist. He listens to Peter's doubt without being tempted to give him a pep talk. It's time for the next step. When you look at the flowchart, you will see that Peter is still in the searching position: his request for help is too vague to be workable. As we have seen on page 101, the miracle question is a great tool to help him rephrase his goals in more concrete terms. Using the protocol on page 106 helps to ask the miracle question in the most useful way.

Ronald: "Good. Can I ask you a strange question? We're sitting here talking in your office. Later we will both continue with our own work. Tonight you'll go home and spend a quiet evening doing whatever you do at home, and you'll go to bed. While you are sleeping, suppose a miracle happens. You don't know this miracle has happened because you are sleeping. In that miracle all your problems have been solved sufficiently that they don't bother you any longer. Tomorrow morning you wake up. How would you know that this miracle happened? What would you do differently?"

Peter: "Well, that *is* a strange question. I don't believe in miracles."

Ronald: "I don't either, but let's just pretend that miracles exist. What would be different?"

A little persistence comes in handy when asking the miracle question!

Peter: "Well, I would feel refreshed and hop out of bed. I wouldn't fuss over work while I shave. Instead I would think about how I will spend the coming weekend with my two sons. During breakfast I wouldn't listen to the news on the radio but put on some classical music. Instead of reading my newspaper, I would talk about bridge with my wife. Heck, talking about miracles, instead of taking the car I would cycle to work!"

Ronald: "Great, go on. What would you do differently at work?"

Peter: "Instead of immediately locking myself in my office I would first walk around and talk to my staff. I would find out the latest news and gossip. Gee, I just realized that if a miracle had occurred, I would ask my secretary to pre-sort my mail for me. Instead of diving into the first dossier that I find on my desk, I would prepare my schedule for the day. Give myself some time to get organized. Then I would start to work on my mail while drinking coffee."

Ronald: "That's excellent. What else?"

Peter: "Maybe I'd go to John's office to say good morning — but believe me, Ronald, that would be a real miracle."

Ronald: "Now that's an excellent idea. What else?"

With supportive words like "great" and "excellent," Ronald confirms Peter's useful ideas without trying to push him to actually do them. He allows Peter to continue speaking in the "as if a miracle happened" mode. This style of speaking helps to avoid resistance — it doesn't have to happen, it could happen. Of course, it is obvious that some of the answers to the miracle question can become real options. Ronald just has to endorse these possibilities. He particularly stresses that visiting John is a good idea.

Peter: "Furthermore, I would do the thing I do every day: work."

Ronald: "Wouldn't something also have changed in your work? Will you do it in a slightly different way now that this miracle has occurred?"

Note that Ronald now shifts from "would" to "will."

Peter: "I don't know. Maybe I would spend my day in a more relaxed manner, not as hurried and jumping from one matter to the next. I don't know. Or maybe I do. Instead of running back and forth all day, I would take time to listen and talk to my staff."

Peter has actually begun prescribing constructive behavior for himself! Without realizing it, he is gradually helping himself to move forward towards solutions.

Following the miracle question protocol from page 106, it's now time to involve others in the miracle.

Ronald: "How will your colleagues know that this miracle happened? What will they see you do differently?"

Peter: "I don't know for sure how they see me lately but it sure would be different. In the last months since the merger I have been grumbling more than in all the years before. They would probably see me more relaxed."

Ronald: "What else would they notice?"

Peter: "My secretary would be happy that I allow her to pre-sort my mail. She has suggested this over and over in the past. My employees will be content that I spend time with them again. Since our first meeting, I have been able to focus more on the planning of the dismantling project. Some of my people are real experts on this topic, and I started involving them in the planning. Let me think if there are other ways that they would notice the change. Yeah, of course, how could I forget? When they invited me for that drink last Monday evening, I immediately said yes. Actually, all these things are already happening for the better."

Ronald: "What would they be doing differently when the miracle has happened?"

Peter: "The most important change would be if the people from the old Solutions Focus Inc. started to be less reserved with the newcomers and talked more openly with them. At the same time, the newcomers would act less self-sufficient and make more use of the experience that is in house by asking for information when they need it. Or to use the words of our HR manager, communication would be facilitated. (Giggles.) My department would come on track again if that happened."

Ronald: "Excellent, Peter. Interesting miracle! Are there elements from that miracle that you could try out in the next twenty-four hours?"

Now Peter is really surprised. It has never occurred to him that you can act out miracles! Ronald just plants the idea in Peter's mind without pushing him to do anything. Experience has taught Ronald that pushing isn't as effective as letting the other take the initiative. By simply asking this question, Ronald suggests that Peter can try out some of the constructive things that he himself brought up. This has the power of a hypnotic suggestion. The beauty of it is that it is failsafe — if Peter gives it a try, it's OK. If he doesn't, it's equally OK. Nothing can go wrong since it is Peter's choice to do whatever he thinks is useful.

Ronald: "Shall we take this a little step forward, Peter?"
Peter: "Yes please."

"A little step forward" implies that some steps have already been taken (see page 35 on underlying implications in solution talk). Ronald guides the conversation in such a way that Peter has the impression that it is he who is setting the rhythm. This "leading from behind" is an elegant and powerful form of leadership that enhances cooperation.

Ronald: "In our first meeting you told me that you would like to see everybody work together again in the old style. You would like to see people less self-interested and focused on their own career. Instead, you would like to reinstall a team spirit so that work can become enjoyable again, like in your pioneering days. That certainly would make your team more effective. By the way, Peter, you know the acronym T.E.A.M?"
Peter: "I haven't got a clue."
Ronald: "T.E.A.M. stands for Together Everybody Achieves More."
Peter: "Wonderful! Can I quote you on that? It's a good slogan. I will use it."
Ronald: "Sure, Peter, feel free to use it whenever you think it's useful for Solutions Focus Inc."

Ronald doesn't lecture Peter on what he should or shouldn't do as a leader. Instead he uses this acronym, which then works as an eye-opener for Peter. This "economy of words" saves you lots of rational explaining and lots of effort in getting the message across. It simply works better. The right word in the right context can work miracles!

Ronald continues: "So when this miracle happens, your project teams will be more focused on the good of the company instead of being preoccupied with their own career. What do you as the leader of your team need to do differently to accomplish this refocusing? How could you achieve this? After all, someone has to set an example."

Peter: "Right. I do realize that I can't change the others but that I can only change myself."

Ronald: "Exactly."

Peter: "But how am I supposed to do that? John doesn't trust me with the new project. By the way, he abolished the 'milestone meetings' that were essential for having an overall view on all running projects. I really don't see how I can get all the new employees on the same wavelength without those meetings, let alone how I could re-install a minimal team spirit."

We can see Peter moving on the flowchart towards the buyer position. Now his request for help is workable but he doesn't know how to apply his resources. Peter did a good job at building effective teams in the past. That indicates that he has the resources to solve the problem, but for the moment he doesn't know how to access these resources. Peter doesn't have a clue what to do. So now, Ronald's job is to help Peter tap into his resources. More solution-focused questions will do the job.

Ronald: "Don't worry, Peter. You will find a way. Maybe there are some possibilities that you just don't see for the moment. Let's take a little step back. How did you manage to do this in past projects? What method did you use in the past when you had to start up similar projects?"

Ronald helps Peter to focus on what worked in the past. In other words, he helps Peter to discover solutions from the past that, if adjusted, are useful possible solutions for the future (see page 148).

Peter: "Like I said, we used to have these big meetings in which all project teams in the department were involved. These 'milestone meetings' allowed us to have an overview of what was going on. But John is against that. He thinks it is unnecessary and too expensive. He insists on one-on-one communication, which I don't think is the most effective thing to do."

Ronald: "What else, besides your 'milestone meetings', did you use in the past that was useful?"

Ronald doesn't go into Peter's problem-oriented approach. Convinced that Peter will eventually generate solutions, Ronald continues to ask him solution-building questions.

Peter: "We used to have a lot of informal contact. We talked about our projects in the corridors, at the coffee machine, wherever. We hung out together in the late afternoons. Plus, I often cut big projects into pieces."

Ronald: "I don't really understand that — what do you mean?"

Peter: "Well, I designed an overall project plan that overarched all projects that my department was doing simultaneously. Even though in reality this master plan was never executed the way it was designed, it was the general guideline for everyone. Then I used to cut every single large project into small, quasi-independent projects and got the different teams going at their piece. It looked pretty chaotic at times, but we learned to let go of the strict project planning. Allowing unpredictability was tough, and I am sure you can understand that, being an engineer yourself. As the projects moved slowly down the tracks, the pieces of the puzzle would eventually fall together. This sounds rather complicated, I know, but it worked in the past."

Ronald: "Wonderful. What stops you from doing that now?"

Peter: "I don't know, with all the new employees who don't really know Solutions Focus Inc. that well, it could be very difficult. And John would never go for it — he wants to survey everything and keep it under control himself."

Peter just described several resources and tools that he used successfully in the past. However, he doesn't know how to use them at the moment. He is now clearly in the buyer position (see page 148). Peter needs help to enable him to use his own resources again. He needs advice. Because advice and suggestions followed by a question mark work better then telling people what to do, Ronald will simply ask suggestive questions.

Ronald: "OK, but that doesn't have to be a problem. Couldn't you hold small, informal meetings again like when you celebrated your employee's birthday? Show up at the coffee machine more frequently, stuff like that? During those occasions you could talk about the dismantling project. I am sure that there are enough employees, including some of the new employees, who would very much like to participate in these chats. Furthermore, without telling anyone, you could design a master plan for the dismantling project and cut it down into small pieces. You have done it before so you know how to do it, and it sure was successful! You could do this in a few days, couldn't you? When you are ready with it, you casually mention your plan during a coffee break or lunch, and you just wait and see how your team mates react to it. What do you think, Peter, is this feasible?"

On the surface, it seems like Ronald is asking questions which Peter can answer freely. But in fact Ronald is suggesting to Peter how to behave. There is little chance that Peter will resist these prescriptions, for the simple reason that he himself proposed them. This is a fine example of co-creating solutions and building on them by asking solution-focused questions.

Peter: "I would really like that idea if it weren't for John, who, I'm pretty sure, will interfere and block me. Then I'm back to square one and I don't want that to happen."

    Ronald: "You are absolutely right. However, I don't think it has to be like that. You've told me that everyone, including you, is impressed by the way John is able to keep everything under control. So then it only seems logical to me that he will want to control this project as well, whether you like it or not. So you have to find a way to let John do his job without you being bothered by him."

When it comes to discussing working with his team on the project, Peter is on the buyer position. On the topic of his working relationship with John, Ronald acknowledges that Peter is still on the passer-by position: Peter believes that John is the one who has to change and he doesn't see what he can do to change that. Therefore, Ronald uses an intervention that is suitable for passers-by. He negotiates about an alternative goal (see page 125). What does Peter have to do differently to get John off his back?

    Furthermore (and this is an example of a "high-tech" solution-focused intervention), Ronald sees John as a passer-by: John will not change by himself and will keep his controlling method. Now Ronald begins teaching Peter how to deal with passers-by effectively: by giving Peter a seemingly logical explanation about why John couldn't do more than he is doing now (namely controlling and having too little confidence in others), he helps Peter to accept John's way of working. At the same time, he offers Peter an alternative idea that will help him get around John's resistance to let go of his controlling method. This is of course not easy, but let's see how it can be done!

Peter: "Well, I'm curious. How are you going to pull that off?"

    Ronald: "It isn't a matter of 'pulling something off', and by the way, I'm not going to do anything — you are. Imagine yourself in John's position. After all, he is the boss and so he has the final responsibility for the project department. It is his task to make sure that the entire project department runs perfectly, or, at least, as well as possible. John knows — as you would if you were in John's shoes — that he is good at this, but he is also very worried because he can't do everything himself. He simply has to let others do a big part of the work. Imagine yourself in John's position, Peter. What would you need to see happening so that you would be sure that everything goes OK?"

Peter: "I never looked at it that way. I always thought that he acted like a control freak to improve his own career. But I guess John is actually in a very tricky situation. After all, he is new to this company, and he is a lot younger than I am and his lack of experience maybe makes him a little insecure. Insecure people tend to overreact. I know that because I have been there." (Smiles.)

Ronald: "Correct. Wisdom comes with the years. How could you reassure him in such a way that he would no longer bother you?"

Peter: "I would probably have to give him more information so that he would know the project is going smoothly."

Ronald: "I don't think that that will be enough. Wouldn't you become suspicious if your employees only brought you good news? Wouldn't you start to think that they were hiding something from you?"

Peter: "Probably ... I recognize that. Maybe it will help if I also consult with him about some minor problems. It's maybe a little cynical but that will give him the opportunity to indulge his need for control. Since I know in advance what will happen, I won't be irritated. Yes, that's it. I will regularly walk into his office and update him on how things are going. On these occasions I will tell him some problems that he can tackle with his expertise. Now that I say it out loud, I realize that some of my employees use that trick on me too — and it does make me feel better. Maybe it will work on him too. It sure is worth trying. What do you think, Ronald?"

Ronald: "Excellent, Peter, just do it. You do realize that you will have to talk to John instead of avoiding him?"

Peter: "Yes. But if we want to keep working for Solutions Focus Inc. we have to work together. So we'd better cooperate. Hey, I am starting to talk like you. (Giggles.) Anyhow, if that burden lessens, I will find the energy to busy myself with my team."

Ronald: "Go for it, Peter. Good luck. When do you think it will be useful for us to meet again?"

With this intervention Peter reaches the position of co-expert (see page 152): he has a workable request for help and has access to his resources. The fact that he comes up with this last proposal by himself is an indication to Ronald that Peter is now able to help himself. From here on,

Peter only needs supervision in order to continue on the solution-focused path.

What about John?

Ronald had one meeting with John at the beginning of his intervention. John made it clear to Ronald that he wasn't interested in Peter's position: "Because of my job, I have to think about so many things and people that I really don't have time to worry about this man. After all, Peter is in a pretty high position — he should live up to that position. In order to do my job well, I need colleagues who know what they have to do and how to do it. I have no control over the fact that Solutions Focus Inc. is going through all these changes. As a company we need to prepare for the future. If Peter shows me that he is capable of carrying out his job properly, I won't bother him. But I'm afraid that he's a man who is gradually getting older and who doesn't have the flexibility one needs to keep up with the times. However, I can't deny that Peter seems to have done well in the past."

During this one conversation, Ronald didn't do much else than praise John for his dedication to the firm. In between his meetings with Peter, Ronald emailed John and informed him when the next meeting would be. He copied these emails to Peter and Jeff.

Meeting 3

Their third meeting is held at eight o'clock on a Friday morning in Peter's office.

Peter: "Come in, Ronald, how are you? Everything miraculously seems to be turning around. Would you believe that I had forgotten how useful it is to walk around in the morning and talk to my staff? I even believe the new people are finally starting to settle down. Do you have anything you want to discuss today? Because if you don't, I have some things I'd like to discuss."

Now Ronald is pleasantly surprised! Peter's tone has changed completely. He is cheerfully taking the initiative of the meeting. With his opening remarks, Peter confirms that he is still in the co-expert position. Now Ronald's task is simple: he has to encourage Peter to "do more of the same."

Ronald: "Good morning to you, too, Peter. You've taken me by surprise. What a difference! Everything seems to be going well. Congratulations. So, can I ask you that same scaling question again, where zero stood for 'the mess I was in' and ten stands for 'perfection doesn't exist but, for my part, the way we now work as a team comes close,' which number do you already stand on now?"

Notice that this again is a different scale. The way this scale is phrased indicates that the zero belongs to the past, while the ten is feasible in the near future. The word "already" implies (see page 35) that big progress has been made in a short time. This phrasing is supportive and is giving hope for even more progress. The zero is defined by Peter alone while the ten goes for the team. The power of words...

Peter: "Well, apart from some minor details that I would like to discuss with you later on, I'm at a seven."

Ronald: "Wonderful. What is in your seven?"

Peter: "I had some interesting chats with my employees. Two of the new guys really surprised me. I talked to them about my 'cutting down' method that I used in past projects. Guess what? Two days later the two of them asked to see me. They presented me a detailed schedule of how they think that the first phase of the dismantling could go. Everything was in there: timing, manpower, machines, and safety procedures. I had to compliment them on their excellent work. They liked that, and they asked for my permission to get the old architectural plans from the archives."

Ronald: "Wow, that's great. What else is in your seven?"

Peter: "Guess what. Just like you suggested, I did walk into John's office one day. I wasn't unhappy to see that he wasn't in."

This is not correct: Ronald never asked Peter to walk into John's office. It was Peter himself who came up with that idea (see page 185). Strange how people sometimes transform their own ideas into commands made by someone else. Equally strange how people sometimes take suggestions from someone else and make them into their own. It is all very human and recognizable.

Ronald: "More?"

Peter: "Well, my wife and I played bridge, for the first time in a long time. I had fun... and we won. I am sleeping better. God knows why. But mind you, Ronald, it's only a seven. I have a long way to go."

Ronald: "Sure, Peter. You have made the first steps. Now keep walking. So, what is it that you want to discuss with me?"

Peter stays in the co-expert position. He is using a lot of his resources and is making progress. Although he reports many useful and even surprising things, he stays on a seven. Ronald accepts that and does not push for a higher number. The language style Ronald is starting to use now becomes more businesslike. In the beginning of an intervention, when the working relationship is still low on the flowchart, it's often more suitable to use permissive language. As you move towards the co-expert position, you can use businesslike language: concise, witty, sharp, precise, and shorter.

Peter: "Well, two things actually. One has more to do with the business than the other. To start with, I would like to talk about the external contractors for the project. John thinks that I am too soft and informal with them. I don't agree with him. I am as courteous to them as is necessary. You can imagine that these projects are very complex. It is customary to set eighty percent of the price up front and the rest as the project moves on. Experience tells me that contractors play with the pricing of the last twenty percent according to the complexity of the project. But it also depends on the way they are treated by us. They are businessmen too, and they know how to count. If they get the impression that we are milking them dry from the beginning, they will recuperate their losses during the last part of the project. Then it turns into a legal war that costs a lot of time and money. I want to discuss how I can avoid this during the course of this project. Second, Ronald, I am tired of the argument I have with John. As colleagues we have to be able to deal with each other in a normal way instead of constantly avoiding each other. I am really fed up with that. If we don't change something here, it will get worse in the short term. I don't want to risk having my team members use our discord to hide their own responsibilities."

Ronald: "Perfect. What would you like to start with — the contractors or John?"

Peter: "It doesn't really matter."

Ronald: "OK, then we will start with the contractors because the matter with John is a lot simpler."

This is a tricky statement. Clearly Ronald tries to de-dramatize the situation between Peter and John but he can't possible know if it will be as simple as he suggests. Yet it is a fine example of Ronald's linguistic cleverness. He sets the art of implication (see page 35) to work. Ronald defines the cooperation with the contractors, with which Peter is familiar and has a lot of experience and expertise, as the most difficult. Peter's relationship with his colleagues — something that is vague and unfamiliar to him — is defined as simpler. With this linguistic maneuver Ronald suggests that Peter has the capacity to find a solution for both matters. After all, if Peter can find a solution for the "difficult" matters (that actually are the simplest for him) he will definitely be able to find solutions for the "simpler" matters.

Peter: "Ronald, you are a born optimist, aren't you, to call the matter with John simple."

Ronald: "Yes, I am, but I didn't say 'simple' — I said 'simpler'. I didn't say that it will be easy. Sometimes simple things are very complicated, until you find the solution, and then you could kick yourself — why haven't I thought about that before? That is something that you as an engineer know much better than I do, Peter."

Ronald teaches Peter about the concept of simplicity. He also uses the opportunity to define Peter as an expert in simplicity. The average competent engineer will mostly interpret this as a compliment.

Ronald: "OK, about those contractors. Describe firstly how you assess the possible problems with them."

Peter makes a list of the things that could go wrong, including, among other things, loopholes in the contract, bad weather conditions, unreliable subcontractors, unforeseen environmental issues and accidents.

Ronald: "Well, it's clear that you know what you are talking about. What was most effective with the external contractors in the past?"

Peter: "For the least expected calamities, you can only prepare in general. That is covered by our crisis management team. It is their responsibility to deal with this kind of stuff. Our job in operations is to make sure that the projects proceed on time and on budget. Nowadays the cooperation with the contractors has become much stricter. In the past, I could make direct deals with the contractors' bosses when they showed up in the yard. I remember, some years ago, during a crisis in the construction business, that I bargained unbelievable prices on the last twenty percent of the project. No written contracts there. We just needed a firm discussion and then a handshake. I don't think that is possible any longer. At least I don't see how I could do the same now. That brings me to my issue about the relationship with the contractors. How can I avoid trouble?"

Peter's unclear answer shows that he falls back on the buyer position: he has a workable goal (optimal cooperation with the contractors) but no access to his resources (how to handle the negotiations during this project). This moving up and down on the flowchart during a conversation is very common (see page 163). It's just an indication that Peter needs some additional help on this issue.

Ronald: "OK, Peter, times have changed. It hasn't become easier. So tell me again what worked best in the past. How did you avoid trouble in those days?"

Again, a little persistence comes in handy. Ronald decides to test Peter's position on the flowchart by asking the same question again. If Peter gives a more useful answer, that will move him down on the flowchart again. If no useful answer comes, Ronald will have to adapt his intervention. Let's see how it goes.

Peter: "Sometimes it helped to, in a manner of speaking, bribe the employees of the contractors by taking good care of them. Give them coffee in the morning, soup at noon, and a beer after the working day. Actually, I sort of cajoled them towards better performance by giving them compliments on their good work. Sometimes it just worked better to yell and threaten. Usually a cocktail of these methods was the most effective. And of course stringent contracts are also a good thing, preferably with big fines."

Peter's answer now shows that he has access to his resources again. He is back on the buyer position. Although phrased in a slightly cynical way (bribing, cajoling) he also shows that he understands the power of a good working relationship when he talks about giving compliments (see page 79). No need for Ronald to adapt his intervention. He can go on with doing what works: asking solution-building questions.

Ronald: "Good, what else would help in the upcoming project?"

This little question both implies that the things Peter just mentioned are useful tools for the coming project and invites Peter to do more of what works. This economical use of words again shows that less can be more.

Peter: "More of the same, I guess. But now things are more complex, especially for the dismantling. The contractor and my people will be working together closely. I have confidence in my own people, but given the degree of complexity, I really have to find the best contractors for this project. However, I'm afraid that if I put too much emphasis on the degree of complexity, the contractors will think twice. They might charge so much that we'll definitely run over budget."

Ronald: "This seems like a good start. How could you turn the contractor that gets the deal into a strategic partner? I mean, should we design the agreement in such a way that the contractor will face disadvantages if Solutions Focus Inc. is faced with disadvantages but will reap benefits if Solutions Focus is in a good position?"

Peter is on the verge of a new idea without realizing it himself. Being an expert in the solution-focused model, in which cooperation between all parties concerned is crucial, Ronald suggests the idea of "strategic partnership." He demonstrates again that suggestions in the form of questions work the best.

Peter: "Yes, we'd better team up with the contractors. Or even better, 'T. E. A. M.' up with them. (Giggles.) This reminds me of an idea I've played with in the past but which I have never used. I'll tell you about it, but you have to tell me immediately if you think it's stupid. Anyhow, a lot of internal lobbying would be needed to carry out this idea because Solutions Focus Inc. has never done anything like this."

Stepping out of the problem fixation helps you to think out of the box. The insights and techniques of the solution-focused model provide mental space where creativity can bloom. The constructive working relationship allows for ideas that you did not dare to think, let alone talk about, before. Using solution-focused questions will lift the self-censorship barrier. Managers often have "wild" ideas that they never bring up for fear of making a fool of themselves. Yet these ideas are often quite valuable!

Ronald: "Wonderful, Peter. Now you are really making me curious. Tell me."

Peter: "Of course, I still have to work out the details, but roughly it comes down to this. Before the negotiation of the contract starts, we stipulate that bonuses and fines can be given to the contractors, just like with car insurance. Fines are easy — if they go over budget, miss the deadline, or fail to meet quality standards, we can fine them. This is a classic, nothing new here — except for the quality part, those initiatives have already been adopted at Solutions Focus Inc. But the bonus side is new for us. Paying extra is not something that is a custom in this company. It will be very difficult to convince Solutions Focus to accept paying these bonuses, even if we as a company benefit from them. Basically, the contractor could earn a substantial bonus if he meets the defined goals regarding time, budget, and quality. The only thing we have to do in advance is work out how we can calculate our profit if we find ourselves in the fortunate position of having to pay the bonus. How much do we gain when the project is on time and on budget? The faster the dismantling is done, the faster the new product line can be set up and become operational. That's when the money starts pouring into Solutions Focus's pockets."

Ronald: "That's great, Peter, I'm impressed. How did you come up with this idea? It's excellent."

Peter: "Thanks! Well, it isn't that new. I read an article about it in a business magazine some time ago and I started thinking about a way to implement this idea in Solutions Focus. I think I even have some drafts on it somewhere. I hope I can still find them."

Ronald: "I have to congratulate you. Find those drafts and work out all the details. The idea of recovering the costs of the bonuses is especially wonderful. That way you create a win-win situation between Solutions Focus Inc. and the contractors. T.E.A.M is the correct word to use here! If you need any help selling this idea to the management, I'll be the first to lend you a hand."

Now Peter is firmly in the co-expert position: he is using his own resources to solve his problem all by himself. But there is more! Peter also comes up with a way to put the future contractor in the co-expert position as well. This shows that he has internalized the solution-focused approach without either of them saying one word about the model. The solution-focused model is about solutions, not about theory! Let's see if Peter finds a similarly useful way to tackle the "simpler" problem with John.

Ronald: "Now Peter, let's talk about how you will handle the problem with John."

You probably notice the implication in this sentence that Ronald trusts Peter's ability to solve this issue. By the way, it's not because Peter is in the co-expert position regarding the contractors' issue that this means he is in the same position when it comes to the problem in his relationship with John. Ronald assumes that it is safe to go one step back and do a little preparation.

Peter: "I'll do my best."

Ronald: "From what you tell me, it seems that the rough edges have softened somewhat over the past few weeks. Maybe the fact that you haven't been seeing each other much lately accounts for this. But still, you have already popped into his office once. OK, he wasn't there, but nothing stops you from trying again."

Peter: "Yeah. Avoiding each other doesn't help us much."

Ronald: "True. In our previous meeting you told me that you understand his position a lot better than before. You realized that John has a lot on his mind. After all, he is fairly new to this company and he has to prove himself."

Ronald carefully chooses his words. He quotes Peter from the previous meeting (see page 185). It was Peter who suggested the hypothesis that insecurity and lack of experience may account for John's overly controlling behavior. Therefore, John's behavior is not so much a direct personal attack on Peter but more a personal issue for himself. If Peter can feel that John's behavior is no attack, he will no longer be tempted to defend himself. Instead of resisting John, he can start cooperating with him.

Peter: "That's true but it doesn't allow him to treat me the way he has been treating me up to now."

Ronald: "I understand. Wisdom comes with age."

Peter said that he himself had been insecure in the beginning of his career and that he behaved like John in those days (page 185 "I have been there..."). The expression that "wisdom comes with age" contains a subliminal compliment to Peter. It implies that Ronald sees Peter as a person with experience and self-confidence. This simple sentence invites Peter to use his wisdom to solve the problem at hand.

By the way, you probably noticed that Ronald said "I understand" and not "I agree." Do you see the difference? Ronald wants to make sure that he never gives Peter the impression that he favors him over John. Yet Ronald acknowledges what Peter says. This again shows Ronald's linguistic art in using solution talk. We don't need many words to say a lot!

Peter: "Thanks. What's your suggestion?"

Ronald: "None. I prefer your own suggestion from our last meeting. Last time you explained to me that you had found an elegant way of killing two birds with one stone."

Peter: "What do you mean?"

Peter is not using his own resources and therefore is on the buyer position. Ronald gives advice by using information that comes from Peter himself.

Ronald: "You told me that you could do two things at a time. While at the same time keeping him informed about the positive progress you and your team make, you can slip in minor problems for which you ask for his advice. That way John will have a finger in the pie without interfering too much."

Peter: "Isn't that unethical?"

Ronald: "Not necessarily. It's not like you are cheating John or the company. On the contrary, this requires you to make the first step. You have to take the initiative to go and talk with him."

Peter: "I see. So maybe I have to find a neutral topic to talk about."

Ronald: "Maybe. But why beat around the bush? Both of you have more than enough topics to talk about. Maybe your excellent bonus idea is a good starter. You could work out this idea together with someone from your team. In order not to confront John with a *fait accompli*, you might present him this plan with some gaps in it and ask him for supervision. That way, he gets a chance to add some of his own ideas and the plan becomes a joint plan."

Peter: "I think John will be more likely to accept the plan if I work it out in concrete numbers. I'll calculate the estimated costs and profits of the proposal. I'll also calculate the cost of carrying out the project the traditional way. Then John can compare both results. If I can get him interested enough, I'm pretty sure that he can and will add interesting points of view."

Peter picks up on the suggestion and is now using his own resources: he is in the co-expert position. Ronald only needs to encourage him to do more of the same that works.

Ronald: "Correct. If you can show him hard data that supports the new method, chances are high that he will buy into it. You know that John is always interested in something new, and you know his remarks about 'dinosaurs'."

Peter: "OK, I will give it a try. I believe he might buy into my new method but only if he sees the hard data. However, cooperating with me, now that's an entirely different matter. Certainly after the mess we made of our 'cooperation' during the last few weeks. How on earth will I get cooperation from John?"

Ronald: "That might be pretty simple, although it won't be easy. Again, you will need to take the first step. You could start off the meeting by telling him that you are convinced that his contribution and improvements will be essential for the success of the plan. That would be a nice compliment, don't you think?"

Peter: "Yes. Plus it shows John that I am willing to bury the hatchet. Actually, it will not be that difficult because I really think that his contribution is valuable."

Ronald: "When you do this, you are already cooperating."

Peter: "Good idea, I can use your T.E.A.M. concept. Solutions Focus will gain from this, as we all will. This is an elegant solution that won't oblige me to go down on my knees before John."

Ronald: "Sure Peter, no use for that. This is not about going down on your knees for each other but about cooperating for results. You can be sure that the board will appreciate and endorse your joint project plan. Good work and good luck."

The outcome

The weeks go by in a mad rush. Peter makes a habit of saying "Hi" to John every morning. Initially John was surprised by Peter's friendly behavior, but he really appreciated it and told Peter so.

Over the course of three Saturday morning meetings, Peter finalizes his plan with the help of some of the new employees. Then he invites John to have a breakfast meeting, saying that he needs John's supervision with some matters. This meeting goes smoothly and is very successful. Both are pleased and surprised to find that they are able to talk to each other in an entirely different style than before. Ronald is updated over the telephone. He receives the project plan by mail and is pleased to note that both men signed the document.

The evening of their last scheduled meeting, Peter calls Ronald at home to cancel and apologizes for canceling so late. He tells Ronald that John has invited him to come along on a working visit to a sister company. Ronald congratulates Peter on the project plan and on the cooperative style that he and John have developed. When Ronald asks if Peter thinks it necessary that they meet again, Peter says, "I don't think so. We are all set now and I can manage on my own. But thanks for the help."

In the following months John and Peter slowly but gradually replace their battle with a growing mutual respect. They never became best friends, but that isn't really necessary anyway. As long as they respect each other as colleagues they can work together successfully.

Chapter 6

Frequently Asked Questions

Finally, in chapter 6 we talk about special issues you might run into when you are a manager in a non-perfect company and work with non-perfect people.

For your convenience, we have gathered our most frequently asked questions and provide you with possible answers in which you will recognize all the insights and techniques explained in this book.

For those readers who choose to start out with this chapter: welcome. We hope that it will motivate you to spend some time on the other chapters as well.

For the readers for whom this is the final chapter: congratulations, you are almost there now. Especially for you, we have chosen to use a light style in this final chapter and hope it will offer you a few smiles!

What is the solution focus all about?

Three-minute explanation

Imagine you are in the elevator with your CEO and he gives you three minutes to explain what this solution-focused mumbo-jumbo is all about. This is what you might say.

To set the right tone and get him in the mood for what's coming, you could start by saying:

"Good morning, Mr. CEO. Thanks for asking me about our solution-focused project. I'm glad to get a chance to talk to you about it."

And of course, business comes first, that's what the CEO is interested in:

"This project is on time and within budget, and this is mainly due to the efficiency of the solution-focused management approach."

While you look him in the eyes to get his attention, you use a little yes-set:

"It also fits very well with our culture. Here at XYZ company, we have always been pragmatic, haven't we? At XYZ, we aim to get results as fast as possible."

Now prepare the CEO for the more difficult part while at the same time you reassure him that you are really talking business:

"Well, being pragmatic and achieving the company goals fast and efficiently, that's what solution-focused working is all about. The extra edge that the solution focus gives us lies in cooperation, the concentration on our strengths, and working on goals rather than spending too much time analyzing problems.

We don't go searching for the causes behind problems because if you do that, more often than not, you end up with a situation in which you are looking for the person to blame rather than getting the problem solved. Just like when you have a flat tire — you don't spend too much time trying to find out why it is flat. You get a new tire and try to make sure that it stays inflated.

Concentrating on our strengths enables us to utilize the company's resources, both the personal resources of our staff and the resources of the company, optimally. To access the personal resources of our staff, we as managers ask them solution-building questions rather than providing them with all the answers. This way, we develop their competency and get customized results.

When a new solution is developed by our staff, we make sure it gets passed around so that everybody in our team and the company as a whole can benefit from the learning. You know the old saying: T.E.A.M. — together everybody achieves more."

So far this all sounds well and good to the CEO — however, is it credible? It's time for an example:

"Last week, two of my sales managers were arguing with my project engineer about our new product. They told him that one of the clients complained, not about the quality of the product, but about the difficult technical manual that goes with it. The engineer started defending himself and the sales people kept going at him. Soon they were accusing each other of all kinds of mistakes. In the heat of the argument one of their colleagues came in and got involved in the discussion. He complimented both parties on their commitment to the company and on their efforts to do the best possible for the client. This took away some of the heat of the discussion. He then asked them if they had had similar problems in the

past and how they had solved them then. It soon came out that in the past they had solved similar problems by writing an additional "getting started" manual and by putting the engineers in contact with the client to explain all the technical features. The project engineer said that his people would love to do that again, and the sales managers immediately saw a commercial opening towards the client. They agreed to propose this as a new procedure at the coming meeting for the complete team."

Add a little clarification:

"Our people all encounter problems of some sort. This is perfectly normal, and it comes with business life. Working in a solution-focused way does not mean that we are problem-phobic nor that we are naive optimists. On the contrary, problems are there to be solved. The major difference is that we deal with problems from an entirely different viewpoint. We solution-focused managers see problems as golden signposts to possible solutions. This model offers lots of insights and simple, ready-to-use tools to enhance the productivity of our human resources."

Time to go in for the kill:

"You see, working in a solution-focused way is hugely practical and hands-on, no mumbo-jumbo involved. It's about enhancing the ability to create sustainable solutions quickly, and this is essential for economic success. In the end, everybody benefits: our employees, we as managers, and the company as a whole. To put it in one sentence: "Simple works best."

PING: The sound of the elevator at the top floor.

Work smart, not hard!

How can you manage to work less hard as a manager, and still get your employees to work smarter?

Dear reader, this is your captain speaking. Please look at the instructions in the seat pocket in front of you. What follows is crucial information, so please sit tight and listen carefully. Because of your lack of time, I will say this only once.

For those readers that, instead of reading the whole book, were lured to this paragraph because of its enticing title, congratulations: you are the truly lazy ones! Why read a book when you can learn from reading one paragraph? Now, if you want to learn how to use the simple solution-focused tools in the easiest way possible, read the rest of this paragraph and then jump to chapter 5, *The Man in the Middle* (page 165). There you will find a real-life case study in the form of a story. However, beware: after reading chapter 5, you might — and this is our sincere hope as authors — be lured into reading even more of the book.

For those readers who took the effort of working themselves through all of the preceding pages: congratulations and thank you for your time and effort. If the title of this paragraph makes you think that what you are reading now contains the ultimate secret of the solution-focused model: again congratulations. This means that you truly understand what the solution-focused model is all about, and you already know the secret by now! This secret is: More is less, and less is more.

But hey, I thought that managers are supposed to work hard, or at least harder than their employees. Are we not paid for putting in the extra hours, the extra stress, the extra mile? Sure, but sweating when you work does not necessarily mean that you work efficiently, especially not when you are a manager. Managerial sweat ought to be reserved for the gym! Remember, management is the art of getting things done through other people. Doesn't this imply that you are not supposed to do everything yourself? Instead, your job is to create an environment in which your employees perform optimally. Your job is to help them work smart, more than just hard. Now, what is working smart?

You all know the famous acronym for the description of goals, of course. Classically, "S.M.A.R.T." stands for: Specific, Measurable, Ambitious, Realistic and Time-bound. And as you know, a lot of smart management involves goal-setting and making sure that goals are attained whilst keeping a resource focus. With our adage "simple works best" in mind, working smart is defined by a precise balance between input and output: maximum results with minimal effort.

Tips from the hitchhiker's guide for the lazy but efficient manager:

- Set clear, concise, and obtainable goals for the short, mid, and long term and make sure these are in line with the overall goals of the company.
- Make sure to involve your employees when setting goals: the more involvement, the more ownership, the more motivation and the better the results.
- Make sure to demonstrate the four tenets (page 22) of the solution-focused model in everything you do as manager.
- Be a hunter for exceptions to the problem, for these open doors towards solutions.

- Prefer resource-drive over goal-drive.
- Encourage your employees to be as open as possible with themselves and each other about their own resources.
- Indulge in what goes well in the team, and make plenty of compliments about everybody's contribution.
- Don't be shy when it comes to giving compliments.
- Don't be shy when it comes to criticizing.
- Don't be shy when you take decisions. Just keep everybody involved in the consequences of your decisions.

How do I manage myself?

It's lonely at the top

The way to the top — every top — is long and often crowded. Yet only few really make it there, and the way up is never ever easy. You have been working hard and intelligently to get into the position you are in today. But that doesn't finish the job! Getting to the top is one thing, staying there and achieving great things for your company is another. You are shrewd, hard working, persistent, self-confident, wise at some moments and a risk taker at others, well educated, emotionally and intellectually intelligent, and maybe you have been lucky at times. Yet, as the saying goes: luck favors the well prepared.

Being a manager, you have surely used all your resources and self-confidence while avoiding the trap of over-confidence. In reflective moments, you probably once in a while say to yourself: "I got the top job because I was able to play the corporate game to this level. Of course I am competent, of course I am intelligent, of course I am an expert in handling business as a top professional. I earned it to have been selected for this top job, and the people who supported me on my way up are no fools. They are in for shareholder value, and I am good at providing just that. Sure, the pay and everything that comes with my top position is good. Of course, it is a stressful job, but hey, pressure comes with the territory."

Once in a while some managers feel loneliness at the top. If you don't recognize this feeling: congratulations, how did you do that?

However, occasionally feeling lonely at the top is all too common. Some even say that this is the toughest feeling that comes along with the top job — the cliché is correct: it *is* lonely at the top. "I don't belong to another group anymore. I am the top manager, and there is just one spot at the top. Being a CEO is no T.E.A.M. sport: there simply is no team that provides me with shelter from the storm. If we hit success, success shines on me, and I have learned that distributing success among my employees makes me a better leader. If we hit trouble, trouble lands on me personally. Being the acting CEO feels like a one-man show with an audience of hungry wolves staring at me and waiting for my first wrong move. As a CEO, I sit high in the corporate tree, but the storm wind is howling. I'm visible, and I do feel vulnerable. On top of that, I'm afraid and convinced that if I show my vulnerability, the wolves are out there to get me. I sometimes feel scared, but am afraid of that feeling, even a little ashamed. That is not something a top manager ought to feel. If only the others knew how much I sometimes feel like an impostor..."

What can you do?

You may feel lonely but the fact is that you are not alone! Rest assured that you are not the only person in a high position with these thoughts and feelings. No matter how difficult it may be at moments, having self-doubts, feeling scared and overwhelmed by certain difficult decisions that you have to make alone is normal. Virtually no one will ever admit it in public, yet practically everybody recognizes these negative moments. Furthermore, a person who never doubts him- or herself is so self-centered that he or she has no openness to what happens around them. That is not the stuff successful managers, let alone CEOs, are made of.

Now it's one thing to have these doubts, it's entirely another to nurture them. Here are a few insights that you might want to try:

- Think of moments in the past when you were doubting yourself: what did you do to stop doubting and start acting? What worked best then?
- Remind yourself of your resources and the way you have used them on your way to the top.
- Remember the people who helped you on your way up: how did they do this? What was most helpful then? Can you find a similar person now?
- Write these thoughts down in as much detail as possible and keep this document in a safe place. The next time you find yourself in doubt, reading this personal document, written when your emotions were not clouded, will help you to recover faster.
- Talk to someone you trust and respect who is not involved in your organization and has no stake in your professional life. Being able to vent your loneliness and doubts, and just being listened to without getting advice, is often the shortest way out.
- Beware of the inevitable corporate yes-men and flunkeys, hear what they say but don't listen. Instead, keep searching for authentic opponents and counterparts, who have no stake in opposing you but sharpen your ideas by their opposition.

To summarize:

- Guard your self-confidence as your most valuable weapon.

The perfect manager — superfluous?

What is left for you as a manager when your employees can help themselves?

In your career as a manager you may well have dealt with a boss that suffered from the *horror vacui*: the feeling of anxiety that befalls someone when he or she thinks that they do not have much to contribute, or when they are not in control. People suffering from *horror vacui* have a counterproductive tendency to make themselves feel important by keeping themselves busy with all kinds of stuff that isn't that important. To fill the vacuum, they invent new things that they think will make them indispensable. To cut this illusion short: throughout the world, the cemeteries are full of indispensable persons…

It's normal practice to see yourself as indispensable and fully in charge, working long hours and interfering with almost everything your staff is working on. Isn't that the self-image of the modern manager? Isn't that what we all craved for when we first wanted to become a manager? Isn't that the big illusion the corporate world wants us to believe and adhere to? It often sounds that way. However, reality teaches us a different, although less traditional, lesson: being on top of everybody and everything at all times is not only impossible, it's counterproductive. In addition, our staff are intelligent people who come up with interesting ideas themselves without always needing their managers. Our staff — like you — like to do things independently and crave acknowledgment for their efforts. So, if we make the mistake of thinking that as managers we are the center of the universe, while we are confronted with an entirely different reality, then it's pretty normal that we have to fight feelings of being superfluous once in a while.

Now relax, actually, there is nothing wrong with feeling a little superfluous! If nothing else, it keeps your feet on the ground.

Let's look at this topic from a more constructive and solution-focused point of view. If management is the art of getting things done through people and you notice that your employees take care of themselves, then the simple conclusion is that you are a very effective manager. Instead of feeling superfluous, you should give both yourself and your employees a big compliment.

However, there is still a lot left for you to do and maybe the following tasks are the core of your job as manager.

One, if what they do is working, your job is to help them do more of the same that works, by encouraging them.

Two, while your staff are doing a good job, you have time to look over the horizon of the future and make plans for the longer term. In short, your staff is acting and you can be proactive.

Here is a non-exhaustive list of what you can do when your staff are operating well on their own:

- Help your employees to grow by coaching them (not because they're deficient but to ensure that things stay the way they are).
- Facilitate meetings.
- Manage by wandering about.
- Socialize and take care of the good working relationships throughout your team and company.
- Be the interface with other departments.
- Provide your staff with resources where needed.
- Listen.
- Encourage people.
- Give compliments on what your staff do well.
- Smooth out potential conflicts.
- Speak up for your team towards the outer world. (Be the "foreign minister.")
- Think about long-term strategy.

To conclude: it's a great honor and pleasure to be the manager of a team that is able to do its work independently of you. It enables you to concentrate on your core task: helping them to do more of what works.

Coach hat — manager hat

What if wearing different hats as manager and coach gives you a headache?

If this happens, it is very unfortunate because wearing more than one hat comes with your double role as manager-leader and manager-coach. When it is not clear to both yourself and your employees that every manager has (at least) two different roles, confusion is likely to occur. With confusion comes tension and with that tension comes your headache.

It helps if you are not wearing both hats at the same time. Just make sure that your employees understand that in your position you have several hats, and when you are wearing the leader's hat, you keep the coach's hat in your hand and vice versa. That way nobody gets confused.

Once you have said and done what needs to be said and done as manager-leader, your employees know the direction and the boundaries of what you expect from them. For example, you give them budget constraints, sales targets, allocate resources to their teams, etc. When that is clear, you can take the manager-leader's hat in your hand and put on the manager-coach's hat. Now they know that you will be supporting and encouraging them to do what is useful to meet their goals and the goals of the company. When the confusion is gone, your headache is likely to disappear along with it.

Of course, doing your best to make things clear doesn't solve this problem forever. Since both your roles are intimately connected, they cannot always be separated so neatly, even though you try. The two roles are different sides of your managerial coin, so there will always be a little overlap where both roles are at play. You may sometimes hear your employees saying: "I thought you were coaching me, and now you tell me that I was wrong in doing X." Or, in contrast: "I thought you had given me an order and now you tell me that I have to come up with my own proposals for action."

This overlap is unavoidable for different reasons. The first is that people always make interpretations about what they hear: "I thought this is what you meant..." These interpretations might or might not have anything to do with the hat that you had been intending to wear in a given situation. So, even if you had intended to wear the coach's hat, people might perceive you as leading and vice versa. Secondly, some employees will use these interpretations to serve their own purposes, and this can be a challenge for your leadership. For example, while you are coaching your sales team to help them reach their targets, they might interpret your helping attitude as opening the door for a bigger budget. Thirdly, both you and your employees work in an ever-changing context. This forces you to shift your role and position constantly.

Let's look at an example. As a sales manager you probably do some field coaching. You sit in on meetings with clients. The clients see you as the leader, and now that they have the opportunity to talk with the top guy, they may ask you to make decisions. These decisions may run counter to what your salesman has promised them. You neither want to cut his decision short nor do you want to say to the client: "Hey, sorry, but I am only coaching my staff for the moment." So you adapt on the spot. You consult with your salesman as if you were on the same hierarchical level, and you jointly take or postpone decisions. After this meeting, you shift back towards the coaching position and discuss the lesson learned by both of you.

To summarize:

- Wearing two hats is unavoidable.
- Make it clear when you are wearing which hat.
- Accept a limited amount of overlap.
- Talk constructively about these gray areas so that your employees know where they are.

How do I manage my employees?

A little note on the concept of resistance

Resistance is a peculiar form of cooperation.

How often do you hear: "I would like to … but no one will support me" or "If it were up to me, that would have been finished a long time ago but the others don't want to…" or "The top/middle/lower management isn't prepared to accept my proposals, so there is nothing I can do" or "They are against me" or "There are too many opposing forces" or "If that wasn't the case, I would…"

When they don't achieve their goals, some people even use the concept of resistance as an explanation: something or someone else is the cause of their failure. Furthermore, it is not their failure, they are not to blame. It is someone else's fault. "Well, it wasn't possible anyway. The odds were stacked against us."

We often have to work with people who don't ask for our help, don't allow us to help them, or sometimes openly oppose our offer of help.

All the above-mentioned attitudes and behavior styles are called resistance to change, in the classical problem-oriented approach. Resistance is seen as a negative characteristic of a person — as if people prefer not to change or refuse to acknowledge the possibility of change.

When we meet resistance, we are tempted to keep repeating our viewpoint in other words. If we don't watch ourselves, we get excited and annoyed. We might even become angry. But reacting with anger won't help us to reach a solution — in fact, it will probably make things worse.

To summarize, in the classical problem-oriented management style, resistance is seen as "a thing, a virus" that exists in the world. In the solution-focused view, resistance is merely a concept in the mind of the one who defines certain behavior as resistance: it has no "objective truth" whatsoever.

Steve de Shazer showed that resistance in the classical interpretation is just a *concept*, not more, not less, and in addition to that a rather useless concept. The solution-focused model takes an entirely different stance on this topic. It defines resistance as "every interaction that initially doesn't seem useful for achieving the goals, but that nevertheless offers information." The word "seem" is crucial in this definition because it indicates that one can do something else with this information rather than just discarding it as negative.

If resistance is no longer seen as opposition, then we do not have to oppose it. Instead, if resistance is seen as information about a peculiar form of cooperation, it becomes a useful concept. Resistance is no longer a dragon to be slain. Resistance is a signpost guiding our behavior.

When you offer your best advice to someone who doesn't ask you for advice, it shouldn't come as a surprise that that person doesn't listen, let alone follow your advice. Is that a resistant person? Or is his behavior of not accepting your advice his way of informing you about your less than appropriate action?

Seeing resistance as useful information isn't easy. Therefore we offer you a list of "the classics in the repertoire of resistance" and show you on page 208 how to translate them into more useful concepts. Learning this novel and innovative view of the concept of resistance will make you into a master of cooperation!

Sailing around the cape of resistance is a technique but with enough practice it becomes a skill.

Beware of corporate sabotage

Some forms of resistance can't be seen, let alone tolerated as information: insubordination, sabotage, deliberate and excessive criticism, (sexual and other) harassment, theft and other criminal actions, etc. Such acts of "corporate terrorism" are unacceptable, and swift action must be taken. Treating people in a respectful way does not mean that everything is allowed.

In cases of corporate sabotage, you will take off your manager-coach hat and put on the hat of the manager-leader who is also responsible for keeping good order. Of course, you will first make dead sure that you are not making a wrong judgment about the behavior of the employee concerned. You will probably consult with others about the issue. But once you are one hundred percent sure that their behavior is deliberately geared to doing harm to their fellow employees and/or the company, you will take action to remove these people from the payroll. The best

Resistance: classic concept		Solution-focused translation
Not keeping agreements in spite of repeated promises.		Find out what would help the employee keep agreements.
Fostering unrealistic expectations and then being disillusioned when they aren't met.		Help to make the expectations realistic and link them to concrete behavior that the employee can try, to begin meeting those realistic expectations.
Giving too much or too little information so that disinformation emerges.		Help to structure the information so that it is clear, concise and useful.
Excluding colleagues from information or meetings.		Design the organization in such a way that teamwork is hard to avoid and/or the alternative is that one person has to do a task on their own.
Acting so docile that the employee only does what he is told to do, not more or less.		Stimulate initiative by offering small assignments at first and then gradually change these into more open-ended tasks. Combine this with a stringent but respectful control on the outcome of the tasks.
Having such a low self-esteem or on the contrary being so totally self-confident that it prevents openness toward others.		Compliment the employee with low self-confidence on the small things he or she already does well. Compliment the employee with excessive self-confidence on his or her great amount of energy. Then assign a task that can be carried out only with the cooperation of others.
Always blaming others instead of accepting responsibility for what goes wrong.		Compliment the employee on his or her great insight into the failures of human nature and ask if he or she dares to use that insight on him- or herself. If that doesn't work, isolate the employee and assign tasks for which only he or she is responsible. If that doesn't work either, resign yourself to the fact that you are dealing with a veteran grumbler and refuse to be bothered by this.
Always leaving the initiative to superiors because "they are being paid well to handle that."		Compliment the employee on his or her modesty, and invite the person to think about ways of making him- or herself (even) more valuable to the company.

removals are swift removals. And it is always good to inform the remaining employees about the facts behind this removal so that nobody is left in the dark. This sets a good example for everybody and, at the same time, it allows you to show your respect to the employees who are loyal to the company.

Who do I coach first?

Who do I coach best as manager: the stars or the underperformers?

Now this is a tricky question. First, you need the courage to admit that your team is not perfect while at the same time you need some wisdom so as not to blame yourself for your non-perfect team. Then you have to fight the misapprehension that everybody in business must be a star. This is simply not true: all corporations all over the world are filled with a mix of stars, average people, and slow movers.

Dividing your staff into three categories and then putting a label on each of them is dangerous. Labels tend to become reality and reduce people to the label they have on their foreheads: this may lead to "corporate racism." Labels describe the intrinsic (lack of) qualities of people. But, they also say something about the one who applies the label. If your company only uses three different labels, then the company itself is rather simplistic in the way it treats its staff.

It is even more complex when you realize that someone can be a slow mover in one area of work while he is average in another. The lowest performing engineer may be good in administrative procedures while your best salesman is a below-average administrator.

To add another level of complexity, you could argue that companies have a responsibility to helping their staff to become better in what they do. This implies that the company (read: you the managers) has the responsibility of managing all staff towards better performance. Limiting labels are no help here.

What does help is to define the requirements you make of your staff in terms that are as detailed and concrete as possible. One can only be called slow if measured against a specific norm. A Ferrari is a fast car when compared to most cars, yet slow when compared to a plane. However, you can go shopping in town with a Ferrari and not with a plane.

Now, this being said, with all levels of complexity added, it still remains true that some are more equal than others. Even if you have distributed tasks optimally, described them well and allocated the resources accordingly, you will still have some staff members who are faster and more efficient than others. In an ideal world, everybody is perfect or at least more then good enough. But perfection is a myth, and managers have to deal with imperfection. The question of who to coach first remains.

So, let's be practical while keeping the above-mentioned complexity in mind.

As a manager you coach individual employees, and you also coach teams that are made up of a bunch of individuals. In order for a team to be more than the sum of its individuals, they need to act like a cycling team that is competing in a time trial. The team that wins is the team that has the highest average speed combined with a fast leadsman. If the star of the team rides so fast that his slowest team mate comes in too late, they (all) lose.

So, you coach the leadsman to go as fast as is useful for the team, you coach the average cyclists to speed them up a little, and you coach the slowest to go as fast as he can in order to come in on time.

However, there are more people involved. Every cycling team has specialists in it who do not ride a bike. They prepare the bikes, arrange hotel rooms, and coach the sportsmen. During a race, they sit in a trailer, stand on sidewalks, or ride in the car that follows the team. Their sweat only comes from the stress of their commitment!

Make sure to spend time with these experts and show them how important they are, even if they will never cross the finishing line personally.

For the best results, you must coach all of them: the stars, the average, and the slowest. Who you spend the most effort on depends on the situation.

When you need a breakthrough in your team, you coach the person with the highest potential for pushing the limits. However, make sure that you help that person to stay in contact with the rest of the team: they need information about what he/she is doing concerning that breakthrough, so that they can do the groundwork when it's their turn to work on the results of the breakthrough.

Take the example of a high-potential sales engineer working for a major business-to-business provider of logistic applications. His company really needs that new account that he has been working on for months. Winning this account will have enormous consequences for his team: they will need to develop, test and implement a giant new piece of software according to the specifications of the new client. His manager has supported and coached him when times got rough. At the same time, his manager made sure that the sales engineer constantly reported the progress on this account. The goal of this was two-fold: reporting his progress gave him additional support and ideas from his team members. At the same time, it prepared the team for what they would need to do after the sale was closed. Imagine what would happen if the sales engineer closed that deal with all the help from his manager but without any communication with the team.

Laws of statistics tell us that the most frequent subspecies of humankind is the average man or woman. Coaching them is great since they are average: they do not need too much, nor too little attention. They only need the *correct* attention. They have areas where they perform better and issues on which they are not so good. Good managers coach the average person on his well-functioning characteristics and support him to do more of what he is already doing well. The less well-functioning aspects of the average person are probably not so bad as to cause serious concern. Good managers coach the average person so that his less well-functioning aspects put no constraints on his contribution to the team or company. They don't lose time or energy in trying to change the average person into a non-average person: this is idle and preposterous (although politically correct in certain business cultures). The only thing you need to avoid is setting the average as the norm: that will not help you win any business prizes!

Then come the slow movers. You pay attention to the slowest in your team for two main reasons. The first reason is that there always is and always will be someone who is the slowest. When you show your interest in the weakest team member as a manager, this instills a respectful atmosphere for the whole team. Showing interest is, of course, not the same as protecting them, let alone allowing them to lower the team's performance. Secondly, you want to see if there is a way to speed them up a little so that they contribute to raising the average speed of the team as a whole.

There is of course a limit to the effort you devote to the slowest team members. This limit comes in sight when in spite of your coaching (or even coaxing) efforts, the slowest constantly stays too far behind in all aspects of his work. Then they offer neither added value nor useful contributions. If this is the case, they move into the category of chronic underperformers: they stay too slow on all aspects of their work and there is no betterment in sight. To question where their underperformance comes from, from lack of capability or from lack of motivation is actually irrelevant. The fact is that chronic underperformers have a braking effect on team performance. It is up to you as a team manager, if you want your team to ride a time trial with the brakes on. The intervention with these team mates is either to find them a new spot in the organization where they can perform better or to ship them out respectfully. When they are not able to shape up and you have to ship them out, it comes to firing them. Have a look at the paragraphs on how to fire someone (page 219) for the best way to do this.

If you have no time to coach all of them at the same time, you'd better make time to give everybody a little of your attention and make sure to show respect to all the members of the team (which maybe is the most basic form of coaching).

To conclude:

- Perfection is an illusion.
- A perfect team consists of stars, average, and slow team members.
- Stars need coaching to help prevent overperformance, and thus losing as a team.
- Slow staff are an unavoidable statistical part of the population.
- A little extra coaching for the slow raises the average speed.
- The average performer is the most frequent, but cannot be allowed to become the norm.
- When it comes to chronic underperformers you have to make a choice for the good of the company.
- Success is all in the mix of differences.

My employees never do as they are told

You know you are right, but your employees never do what you tell them. If this is correct, then you have a big problem! Maybe you are the problem, maybe they are the problem. Or perhaps — hopefully — you are simply making a mistake in your judgment. Either way, it is a waste of time and energy to analyze the "who is right and who is wrong" further. Arguing with your employees or retreating into the boss-dictator position will not be of great help. The more you insist, the more they will resist. And on top of that, maybe, just maybe, they are correct and then what? It's far more useful to ask yourself what you could do differently so that you get the results you want. This however is more easily said than done, especially if you are ensnared by your own convictions.

The following line of questioning might provide an escape route. In order to avoid the linguistic trap that is hiding in the sentence "My employees never do as they are told," start asking yourself some questions like:

- How do you know you are right?
- What is "right"?
- How often is "never"?

- Who are the people meant in the word "my": everybody, some of them, always the same persons...?
- Are you sure that they receive the same message that you intend? How do you know that? Did you ever ask them their interpretations of what you think you tell them?
- What good intentions might they have for not responding in the way you ask them to respond?

When you have asked yourself all these questions, do you remain convinced that your initial statement is useful, or is your position changing? If these questions only strengthen your conviction that they "should" do as told, your problem grows. If, however, you sense that your conviction starts to erode a little, you know for sure that you are on the road to change for the better.

The next step is to ask yourself the following questions:

- If they don't do what you tell them, what are they doing *instead*?
- Is what they are doing instead useful?

The answers to these questions indicate what it is that your employees are doing already that is useful to your organization, even if you hadn't realized it. Most likely your view on them will become more and more constructive. You will build some trust and allow them to do more of what they are already doing that works.

Of course, there will be things left that you would still like them to do and here is an alternative method:

- Compliment your employees on their contribution to the company and on their independent way of doing this.
- Ask them if it would help if you phrased your demands differently, and ask for their suggestions on how to do this.
- Ask them to help you when they think that the content of what you ask them is not in line with what they think should be done.

This way you show your employees that you have the courage to sidestep your ego, and the human tendency to cling to the "power" of your position. Asking your employees for feedback is a sign of true leadership, and this will certainly be appreciated. This mutual appreciation facilitates the cooperation. This will make it easier for both parties to do things that otherwise would remain stuck in stubbornness.

To conclude: knowing you are right is one thing, getting others to agree is another, and then getting them to act differently is yet another. No manager, not even you, is nor needs to be infallible.

My employees don't accept criticism

When I criticize my employees, they always feel hurt, and that's not very professional.

You have probably heard this remark many times and especially from the mouth of less experienced and seasoned managers than yourself. You might even recognize this remark as something that you have said or thought to yourself in the early stages of your development as manager. This saying is a typical sign of frustration when things don't work as one would like them to work. Although common, it is not the most useful attitude that a manager can have. The reason for its uselessness lies in the words "always," hurt," and "professional." Let's have a closer look.

The word "always," when used in this context, invites you to think in black-and-white terms. It is as if the employees have no option other than to react the way they do. This is of course not true: people react in whatever way they think appropriate; sometimes they do not react at all, and sometimes they react in a totally unexpected manner. When you use the word "always," you wipe out this differentiation. The word "always," just like the word "never," is a short cut to discussions and arguments. Imagine your boss saying to you: "You *always* do as you please, and you *never* do as you are told." What is the effect of such a statement? Most likely, you switch to defensive mode and start arguing why your boss is wrong.

In the world of business, feelings are as natural as in private life. Yet, the saying "when I criticize you, you feel hurt" connects a so-called neutral and professional remark with a negative and very personal emotion. This, of course, triggers another defensive reaction from the person on the receiving end of the remark.

Finally, the words "not very professional" put the icing on the cake of uselessness. Calling other people unprofessional disguises your disappointment that your well-intended endeavors to help them did not hit the mark. Calling someone in your organization unprofessional is not a criticism, it is unqualified blaming. If there is one thing that is guaranteed not to be useful, then it is blaming employees and colleagues.

So you can easily understand how this little sentence can have great counterproductive power.

Does this mean that you can't criticize anymore? Certainly not! Criticism is a must in business for the simple reason that lack of criticism is lethal. Without criticism (towards yourself and others) things just stay as they are, and change for the better is not going to happen.

If you want your criticism to be useful, bear in mind the following ideas:

- The power of criticism lies in *how* you criticize: the packaging of your message is more important then its content.
- The goal of criticism is to get the job done in a better way than it's done now. So along with your remarks, offer alternative possibilities, and thus you create constructive criticism.
- Don't criticize the person but his or her actions.
- Use the sandwich technique: first give a compliment on what goes well in spite of the problem, then deliver your criticism, and end with another compliment.

These people are impossible to work with!

Who hasn't entertained this notion when confronted with difficult people or situations? The people meant in this sentence can be anybody: employers, employees, clients, suppliers, government, family members that work in the same family business as you do. When the going gets too tough, uttering this sentence can be a relief: "It's not me, it's them!!" But of course this exclamation serves no other purpose than to let off some steam.

Actually, what this phrase really means is: "At the moment I do not know how to handle these people. I have tried lots of things, and although I didn't get the impression that something was working, I kept trying even harder. Because that didn't work, I have now come to the conclusion that *they* are impossible." Although utterly useless, this idea that they are impossible frees me from blaming myself on my inability to handle them. The sole potential stemming from this definition is that I retain a bit of energy, and maybe I can use that to do something different rather than merely vent my frustration.

Impossible people do exist but are very rare. What is more frequent are people that *behave* in such a way that the results can be called "difficult." With this insight, you discover that this so-called impossibility is just an interpretation and not a very useful one.

So try to change your interpretation by asking yourself the following questions:

- What are they doing to make me tend to call them difficult people?
- What is it that they are trying to tell me by their so-called difficult behavior?
- What are the advantages of their so-called difficult behavior?
- On a scale of zero to ten, where minus ten stands for total impossibility and zero stands for doable, where are we now? What are we already doing differently so that I can give this number?

- Remember a moment in the past when the number was above zero. What was everybody doing differently at that moment?
- How did I deal with "difficult" people in the past? What worked best then?
- How could I behave differently towards them in order to reassure them that I do want to cooperate with them?
- What is it that I want to accomplish in working with them?
- If I ask them what they would like to accomplish in our cooperation, what would they answer?
- Did I give enough compliments on their tenacity and independent behavior?
- What might be the smallest sign of improvement in our cooperation?

Answering some or all of these questions will most probably reduce the sense of impossibility and allow you to proceed with renewed vigor.

To conclude: the knowledge that it's all interpretation gives you a window of opportunity to act differently towards them. When you change your interpretations and, therefore, your actions towards the others, chances are high that they will behave differently towards you. The vicious circle of self-perpetuating negative interpretations that steer useless behavior is broken.

Help, half of my team are morons!

There is no scientific definition for being a moron. Sure, people sometimes behave like morons but that doesn't mean they are morons. It's just a perception and perceptions are not lethal. Perceptions can be turned around fairly easily, if you are willing to do so. So here is what you could try if you are open to the fact that people being morons is a matter of perception. Ask yourself the question: "When was the last time I witnessed a so-called moron doing something that was a tiny bit useful? What was different then? How did I react to it? Would it be a good idea to watch for useful behavior or do I keep myself occupied with this useless idea that they are and remain morons?"

Maybe the person you call a moron is just someone you don't particularly like. No problem, these are people you work with — you don't have to go on vacation with them! You don't have to be friends with all of your team mates, yet you can learn to behave pleasantly towards everybody. That will result in them acting more friendly towards you. Consequently, your perception might change.

Maybe you call them morons because you *think* that they don't do what has to be done for the company. If this is the case, then maybe the following idea can help you to make a little dent in your perception: unless it's proven otherwise, everybody tries to do their best. Nobody gets up in the morning and comes to work with the specific intention of making a mess out of it. So, if you are willing to look at them from this different perspective, you will find the courage to approach them in a different way.

You might ask yourself what it is that they are doing instead of what you tell them to do. What are the good things they are doing, even if it is not what you asked them to do? How are these things beneficial to the company?

You might ask them what they think is their best contribution to the company. "What are the useful things you do for the company? What else do you think would be useful that you are not able to do for the moment? How could I help you to do these things?"

Whatever the answers are, it is highly likely that you will be surprised how much you learn now that the moron-plug is out of your ears. Encouragement and support will become easier now that you have discovered interesting things on which you can compliment them. Besides, it's only half of your team that you perceive to be morons. How are the others doing?

To conclude: if you are not followed when leading, stop, turn around, and invite. When they come to your position, you let them pass. Then you allow them to walk in front of you and prompt them along the way with the help of solution-building questions. Thus you become "a leader from behind."

In brief: if you are out to change the world, start with yourself.

When do I fire someone?

Let us divide this question into two parts: when do I fire someone and *how* do I fire someone?

The answer to the "when" question is rather obvious but not always easy. The clearest situation is when the economic circumstances force you to cut costs: better less people in the company then no company.

In an ongoing company, the need to fire someone arises when he or she no longer fits in with the rest of the company. This "fit" can mean lots of things of course. If the key no longer fits the lock, maybe the key changed, maybe the lock changed or maybe both changed. The result is the same: the door stays closed.

In general, those people who in spite of coaching efforts (no longer) offer added value of some kind to the company and people who (willingly) inflict harm to the company and/or its members are suitable candidates for being moved out.

Here is a painful example.

The employee, whose career started together with the company some fifteen years ago, has moved up to the position of administrative director. He didn't however evolve along with the company, and his employer discovers — with sadness — that this person's added value is zero in this new function. The employer, who owns the family business, offers his employee some coaching but to no avail. The conclusion of the external coach is that the employee is simply not fit for his function. Of course, the employer realizes that he made a mistake by offering him that job in the first place, but now he has no choice other than a demotion. The employee reaction is first disappointment and then fury. He feels that his loyalty to the company is ignored. His demotion is painful for him, but his reaction to it is a prolonged gossip campaign that downgrades both his employer and the company. When the employee starts spreading negative news about the company to its financial suppliers, the employer puts an end to this by firing him.

The next element is the most important part of the firing issue: *how* to fire staff. Central in this (often painful process) are the words "respect" and "integrity."

It is obvious that firing someone falls into the category of bad news conversations. So rule one is: have a conversation with the person that you are firing. Do not limit yourself to an email and registered letter. Don't beat around the bush but get the message out as soon as possible, and make sure that you explain the reasons for your decision in as concrete terms as possible. Allow for an emotional reaction on the part of your employee. Then make sure that you talk about other things that the fired person contributed to the company, about their resources as a person, about your appreciation of what he or she did that was remarkable or helpful to the company, about your trust in the capabilities of the fired person that will help him or her find a new place in the corporate world. In short, offer compliments on every aspect of the fired person that you genuinely think he or she can use in the next stage of his/her career. Keep allowing for possible emotional responses while you restate the concrete reasons for this firing. If, in the end, you come to a shared conclusion that it is better for both parties to separate, your mission has succeeded. Both the company and the employee can move on with their life and career. It will still be difficult for the one who is fired of course, but chances are high that he or she — at a later stage — will understand that it was for the best for both parties.

Why should I go through this effort when I fire someone? After all, I fire them because they no longer fit in with the company.

There are several good reasons to make this effort. At least three parties are involved when you fire someone: the one you fire, the one who does the firing, and the people who stay behind.

In human interactions, there is a law involved: what you give is what you get. Treating someone respectfully will provide you with respect in return. This is simple and basic human nature. Even when you fire someone because he or she no longer fits in with your company, you are better off letting him or her leave with his self-respect intact. Acknowledging a person's efforts and contributions in spite of the fact that he/she is fired is the best way to accomplish this.

In the macho world of business where expressions like "shape up or ship out" are popular, some people simply overlook the fact that firing people is never pleasant. It is always better to treat people like you would like to be treated yourself. After all, a day might come when you could be on the receiving end and, if so, you would like some respect, wouldn't you?

Perhaps one of the most important reasons for making an effort to fire someone respectfully resides in the fact that people stay behind. Those who stay behind are all affected by the fact that someone has been fired.

If the fired person was perceived as not useful for the company or even as obnoxious, then the reaction can be one of relief. However, the way that person was fired reflects the style of the firing manager. Kicking out an obnoxious person can initially be met with sarcastic enthusiasm, but there an unpleasant atmosphere often lingers: "Sure, he was a jerk but was it necessary to treat him like a jerk?" So, the style of dismissal leaves a residue with the remaining people. When it is accomplished in a respectful manner, there will be a respectful residue.

When staff are removed from the company, it often results in a sense of uncertainty for the remaining people. To avoid the risk of growing uncertainty, the remaining staff members need information about why that person has been fired. This will provide them with clarity on their own position and an update on the health of the company.

Never be afraid to say something positive about the person that you fired. This is not inconsistent with the fact that he/she has been fired. Similarly, being fired does not make someone a bad person who didn't do anything worthwhile. Just explain that the person no longer fits in with the needs of the company. It gives you a great opportunity to show the ones who stay behind that you treat all people with respect, even the ones you let go.

Now what about so-called corporate terrorists, people who have willingly harmed the corporation and/or co-workers? We suggest that you first take care of the legal side of pending issues with those persons and then fire them in as clean as possible a manner. Remove them as quickly and silently as possible from the company. It can feel like a great victory to expose them publicly but in most cases this serves no other purpose then revenge. And revenge is a bad sentiment in corporate affairs: it eats energy and dollars.

What is the best way to handle a large downsizing while keeping the morale high in the remaining group? The solution-focused way to do this runs along the same lines! Showing respect by acknowledging the contributions of the departing group, while at the same time giving a correct and open explanation of the "why" of the collective firing, provides optimal clarity to both the departing group and the remainers. A downsizing is never a fun exercise, and there is no reason to hide this fact. However, this openness does not mean that one should start whining, crying or excusing. For the responsible manager, whose job it is to handle this collective downsizing and who therefore wields the axe, it is useful and comforting to remember the old cowboy adage: "The dogs bark but the caravan moves on."

When the downsizing is done in a respectful manner, chances are high that no "survivor syndrome" will occur. In the heydays of corporate re-engineering, large "quantities of workforce" (read: humans) were sacked for the sake of shareholder value. This hemorrhage of people resulted in the survivor syndrome: many of those who remained struggled with the idea "Why did I survive this corporate massacre?"

People afflicted with this survivor syndrome feel depressed, unsure of themselves, scared, and hurt. They tend to operate in a safe mode that results in sub-optimal behavior: they are more concerned with doing the right tasks than with doing tasks well. In order to become invisible to performance scrutiny, sub-optimal performance becomes the norm. The result of the survivor syndrome can be deadly in the short run for an organization: innovation and initiative are stopped dead in their tracks.

To conclude:

- Firing people is an unavoidable part of life in business.
- *When* to fire someone is less important than *how* to fire someone.
- Showing respect to the people you fire has a positive effect on all parties concerned: the fired, the firing, and the remaining staff.
- Transparency and clarity eases the firing process for everybody.
- Even corporate terrorists deserve respectful firing, not so much for their benefit but for the benefit of the remaining staff.
- The survivor syndrome as a result of downsizing is a side effect that can be prevented by acknowledging the positive contributions of the

fired persons, while at the same time providing information to the remaining staff about the necessity of the action.

- Showing respect earns respect.

How do I deal with my superiors?

My boss sees problems everywhere!

How do you handle a boss who only sees problems popping up everywhere?

Instead of allowing yourself to be bothered by this, you might consider the fact that you have a hard-working boss who is creative about discovering and sharing all his worries with you. So make sure that your boss knows you are listening to his worries. Otherwise, he will keep concentrating on the problem and probably even detect further elements of the ever-growing problem.

However, make sure you stay away from the lure of problem-orientation. Taking one step back helps to avoid inheriting the panicky behavior that results from problem obsession.

Never allow yourself to become irritated, not even by your boss who is a professional worrier. Just stay the calm professional solutions warrior and, at the right moment, ask him: "OK, boss, I see your point. Given your analysis of the problem, what could be the first small step towards a possible solution? The situation as you describe it is pretty cumbersome, but after all our efforts, we can't allow the seriousness of this problem to drown us, can we? There are still some things left that operate pretty well, how about starting there and see how far we get? You surely agree that we must make sure that the things that are still functioning in spite of all the problems are worth continuing!"

Such an intervention has more chance for success then responding in a cynical way to your constantly worrying boss. Of course it's your boss's style to overreact a little and have a penchant for the negative sides of things. Yet, this problem-focused sensitivity can be transformed into a radar that constantly picks up hints of possible solutions. The only thing you need to do is to help yourself and your boss to single out the glimmer of hope that leads to possible solutions instead of staying fixed on the white noise of the problems.

If you are patient and persistent, there will come a time when the doors to the problem attic open up, and a little light of a possible solution will shine in. Carefully put your foot in the crack of the door, or maybe start with a little toe... In order to do this *gently*, make sure to add "even if we still are having many problems" to the following questions. "What would be the smallest signal that we are making a little progress? How would you notice that the problems have lessened, even a little? What would your employees do differently then? How would you react when you see the first small signs of improvement?"

Tips for handling an ever-worrying boss:

- Accept his worries at face value because they are his reading of the facts.
- Refrain from rationalizing and arguing about the wrongness of his worries.
- Show your boss that you value his commitment to the organization, even if this commitment is packed with eternal worries.
- Don't allow yourself to be engulfed by the rising tides of despair.
- Ask questions about those things that still go well in spite of the problem and compliment your boss about his share in this.
- Wait patiently until the veil of negativity recedes and then ask questions about the smallest signs of improvement.

To conclude: an ever-worrying boss mans the observation post that looks out for every possible threat one might encounter. Although at times it is hard to endure, this quality deserves appreciation. After all, you know that your back is covered and that frees you up to explore all possible roads towards swift solutions.

My boss scares me

Although you will never admit this in public, you sometimes feel scared of your boss.

Some of you may recognize this (I certainly do!), and others may find this alien to them. If you reside in the last category: congratulations, you are in no way hampered by these unhelpful feelings.

If, however, you do recognize these feelings of being scared, even if it is only because your partner or colleague mentioned them to you, then it's a good idea to put them in the correct perspective. Feeling a little apprehensive of your boss is absolutely no indication that you are not able to do your job or that you should not be a manager. On the contrary, it indicates that you, or the people you know who are apprehensive, are sensitive people who want to make the best possible contribution to the organization.

Of course, when apprehension turns into downright anxiety that freezes you, then it can become a problem. Lying awake at night while brooding over some problems in your company that you want solved is perfectly normal for managers. Lying awake with the haunting image of your boss staring at you with red eyes and foam on his mouth isn't.

So here is what you might do:

- Ask yourself if being scared is useful, and if not: do something else instead like focusing on another dossier, getting up for a coffee, calling a friend, or concentrate on your last vacation for a moment, visualize your boss naked before an audience...
- Remind yourself of all your resources and the successes that you have had up until now and ask yourself how you did it.
- Remind yourself of a situation in which you were able to conquer your fear. How did you do it?
- Consider the fact that your boss might nurture the same fears as you since he or she is not in total control either.
- When you are focusing on the previous point, consider the fact that there is even more at stake for your boss: he or she needs you to do the job, can't do it in your place and is dependent on your efforts. Now how is that for a fright?
- Remember that nobody is going to eat you alive, not even when the most unfortunate things happen, or when you make a really big mistake.
- Use your emotions to become even better at what you do by redefining your fears into challenges.

My boss never tells me what to do!

Isn't it horrible? You try your best to be a good leader, manager and coach, and your superiors seem to be indecisive, don't have a clue, and don't give you clear goals.

So what do you do?

Let's start with what you shouldn't do, even if this first reaction is very common and human. What you most certainly want to avoid is indulging in speculations and hypotheses of what it all might signify. As unfortunate as their silence might be, their not telling you what to do can have many reasons. Losing oneself in ever deepening hypotheses on the "whys" of someone else's behavior is particularly unhelpful, as you will never find out for sure. Plus, there is a big chance that you get lost in the dark and scary forest of your boss's presumed bad intentions. And in the end, losing your self-confidence will make you a less effective manager and leader.

So, it is better to stay at the surface of the boss's behavior and try not to analyze it too much. Just accept it as a given.

Your boss's silence has as many advantages as it has disadvantages. You will quickly see the beneficial side of a silent boss: he shows his trust that you are doing well and he allows you to proceed with your work as you think is appropriate. Of course, these are also interpretations but they are more useful. So enjoy and keep working.

If, however, this makes you a little uncertain, and/or you are faced with the need to get a decision from him in order to be able to proceed, then you could try this: just kindly ask him for help and directions.

If this doesn't work, not to worry. There are still other ways.

One of them is to offer your boss a wider menu from which he can choose. Provide him with a few possible options, and make sure that your options have all the necessary background information that he will need to make a decision. Of course, you don't want to increase his indecisiveness by offering him too many options and showing indecisiveness yourself. So you can add your own suggestion of what you think might be the best option. Such a suggestion, however, is much more powerful if you wrap your suggestion in a question. "Do you think that doing X is best for the company at the moment?" When this invitational question prompts him to talk with you, be open and ask for his opinion based on his superior experience in the field or with the company. This procedure shows your boss that you are a responsible and enthusiastic manager, that you respect your boss even if he has been silent, and that you respect the hierarchy. This respectful attitude is much more elegant and powerful than a seductive "I know better" posture.

When worse comes to worst, and your boss still does not respond, you might consider using the horror scenario technique: you express your concerns and worries about what might happen if no decision is taken. Then you picture in as vivid a way as possible all the horrible consequences for the company if no decision is taken, and you declare yourself hopeless without your boss's help and expert support.

If he still chooses to remain silent, and you have done everything that you can, then it is advisable to cover your back and send a memo with all the possible options and all the relevant background information that is needed for your boss to take decisions. Make sure that you also express your concerns about the consequences for the company in the memo. Then wait and see while you move on to other work for your company. Chances are high that — sooner or later — your boss or your boss's boss will stumble on your memo and act accordingly. If action then follows, you give credit to the one who has taken action. Your own credit is implicit in your signature under the memo. It is even better to use email because that makes sure that your document is dated (and secure on the company's server).

In conclusion:

- Don't get lost in speculations.
- Trust your boss to trust you.
- Kindly asking for directions works far better than demanding decisions.
- Offer your boss a multiple choice combined with a suggestion.
- Pushing or pulling your boss has a contrary effect.
- A respectful attitude combined with the tenacity of a pit bull terrier works best, especially when you express your concern and commitment to the company.
- When nothing helps, make sure to cover your back while keeping the good of the company in mind.

How do I manage crisis situations

We are in a crisis, so no time for solution focus

Crisis is part of business life, it comes with the territory. That is easy to understand. Change is inevitable, some changes come unexpectedly, and some changes have big and unwanted impacts on your company. It's the manager's job to deal with the consequences of these impacts. Examples range from the sudden departure of key personnel, bad exposure in the media after an incident in the factory, or stocks that have to be reviewed because of a financial scandal, to restructuring of your division after a merger, bankruptcy of a big customer, or a devastating fire at your headquarters. You name it, and it has got the potential to become a crisis.

How to think about this and what to do? To use a metaphor, it is impossible to live in the Caribbean without occasionally having to sit out a hurricane — and your business is surely an island in a hurricane-prone area of life! When you are in the middle of the hurricane, it is dangerous to sit back and observe it. On the contrary, it is safer to occupy yourself with what you need to do for protection. When your house crumbles down on you, don't look at the debris but look for a way out.

The point with a crisis is not to try and fight the causes, because this only makes things worse. It's hard to blow away a hurricane, so it's better to use the energy within it. For example: when a competitor aggressively enters your market, it's not going to help if you just complain about it or ask yourself why this competitor has done this to you. You are better off finding out what your company needs to do for your customers and how you are going to respond accordingly to that threat. But there is more: this threat can become an incentive that helps your company step up its own efforts and enhance your own market drive.

People (including your staff, you and me) are creatures of habit: when something unexpected happens, we tend to react with well-engrained behavior. In order to understand what has happened, we tend to turn into observers of the crisis. Why is this happening to me? What did I/we do wrong? Whose fault is it that we are in this mess? These reflexes risk entrapping us in a paralyzing focus on the problem by which our perception of the crisis is more scary and stressful then the reality of the situation.

Even when you are a well-trained and skilled solution-focused worker, you need to mentally take one step back, in order to keep an overview on how to respond effectively to the crisis you are in.

For example: the merger and acquisitions team of a mid-sized corporate law firm suddenly announces their collective resignation. The CEO-owner of the law firm is knocked off his chair by this news and immediately his lawyer reflexes take over: "Can I sue them?" After some hours of panic, anger, frustration, and counting the turnover that his firm will lose by these resignations, he shapes up. The CEO realizes that there is nothing he can do by suing them and entering into an open war. He works out a plan detailing how his former M&A team can still cooperate with the rest of his specialists, and calculates how both parties can benefit from this. The departing team realizes that they too can benefit from an ongoing cooperation with their former employer, simply because they need some of the other departments to continue their own work.

Tips for staying in the solution-focused mode during a crisis:

- Relax, every crisis is an opportunity that will help you to become stronger (unless it kills you).
- Since you are already in the crisis, it is useless to speculate how it has come about.
- Deal with the crisis in a relaxed and elegant way. If a storm comes, it is better to be a reed than an oak.
- Sit tight, and take time to remember a crisis that you went through before. How did you do it then? What was most helpful at that time? What did you learn then that you could use now?
- You are hardly ever alone in the crisis. So if you manage to keep others calm by showing calmness, you turn bystanders into helpers. And as you already know, together everybody achieves more: T.E.A.M works better.
- Look for a constructive way to deal with the crisis and act accordingly.

Teams at war: how to handle conflicts

Conflicts occur where different parties with different stakes interact. Business life is all about interaction. Conflict is therefore an unavoidable part of (business) life. There is nothing wrong with having conflicts, they just exist. The way you act when you are confronted with conflicting interests can be useful or less useful, even to the point of being potentially destructive.

In economics, resources (time, money, manpower) are scarce. In business life there are two additional resources: respect and acknowledgment. These last two resources are available in unlimited quantities, and yet, they are (too) rare in business life. The classical economic resources are touchable, countable, and consist of hardware. However, respect and acknowledgment can neither be touched nor counted. With them, the essence lies in the *perception* of feeling respected and receiving acknowledgment. The downside is that they need to be delicately handled. The upside is that one needs only a little amount of them in order to be effective. Plus: respect and acknowledgement cost nothing but a little effort.

We have all witnessed and been involved in conflicts in our (business) life, and while you read this example, some of these conflicts might come to mind. Try to think about how you would react when confronted with the following case.

The managing director of a wholesaler in medical supplies starts getting personal emails from customers. These are not happy emails but complaints about promises that have not been kept, deliveries that are late and incomplete, back orders that never show up. She picks up the phone and calls the biggest client who — alas — happens to be the unhappiest client. Luckily she knows the client well enough to be able to discuss what's going on. The client tells her that he has called her sales manager to complain about the incidents. Besides being very courteous and friendly towards the client, the only thing the sales manager had to say is that it's all the fault of the back office and the people in logistics. When the client then called the logistics manager, he got a similar message: "These guys in sales think they can do as they please, they make promises to you that are impossible for us to keep, the only thing they do well is park their big cars in front, come in and yell at my people."

After thanking her client for the useful information, the managing director immediately sends for the three managers involved. You can imagine the ensuing conflict. You can test your business experience by guessing which department voices each of the following complaints:

"You and your people have the nicest job in this company, you sit behind your computer, take some phone calls, email some messages downstairs, and never have to take any responsibility. On top of that, you work nine-to-five. When I come in later in the evening, after a full day of taking care of our clients, your offices look completely deserted."

"You are the lucky guys, driving around in your big cars thinking that the world revolves around you, visiting people and making easy promises without thinking about what's possible in reality. You email out these impossibilities and assume that we can work magic behind the scenes. We are the ones that have to help our clients. We are the real frontline since we deal with the reality of our clients' needs. When you do drop by the office, you just come in to throw complaints about every single one of us on the table, yell some orders, and go for a coffee among yourselves."

"We are the working horses, no nine-to-five here, more five-to-nine and then around the clock. We are taken for granted without ever a word of consideration, you put us in an impossible situation because neither of you needs to actually do anything except pass on commands, and neither of you feels prepared to come and see the mess you make downstairs with your impossible demands. On top of that, when an order goes wrong at our client's office, you both simply pass on the responsibility to my department. You blame us and we can't defend ourselves because we hardly ever meet our clients. You don't need to deny this since I know it for a fact. Our clients tell me this, and you know when? Well, only when they are so upset with the mess you make that they show up at our place."

Now, guessing who said what was not too difficult, was it? and that's only three individuals. Can you imagine the liveliness of this conflict in each department? What do you assume happens at their respective coffee machines? What is likely to happen if you put all of them together in a room with the invitation to discuss their disagreements? How do you handle such a conflict between teams? What would you do?

The classical way of dealing with a conflict is to look for the causes that underlie this conflict. Why are these people behaving like they do? The answer to the why-question in human conflicts often leads to "Who is involved, who started it?" and finally leads to "Who is to blame?" This line of questioning invites all parties concerned to describe their own viewpoint and of course, all the viewpoints are diametrically opposed or they simply would not have the conflict. This method of trying to understand a conflict is a short cut to defending one's own standpoint and results in blaming the others. And we all know what blaming leads to: further escalation. This easily leads to a war in the corporate trenches: consuming time and energy but going nowhere.

There are other, more elegant ways to solve conflicts, however! The following steps guarantee you a more useful way of dealing with conflicts

First it is important to acknowledge the different points of view of all the parties involved in the conflict. It is best to start out from the fact that every party is correct in its own view. No use discussing how real is real because each party has its own reality.

After listening to the three team leaders, the managing director shrewdly says: "I see that each and every one of you has a clear and concise idea about what is going on. You are all very supportive of what your own team does for this company, and you give exact descriptions of these contributions. It's only natural that you favor the contributions of your own team over what the others contribute. And we all know that every team contributes in a different way to the functioning of the company. Without sales, there is no use for a back office nor for logistics. Without logistics, what would be the use of selling our stuff and processing the clients' wishes and needs through the back office? How could the cooperation between sales and logistics be put into action without the intermediate and therefore central interface of the back office? Of course, you are very different teams with different tasks and stakes regarding our clients. This difference is not always easy to live with, and I am glad that all of you realize that it's the cooperation in spite of these differences that creates the power of our company in relations with our clients."

Then give all parties compliments on the way they use their resources when working for the company:

"Now to me it is clear that all of you and your teams are working very hard and trying to do their best to serve our clients in the best possible way."

Look out for and (re-)establish a common ground. Especially when a conflict is harsh, this may seem difficult and sometimes even impossible. But it is not! The common ground is always the good of the company. That is what they all share. Nobody in the conflict is *only* interested in his/her/their own position. They all know that they are parts of a whole, and that the whole is more than the sum of the parts.

"I can readily understand that you are all very uncomfortable when our clients start complaining about our services, even when you all do your best. It's evident that you are aware of things that went wrong in the

recent past. Now, what strikes me most in your disagreements is that all of you are talking about "our" clients. So it's clear that you have a common thing at stake here! We can't allow this company to become divided because of a common zeal, namely serving our clients in the best possible manner. Now instead of delving in the background of the complaints and your respective disagreements, let me ask you the following question."

Ask questions about exceptions. The conflict they are going through has not been there all the time, although when in the middle of it it seems like it's been there forever.

The managing director asks questions like these: "When did you not have this conflict, and what did you do differently then? Have you ever encountered similar conflicts, and how did you resolve them at the time? Is there something that you could use today?"

It is hard for the team managers to refrain from stumbling back into reproaching each other, but here their managing director can help them. She just needs to patiently listen to the reproaches and translate them as well-meant but inefficient ways of making the point clear. Furthermore, she sticks to her solution-building questions. It doesn't take long before the team managers come up with useful answers that form the basis for re-building their cooperation.

Once you help the conflicting parties to turn their noses in the direction of more useful ways of interacting among each other, there remains the question of how they will help their own team members to make the same turn. Giving direct suggestions of how to do this is less powerful than helping them come up with the answer themselves. You already know how to do this: make suggestions in the form of questions so that they themselves "own" the answers. You can kick start this move in the following way:

Managing director: "Now, colleagues, is this a useful way of talking at the moment?"

They will probably all respond with a "yes."

Then she goes on: "What is useful about the way you are talking now?"

They all answer: "This is more constructive. Arguing about who is right and who is wrong doesn't lead us anywhere. We are in this together and we'd better find a way out of our disagreements together."

Managing director: "Correct. Congratulations, that is what I like to see! How will you help your team members to make this same step forward? Would it be useful if you first acknowledge their commitment and their worries? Would it be useful if you tell them again what their contribution to the company is and how well they do in this respect? What do you think your team members need in order to be able to see how their cooperation with the other teams can be restored?"

Together they develop a plan to do this in the coming days.

To conclude:

- Make sure that everybody understands that winning or losing is not personal. If you allow people to make the conflict personal, it becomes more difficult to accept another position.
- Help people understand and feel that mutual respect is at the core of cooperation and that all-parties have to cooperate or they will fail.
- Work on establishing a common base.
- Make sure that in the end everybody agrees that the company is the winner and that all parties who contribute to this, and profit from this, will become winners themselves.

Conclusion

This book is designed like a Rubik's cube: it has six sides (or chapters), and each chapter speaks about the same solution-focused reality but from a different perspective.

For most of you, this chapter is the last one you read.

For some of you it's the first chapter you delved into.

Hence our parting or starting words:

THE END

or for some of you

THE BEGINNING

Bibliography

Adams, D. 1986, *The hitchhiker's guide to the galaxy*. New York: Wings Books.

Axelrod R.H. 2004, *You don't have to do it alone: how to involve others to get things done*. San Francisco: Berrett-Koehler.

Bateson, G. 1972, *Steps to an ecology of mind*. New York: Ballantine.

Bateson, G. 1979, *Mind and nature: a necessary unit*. New York: E.P. Dutton.

Berg, I.K & Cauffman, L. 2001, *From couch to coach: lessons for therapists who want to move into the world of business*. Workshop at Family Networker Conference, Washington.

Berg, I.K. & Dolan, Y. 2001, *Tales of solutions: a collection of hope-inspiring stories*. New York: W.W. Norton.

Blake, W. 1987, *The complete poems*. London: Penguin Classics.

Cauffman, L. 2001, Challenging the family business: the relational dimension. Oslo: *Scandinavian Journal of Organisational Psychology*, 2, 63-62.

Cauffman, L. 2003, Kemphanen/Une Serieuze. Belgium: *Bizz Magazine*, 33, 16-25. (Translation: *Teams at war.*)

Cauffman, L. 2003, Dancing the solutions shuffle. UK: *Amed*, vol 10, 4, 6-11.

Cauffman, L. 2003, *Oplossingsgericht Management & Coaching: Simpel werkt het best*. 4th edition. Holland: Lemma. (Translation: *Solution focused management & coaching: simple works best.*)

Cauffman, L. & Berg, I.K. 2001, *Solutions Inc*. Belgium: D/2001/9314/1. (Editon Korzybski Institute Belgium)

Cauffman, L. & Berg, I.K. 2002, Solution talking creates solutions. Austria: *Lernende Organisation*, 5, 56-61.

Covey, S. 2004, *The 7 habits of highly effective people*. USA: Free Press.

Crichton, M. 2002, *Prey*. London: HarperCollins Publishers.

Csikzentmihaly, M. 2004, *Good business leadership, flow and the making of meaning*. London: Penguin.

De Jong, P. & Berg, I.K. 2001, *Interviewing for solutions*. (2nd edition). USA: Brooks Cole.

De Shazer, S. 1984, Death of resistance. *Family Process*, 23, 11-21.

De Shazer, S. 1991, *Putting difference to work*. New York: W.W. Norton.

De Shazer, S. 1994, *Words were originally magic*. New York: W.W. Norton.

Dolan, Y. 2000, *Beyond survival: living well is the best revenge*. London: BT Press.

Eliot, T.S. 1952, *Complete poems and plays: 1909-1950*. Harcourt.

Freud, S. 1978, *Introductory lectures on psycho-analysis*. London: The Hogarth Press.

Fritz, R. 1999, *The path of least resistance for managers*. San Francisco: Berrett-Koehler.

Furman, B. & Tapani, A. 1998, *It's never too late to have a happy childhood*. London: BT Press.

Furman, B. & Tapani, A. 2001, *Solution talk: hosting therapeutic conversations*. London: BT Press.

Gergen, K.J. 1992, *The saturated self*. New York: Basic Books.

Gibson, R. 2001, *Rethinking the future*. London: Nicholaes Brealy.

Gladwell, M. 2005, *Blink: the power of thinking without thinking*. London: Penguin.

Gleick, J. 2003, *Isaac Newton*. London: Fourth Estate.

Jackson, P.Z. & McKergow, M. 2002, *The solutions focus: the simple way to positive change*. London: Nicholaes Brealy.

Keeney, B.P 1985, *Aesthetics of change*. New York: Guilford.

Kennedy, J. & Eberhart, R.C. 2001, *Swarm intelligence*. San Diego: Academic Press.

Korzybski, A. 1994, *Science and sanity: an introduction to non-aristotelian and general semantics*. New Jersey: International Non-Aristotelian Library.

Lipset, D. 1980, *Gregory Bateson: the legacy of a scientist*. New Jersey: Prentice-Hall.

McKergow, M. & Clarke, J. 2005, *Positive approaches to change: applications of solutions focus and appreciative inquiry at work*. Cheltenham: Solutions Books.

Mandela, N. 2003, *Long walk to freedom*. London: Abacus.

Maturana, H. & Varela, F. 1987, *The tree of knowledge: the biological roots of human understanding*. Boston: New Science Library.

Meier, D. 2005, *Team coaching with the solution circle: a practical guide to solutions focused team development*. Cheltenham: Solutions Books.

Nettle, D. 2005, *Happiness: the science behind your smile*. Oxford: Oxford University Press.

Schmaltz, D. 2003, *The blind men and the elephant: mastering project work*. San Francisco: Berrett-Koehler.

Seligman, M. 2003, *Authentic happiness*. London: Nicolaes Brealy.

Silberman, M. & Hansburg, F. 2004, *Working people smart: 6 strategies for success*. San Francisco: Berrett-Koehler.

Simon, H. 1996, *Hidden champions: lessons from 500 of the world's best unknown companies*. Boston: Harvard Business School Press.

Stam, P. 2004, *Building a solution focused organization*. Opening Lecture EBTA Conference, Amsterdam.

Strathern, P. 2001, *Dr. Strangelove's game: a brief history of economic genius*. London: Hamish Hamilton.

Surowiecki, J. 2005, *The wisdom of crowds: why the many are smarter than the few*. London: Abacus.

Wheatley, M.J 2001, *Leadership and the new science: discovering order in a chaotic world*. Revised. San Francisco: Berrett-Koehler.

White, M. 2000, *Leonardo the first scientist*. New York: St. Martin's Press.

Whitney, D. & Trosten-Bloom, A. 2003, *The power of appreciative inquiry: a practical guide to positive change*. San Francisco: Berrett-Koehler.

Wright, R., 2001, *Non Zero: history, evolution & human cooperation*. London, Abacus.

Acknowledgments

We owe a great deal to our clients and to the worldwide solution focused community we are proud to be part of. Our gratitude goes to all of them. Thanks!

Louis wants to thank Kirsten for her outstanding coaching and support in his struggle to get his twenty years of experience on paper. Without her this book would not be what is has become. Thanks!

I also like to express my heart felt gratitude to my family who allows me to be there while being away so much. Thanks!

Praise for *The Solution Tango*

"Solution-focused" is the buzzword of the day because of the vast advantages that the approach represents. In *The Solution Tango*, Louis Cauffman, an international management expert, presents an eminently readable and practical orientation. Want to be at the forefront of the buzz? Want the latest on being an accomplished manager? The solution is within.

Jeffrey K. Zeig, PhD, Director,
The Milton H. Erickson Foundation, U.S.A

This book is an important one. It is a wide exposé of how to apply the principles of solution-focused psychology to the art of managing people and leading organisations. It is my conviction that the idea of positive psychology in general, and that of solution-focused management in particular, will become a megatrend for all kinds of businesses and organisations. Caring for our own well-being as well as that our staff has already become one of the most important facets in organisational life. This is a serious book of how we all can participate in creating environments that promote rather than tax our well being.

Ben Furman, MD, Director,
Helsinki Brief Therapy Institute, Finland

The Solution Tango is all about solution focused leadership — can it be that simple? Yes, it can. Louis Cauffman's book shows you how: in clear words, underlined with helpful practical examples. Whether someone's leadership life has ever been full of problems before or he has already experienced the solution focus in the past — everyone will find new approaches in this book. Congratulations to Louis Cauffman who has done a great work.

Mag. Sonja Radatz,
CEO, ISCT GmbH, Austria

Louis Cauffman's book *The Solution Tango* makes the bridge between thinking and really, effectively acting. It introduces not only a different way of thinking outside our encumbering boxes, it connects us to the means for effectively acting outside those boxes, too. This book is most definitely not about solving problems, but about crafting solutions."

David A. Schmaltz, USA,
Author of The Blind Men and the Elephant

Cauffman's *Solution Tango* takes the solution-focused perspective out of the therapy room and shows how it may be implemented by managers. The book is a practical guide for managers that recognizes their unique needs and the distinctive challenges that they face. I especially like Cauffman's attention to how effective management involves balancing leadership (setting goals and directing others' actions) with coaching (supporting and encouraging others). He offers realistic suggestions for achieving this balance.

Prof. Dr. Gale Miller full professor of sociology,
Marquette University, Wisconsin, USA

Simple does indeed work best! Louis Cauffman has used his long experience to produce a splendid collection of practical management wisdom. He takes the well established solution-focused approach into the realms of everyday managers in regular organisations with skill, precision and clarity. If you are a manager wanting to build solutions at work, buy this book now!

Dr Mark McKergow, co-author of
The solutions focus: the SIMPLE way to positive change

Filled with great information and easily implemented suggestions, I have already raved about *The Solution Tango* to many of my executive coaching clients and even more so to my coaching colleagues. Recommended for any reader who wants a complete business library as well as a solidly written, highly pleasurable read.

Margaret Krigbaum, J.D., MCC, former Vice President,
International Coaching Federation, USA

Louis Cauffman has succeeded in doing what few manage to do — write an entertaining, practical and, yet, serious book, *The Solution Tango*. Applying the concepts of solution-focused brief therapy which had a tremendous impact on the therapy world, Cauffman has developed what he calls "solution focused management". He offers practical advice and sound theory, while keeping the reader engaged and challenged by the cases that he describes. Full of practical suggestions, like "the miracle question" and the "flowchart", *The Solution Tango* is a must read for managers, executives, owners, and consultants.

Jane Hilburt-Davis, Founding Principle,
Key Resources; President, Family Firm Institute International, USA